SUPERB™

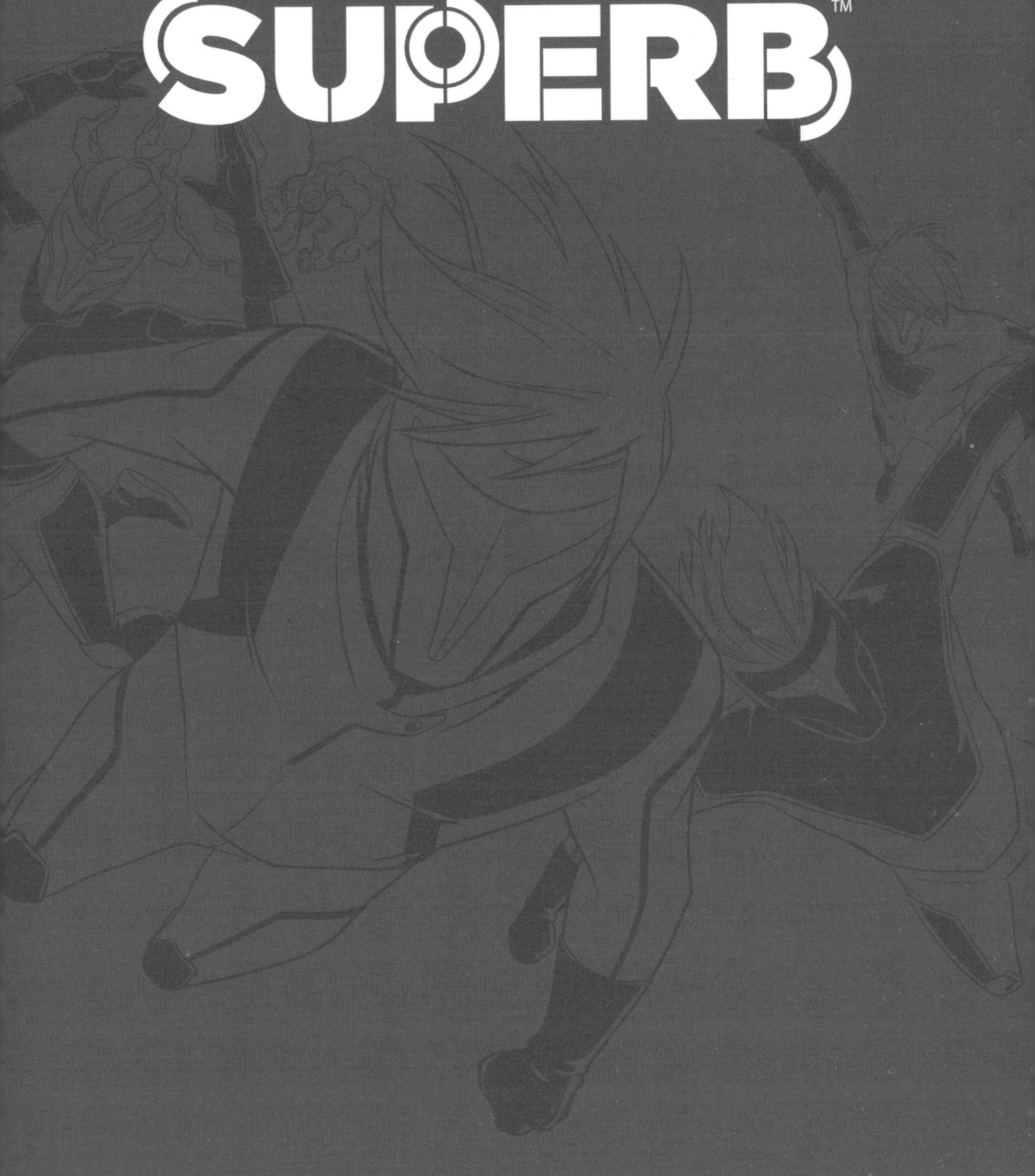

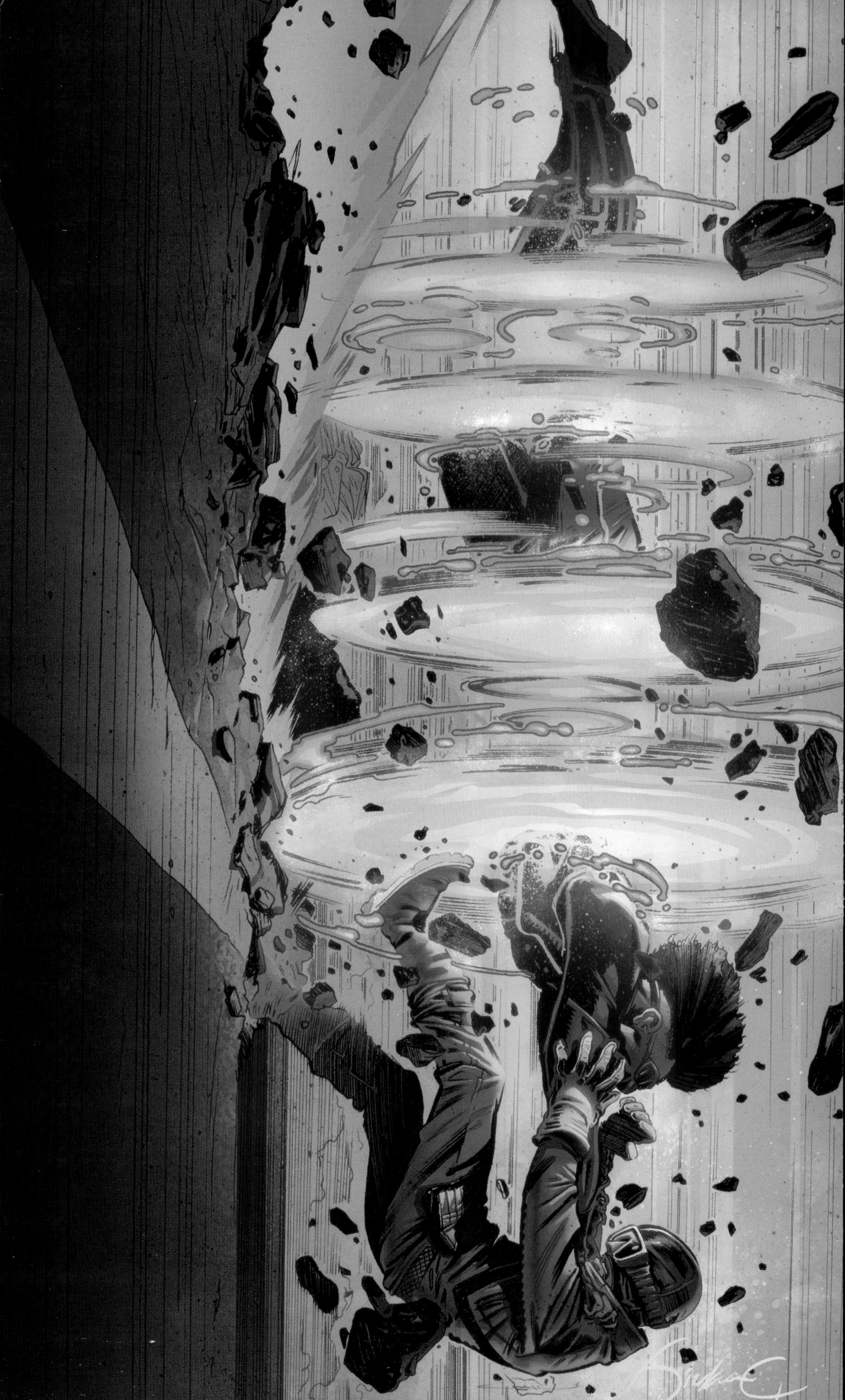

PREVIOUSLY IN SUPERB...

After the Earth survived annihilation from an asteroid which was destroyed by a group of heroic astronauts, the resultant meteor shower turned Youngstown, Ohio into a Level 5 impact zone. Soon after, the Foresight Corporation took over Youngstown to find and regulate any other teenagers with emerging powers caused by the meteor storm.

Jonah Watkins, a young man with Down syndrome, reunited with his friend Kayla Tate, whose parents are scientists for Foresight. During all of this, a mysterious new superhuman named Cosmosis became an Internet sensation and the hero of Youngstown. Kayla eventually discovered that Cosmosis...is Jonah! Based on his favorite comic book hero, Jonah uses secret powers he gained from the meteor shower to help people and oppose crime. But Kayla had some secrets, as well, and to protect Jonah, Kayla revealed her own powers gained from a meteor fragment to fight alongside Jonah as the hero Amina.

When Amina and Cosmosis discover that young superpowered people are being kidnapped and trained to become Earth's best line of defense against the possibility of an alien invasion, the two teenage heroes use their abilities to stop Foresight. In doing so, they successfully captured a dangerous Foresight agent known as Cypher. But they know that with every passing minute, Foresight is planning their next move.

WE CAN BE HEROES
Written by **DAVID F. WALKER**
Illustrated by **ALITHA MARTINEZ**
Inked by **DAVID CABEZA**
Colored by **MAARTA LAIHO**
Lettered by **AW'S TOM NAPOLITANO**

COSMOSIS SHORTS
Written by **DAVID F. WALKER**
Illustrated by **BALDEMAR RIVAS**
Colored by **ADAM GUZOWSKI**
Lettered by **AW'S TOM NAPOLITANO**

JASMINE AMIRI • Editor

Cover by **JOE KARG AND CHRIS BIVINS**

ISBN: 978-1-5493-0288-6

Library of Congress Control Number: 2019930893

ROAR™

CHAPTER ONE

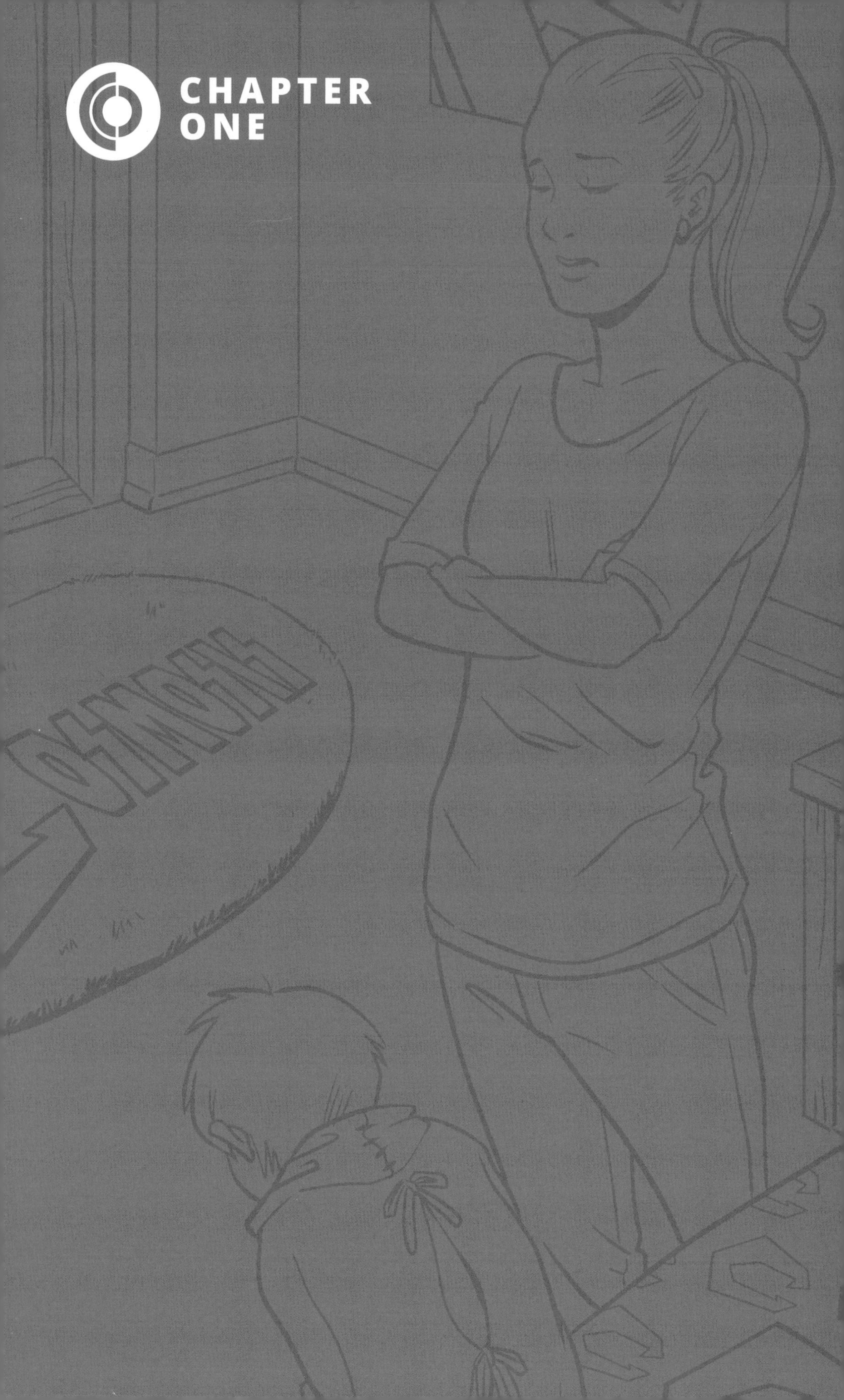

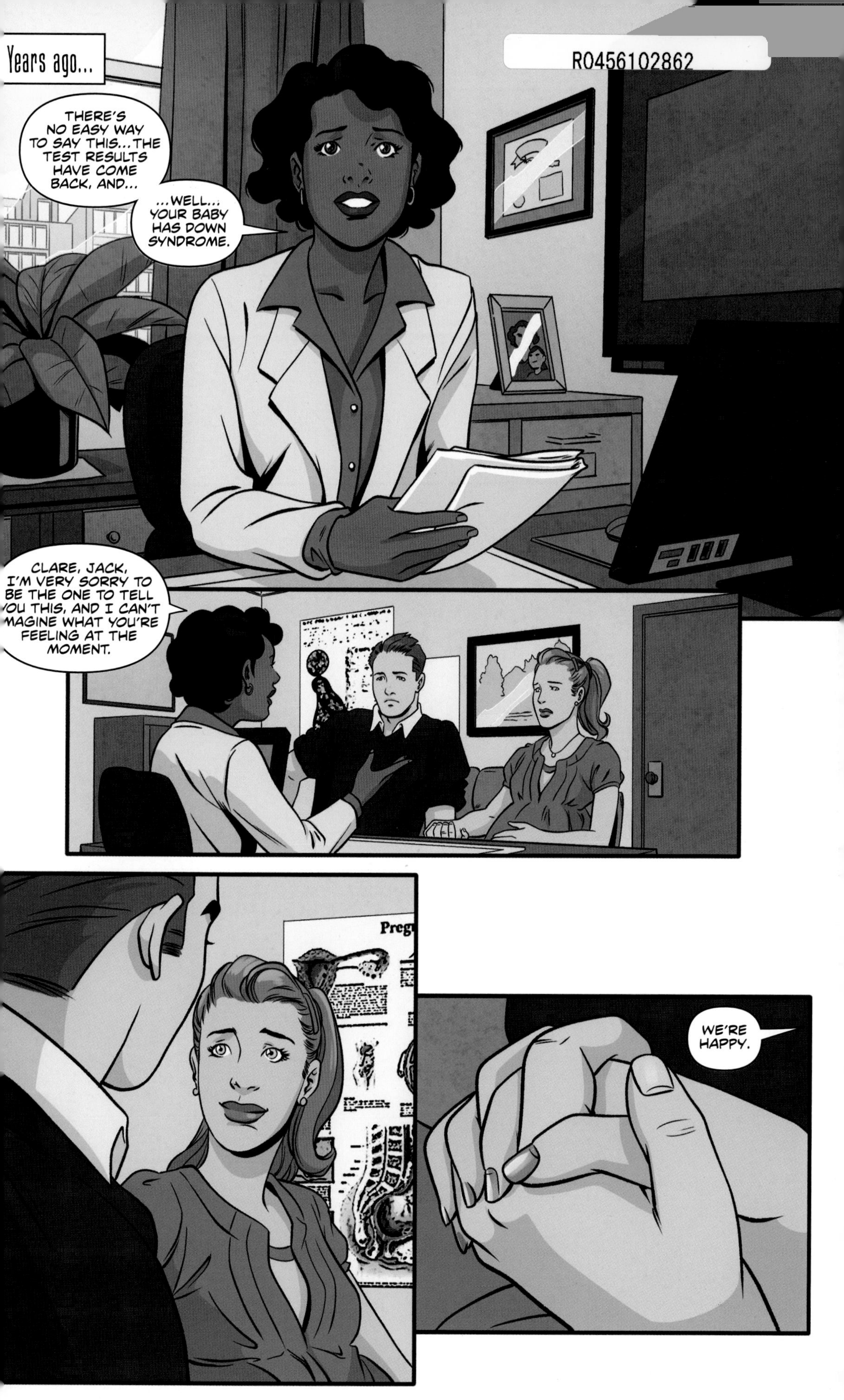
Years ago...
THERE'S NO EASY WAY TO SAY THIS...THE TEST RESULTS HAVE COME BACK, AND...
...WELL... YOUR BABY HAS DOWN SYNDROME.
CLARE, JACK, I'M VERY SORRY TO BE THE ONE TO TELL YOU THIS, AND I CAN'T IMAGINE WHAT YOU'RE FEELING AT THE MOMENT.
WE'RE HAPPY.

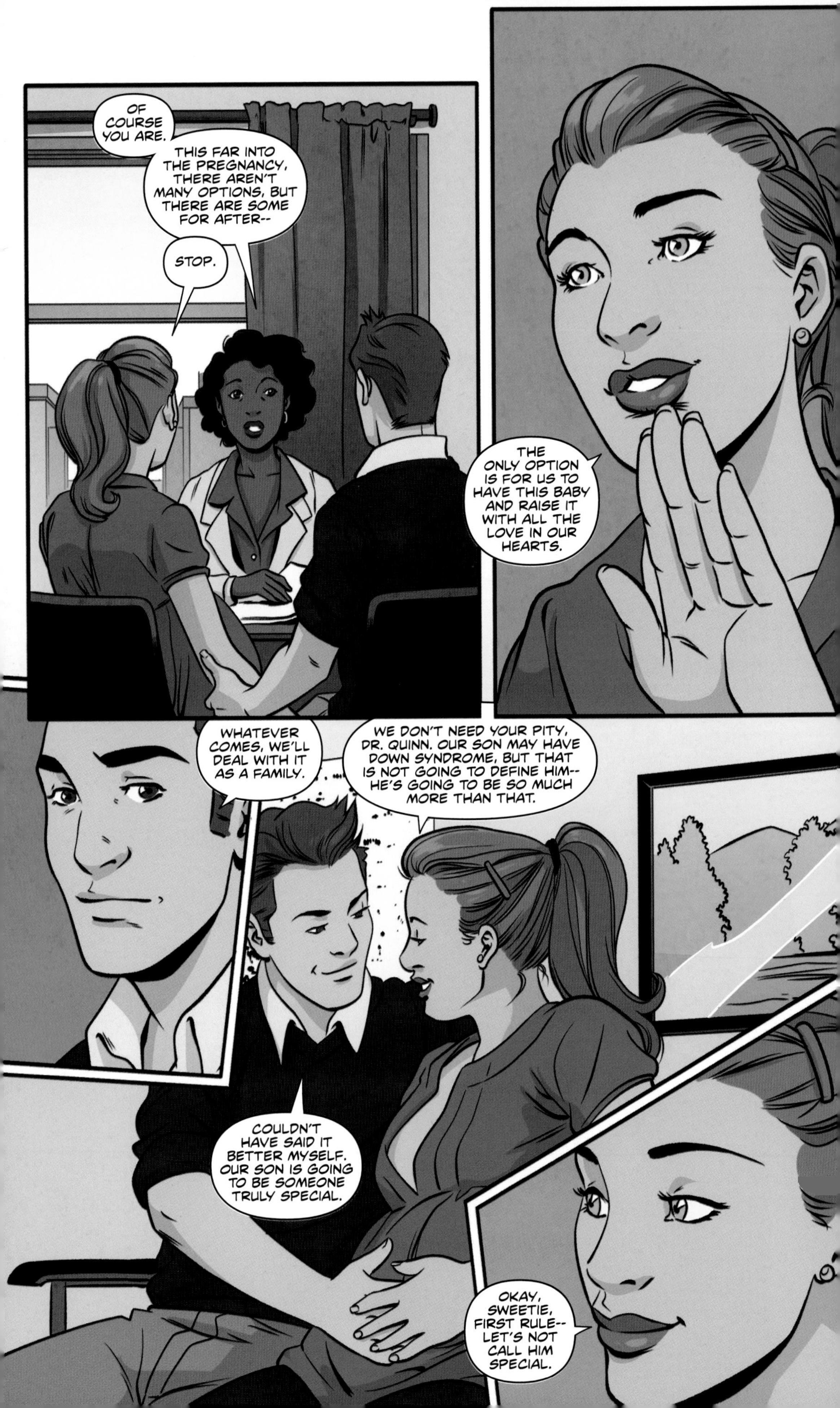
OF COURSE YOU ARE.
THIS FAR INTO THE PREGNANCY, THERE AREN'T MANY OPTIONS, BUT THERE ARE SOME FOR AFTER--
STOP.
THE ONLY OPTION IS FOR US TO HAVE THIS BABY AND RAISE IT WITH ALL THE LOVE IN OUR HEARTS.
WHATEVER COMES, WE'LL DEAL WITH IT AS A FAMILY.
WE DON'T NEED YOUR PITY, DR. QUINN. OUR SON MAY HAVE DOWN SYNDROME, BUT THAT IS NOT GOING TO DEFINE HIM-- HE'S GOING TO BE SO MUCH MORE THAN THAT.
COULDN'T HAVE SAID IT BETTER MYSELF. OUR SON IS GOING TO BE SOMEONE TRULY SPECIAL.
OKAY, SWEETIE, FIRST RULE-- LET'S NOT CALL HIM SPECIAL.

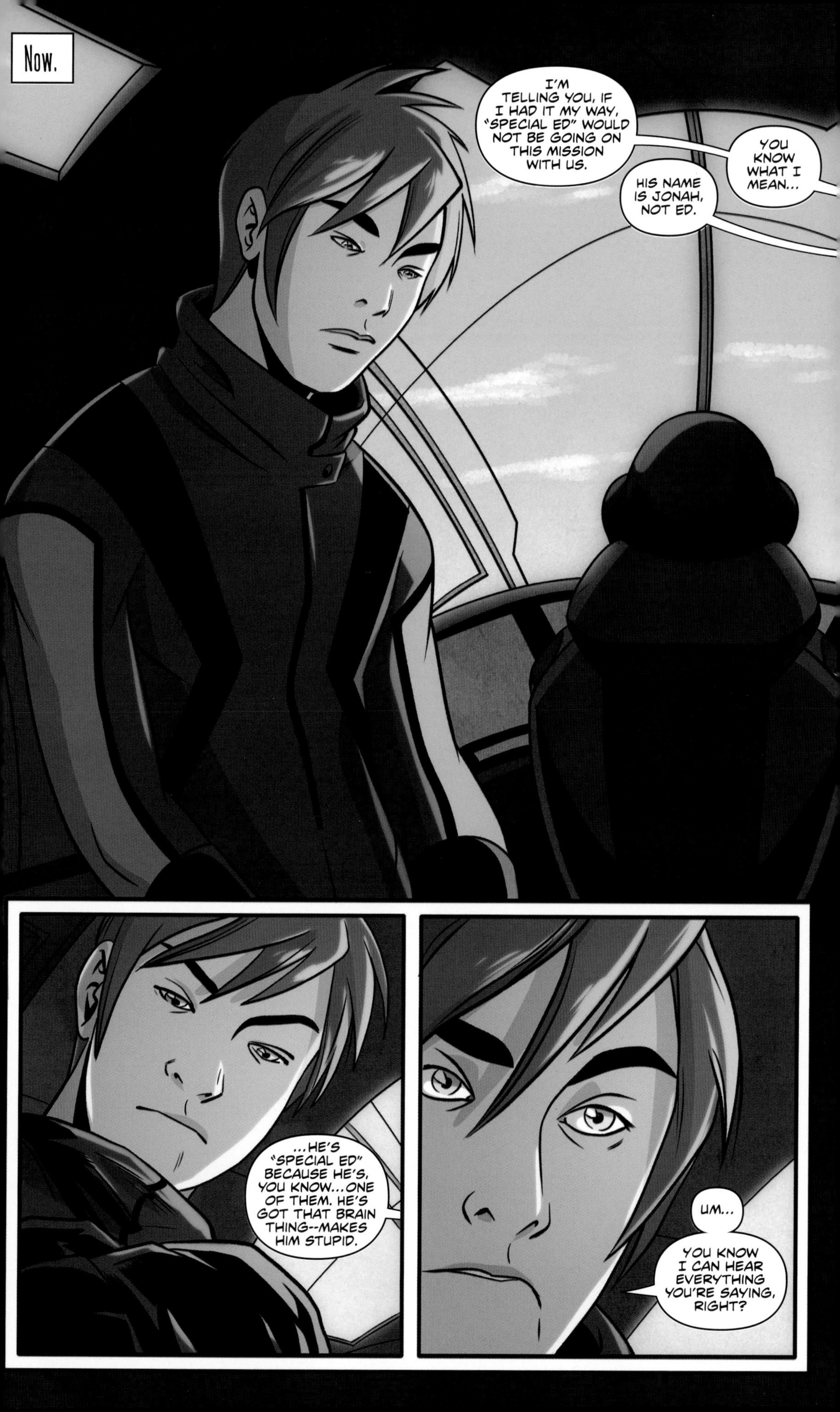
Now.
I'M TELLING YOU, IF I HAD IT MY WAY, "SPECIAL ED" WOULD NOT BE GOING ON THIS MISSION WITH US.
HIS NAME IS JONAH, NOT ED.
YOU KNOW WHAT I MEAN...
...HE'S "SPECIAL ED" BECAUSE HE'S, YOU KNOW...ONE OF THEM. HE'S GOT THAT BRAIN THING--MAKES HIM STUPID.
UM...
YOU KNOW I CAN HEAR EVERYTHING YOU'RE SAYING, RIGHT?

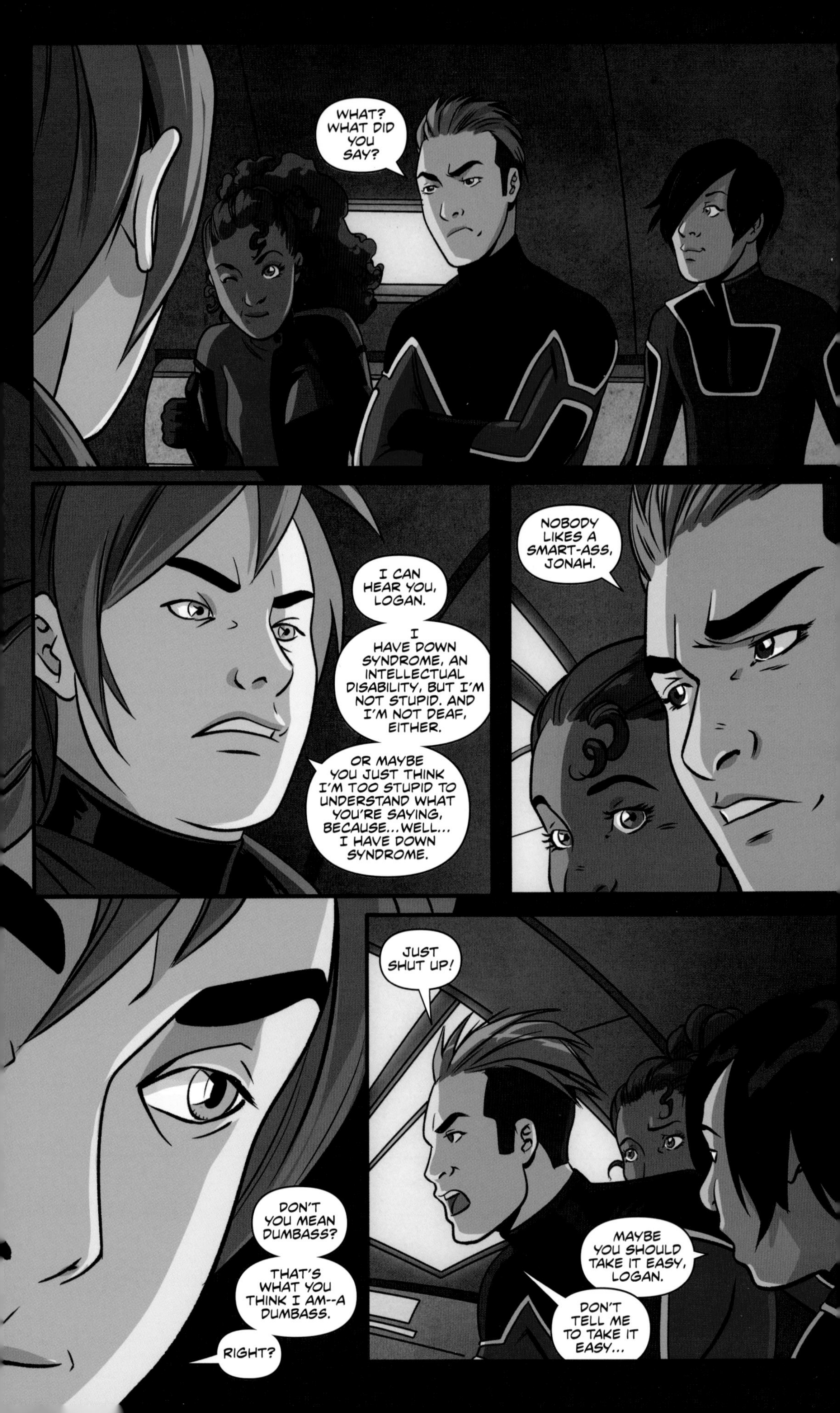
WHAT? WHAT DID YOU SAY?
I CAN HEAR YOU, LOGAN.
I HAVE DOWN SYNDROME, AN INTELLECTUAL DISABILITY, BUT I'M NOT STUPID. AND I'M NOT DEAF, EITHER.
OR MAYBE YOU JUST THINK I'M TOO STUPID TO UNDERSTAND WHAT YOU'RE SAYING, BECAUSE...WELL... I HAVE DOWN SYNDROME.
NOBODY LIKES A SMART-ASS, JONAH.
DON'T YOU MEAN DUMBASS?
THAT'S WHAT YOU THINK I AM--A DUMBASS.
RIGHT?
JUST SHUT UP!
MAYBE YOU SHOULD TAKE IT EASY, LOGAN.
DON'T TELL ME TO TAKE IT EASY...

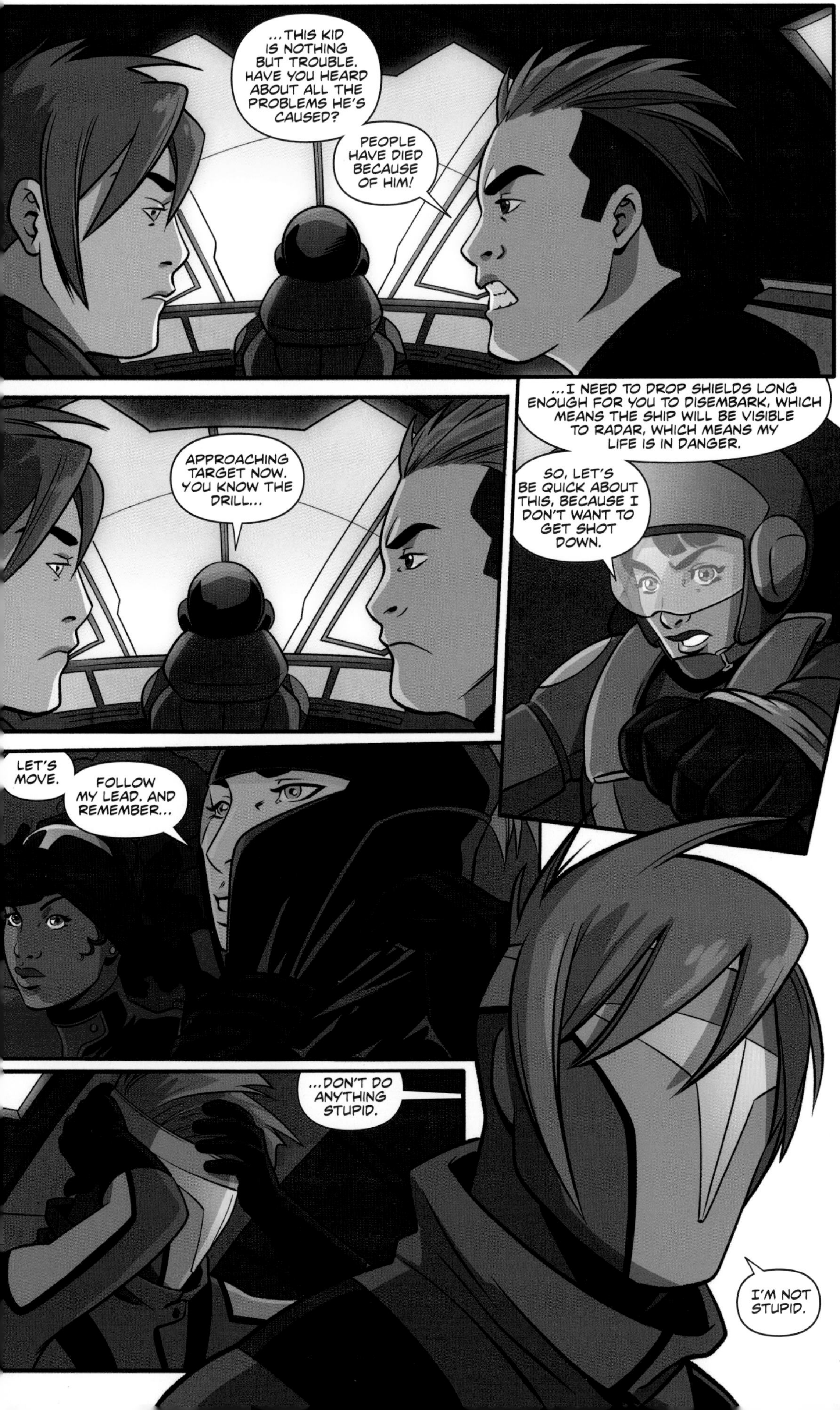
...THIS KID IS NOTHING BUT TROUBLE. HAVE YOU HEARD ABOUT ALL THE PROBLEMS HE'S CAUSED?
PEOPLE HAVE DIED BECAUSE OF HIM!
APPROACHING TARGET NOW. YOU KNOW THE DRILL...
...I NEED TO DROP SHIELDS LONG ENOUGH FOR YOU TO DISEMBARK, WHICH MEANS THE SHIP WILL BE VISIBLE TO RADAR, WHICH MEANS MY LIFE IS IN DANGER.
SO, LET'S BE QUICK ABOUT THIS, BECAUSE I DON'T WANT TO GET SHOT DOWN.
LET'S MOVE.
FOLLOW MY LEAD. AND REMEMBER...
...DON'T DO ANYTHING STUPID.
I'M NOT STUPID.

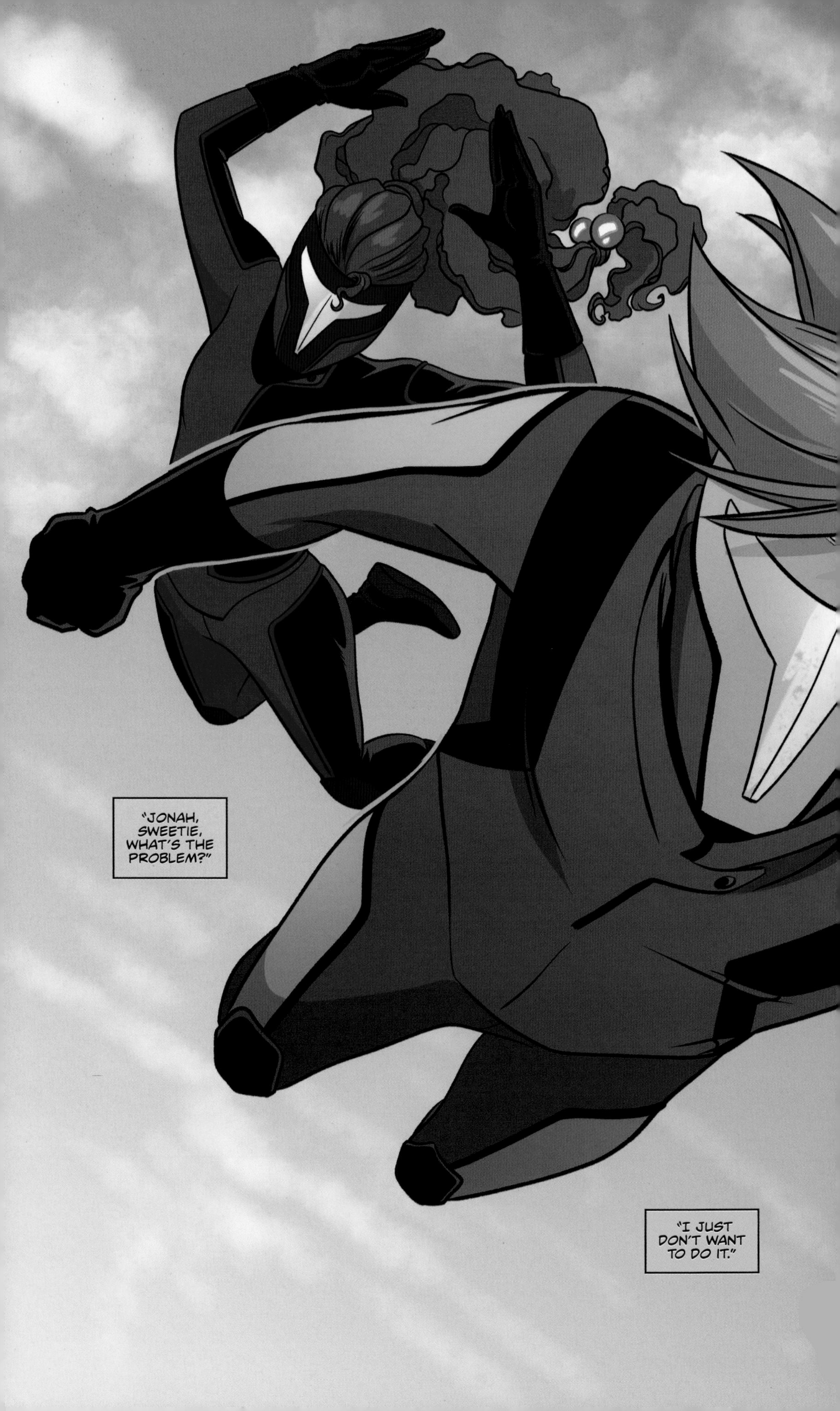
"JONAH, SWEETIE, WHAT'S THE PROBLEM?"
"I JUST DON'T WANT TO DO IT."

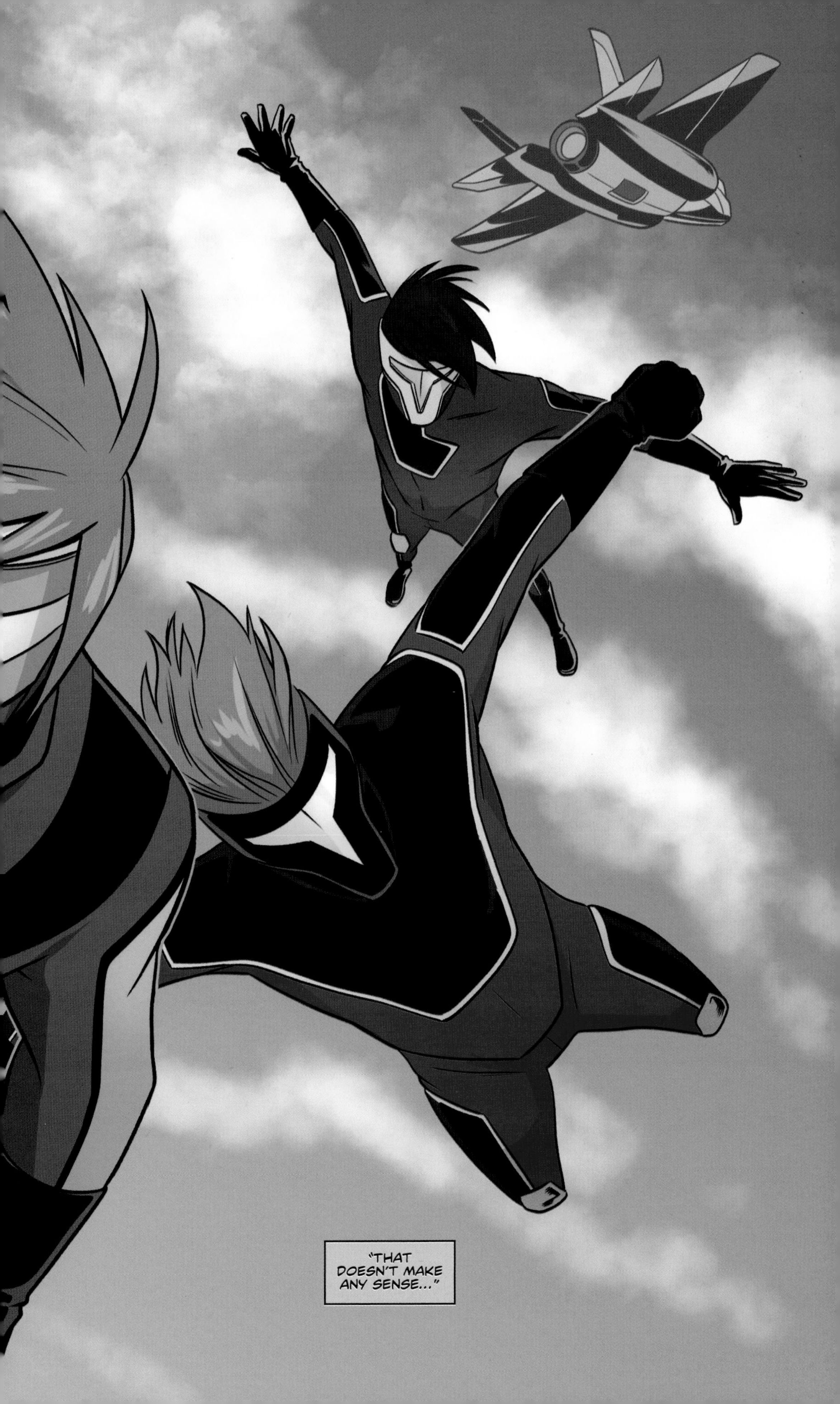
"THAT DOESN'T MAKE ANY SENSE..."

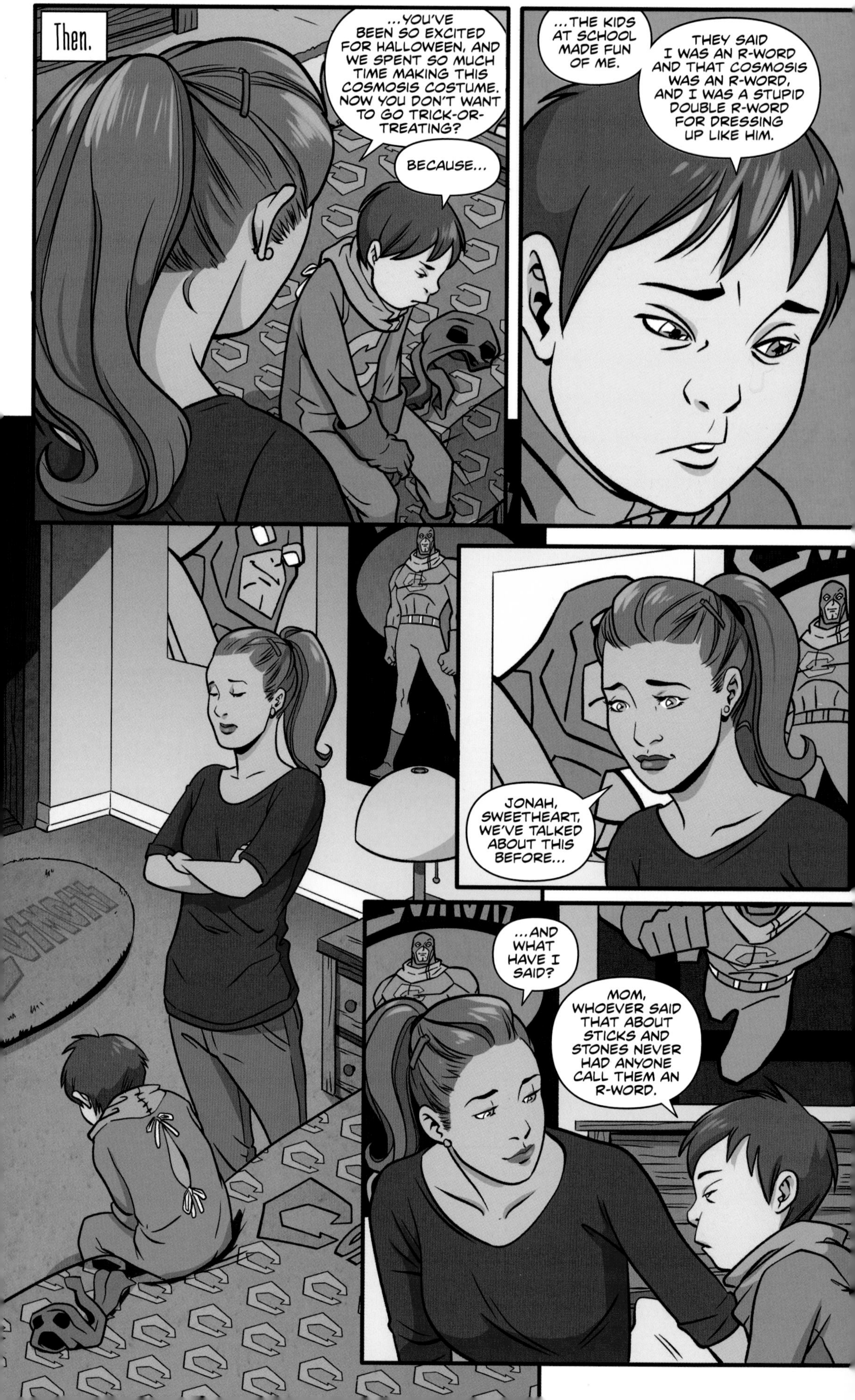
Then.
...YOU'VE BEEN SO EXCITED FOR HALLOWEEN, AND WE SPENT SO MUCH TIME MAKING THIS COSMOSIS COSTUME. NOW YOU DON'T WANT TO GO TRICK-OR-TREATING?
BECAUSE...
...THE KIDS AT SCHOOL MADE FUN OF ME.
THEY SAID I WAS AN R-WORD AND THAT COSMOSIS WAS AN R-WORD, AND I WAS A STUPID DOUBLE R-WORD FOR DRESSING UP LIKE HIM.
JONAH, SWEETHEART, WE'VE TALKED ABOUT THIS BEFORE...
...AND WHAT HAVE I SAID?
MOM, WHOEVER SAID THAT ABOUT STICKS AND STONES NEVER HAD ANYONE CALL THEM AN R-WORD.

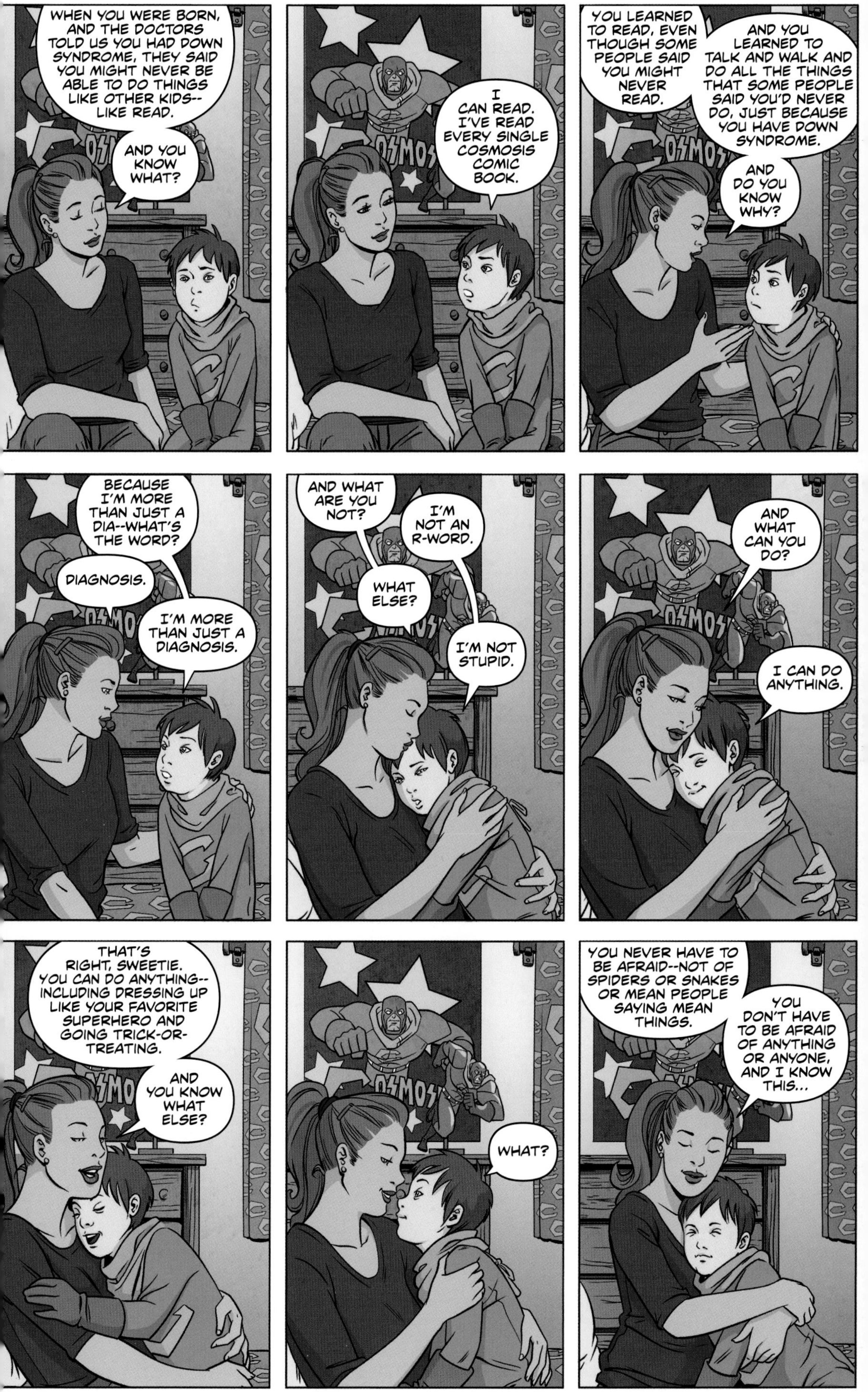

WHEN YOU WERE BORN, AND THE DOCTORS TOLD US YOU HAD DOWN SYNDROME, THEY SAID YOU MIGHT NEVER BE ABLE TO DO THINGS LIKE OTHER KIDS-- LIKE READ.
AND YOU KNOW WHAT?
I CAN READ. I'VE READ EVERY SINGLE COSMOSIS COMIC BOOK.
YOU LEARNED TO READ, EVEN THOUGH SOME PEOPLE SAID YOU MIGHT NEVER READ.
AND YOU LEARNED TO TALK AND WALK AND DO ALL THE THINGS THAT SOME PEOPLE SAID YOU'D NEVER DO, JUST BECAUSE YOU HAVE DOWN SYNDROME.
AND DO YOU KNOW WHY?
BECAUSE I'M MORE THAN JUST A DIA--WHAT'S THE WORD?
DIAGNOSIS.
I'M MORE THAN JUST A DIAGNOSIS.
AND WHAT ARE YOU NOT?
I'M NOT AN R-WORD.
WHAT ELSE?
I'M NOT STUPID.
AND WHAT CAN YOU DO?
I CAN DO ANYTHING.
THAT'S RIGHT, SWEETIE. YOU CAN DO ANYTHING-- INCLUDING DRESSING UP LIKE YOUR FAVORITE SUPERHERO AND GOING TRICK-OR-TREATING.
AND YOU KNOW WHAT ELSE?
WHAT?
YOU NEVER HAVE TO BE AFRAID--NOT OF SPIDERS OR SNAKES OR MEAN PEOPLE SAYING MEAN THINGS.
YOU DON'T HAVE TO BE AFRAID OF ANYTHING OR ANYONE, AND I KNOW THIS...

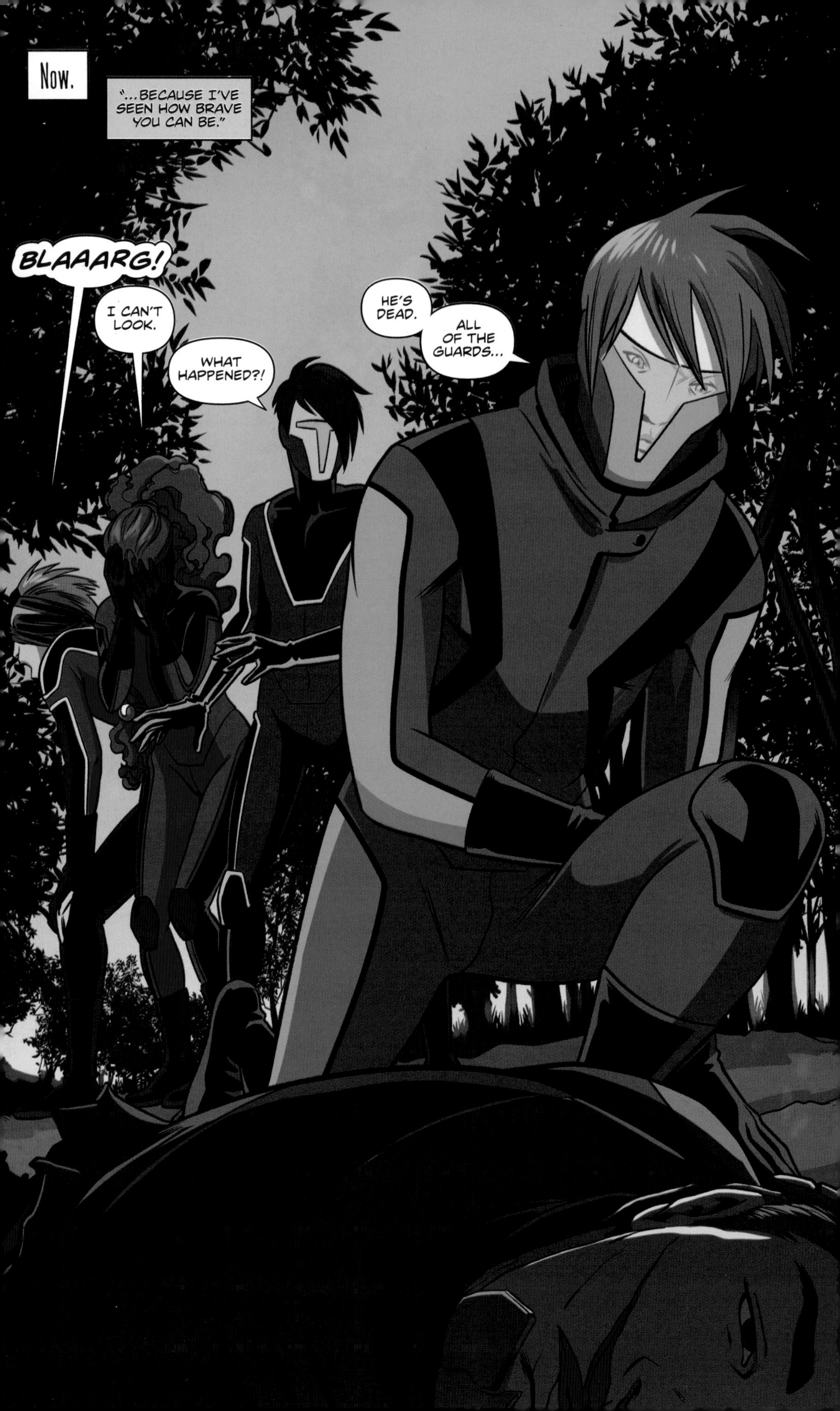

Now.
"...BECAUSE I'VE SEEN HOW BRAVE YOU CAN BE."
BLAAARG!
I CAN'T LOOK.
WHAT HAPPENED?!
HE'S DEAD.
ALL OF THE GUARDS...

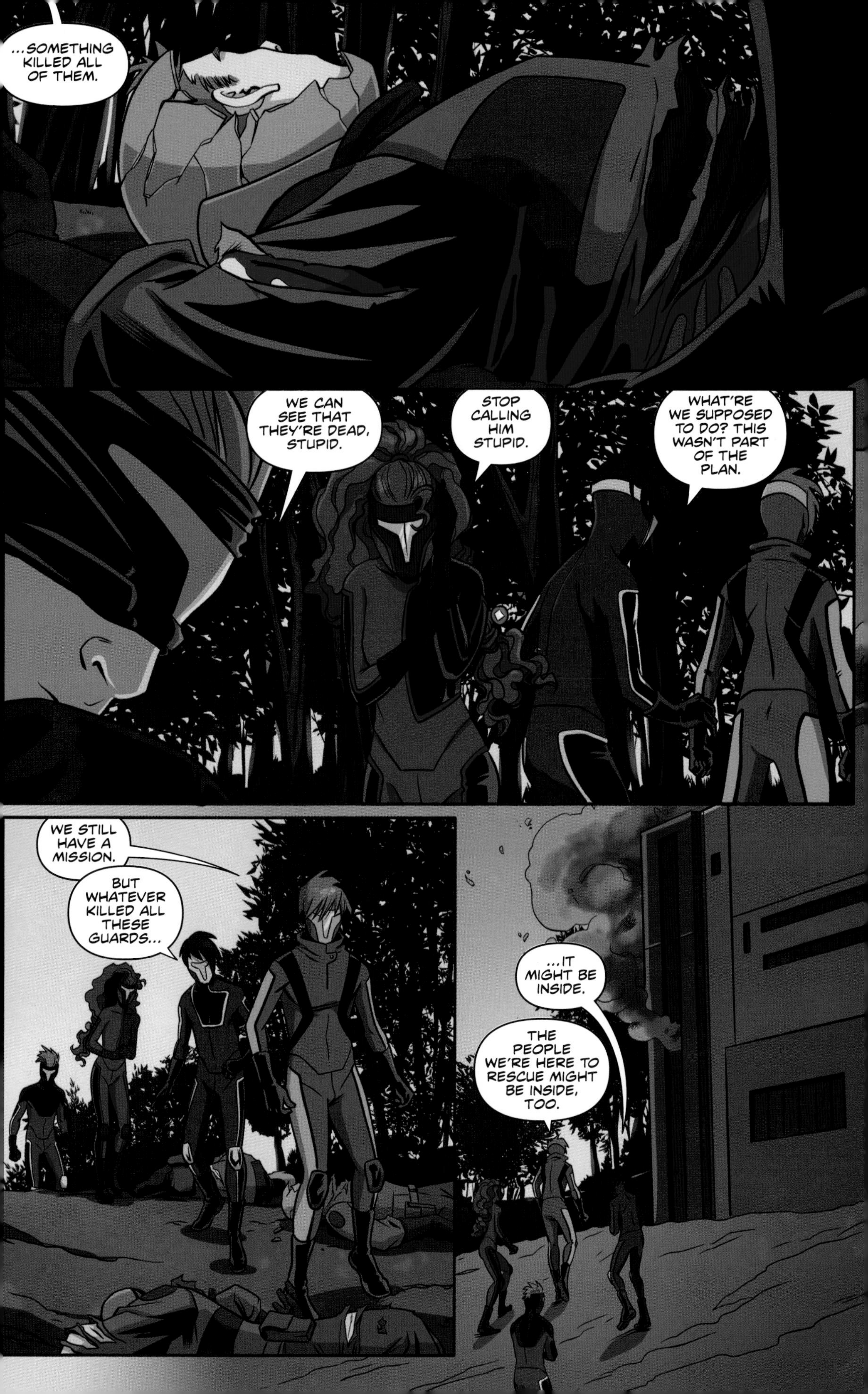
...SOMETHING KILLED ALL OF THEM.
WE CAN SEE THAT THEY'RE DEAD, STUPID.
STOP CALLING HIM STUPID.
WHAT'RE WE SUPPOSED TO DO? THIS WASN'T PART OF THE PLAN.
WE STILL HAVE A MISSION.
BUT WHATEVER KILLED ALL THESE GUARDS...
...IT MIGHT BE INSIDE.
THE PEOPLE WE'RE HERE TO RESCUE MIGHT BE INSIDE, TOO.

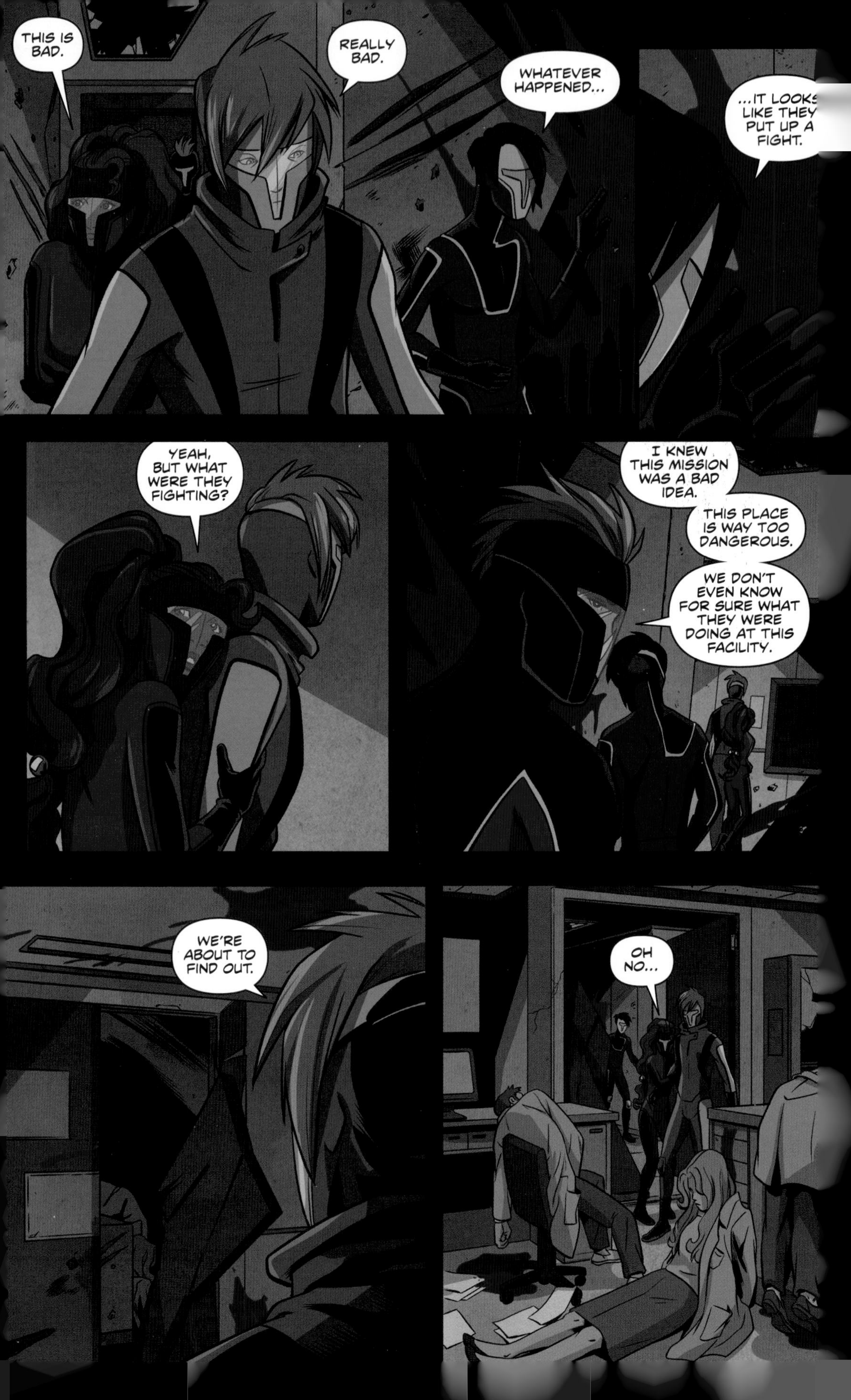
THIS IS BAD.
REALLY BAD.
WHATEVER HAPPENED...
...IT LOOKS LIKE THEY PUT UP A FIGHT.
YEAH, BUT WHAT WERE THEY FIGHTING?
I KNEW THIS MISSION WAS A BAD IDEA.
THIS PLACE IS WAY TOO DANGEROUS.
WE DON'T EVEN KNOW FOR SURE WHAT THEY WERE DOING AT THIS FACILITY.
WE'RE ABOUT TO FIND OUT.
OH NO...

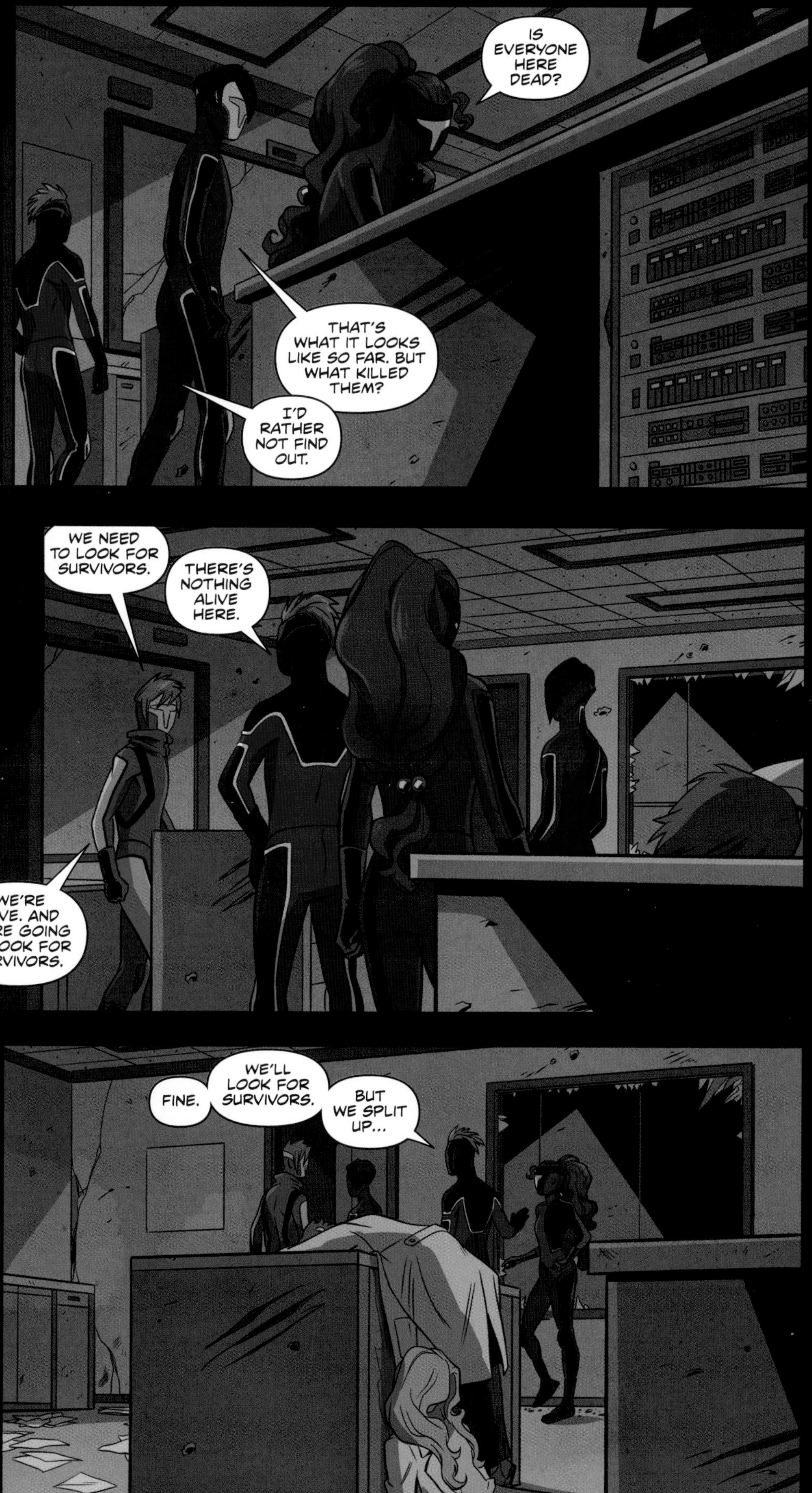
IS EVERYONE HERE DEAD?
THAT'S WHAT IT LOOKS LIKE SO FAR. BUT WHAT KILLED THEM?
I'D RATHER NOT FIND OUT.
WE NEED TO LOOK FOR SURVIVORS.
THERE'S NOTHING ALIVE HERE.
WE'RE ALIVE. AND WE'RE GOING TO LOOK FOR SURVIVORS.
FINE.
WE'LL LOOK FOR SURVIVORS.
BUT WE SPLIT UP...

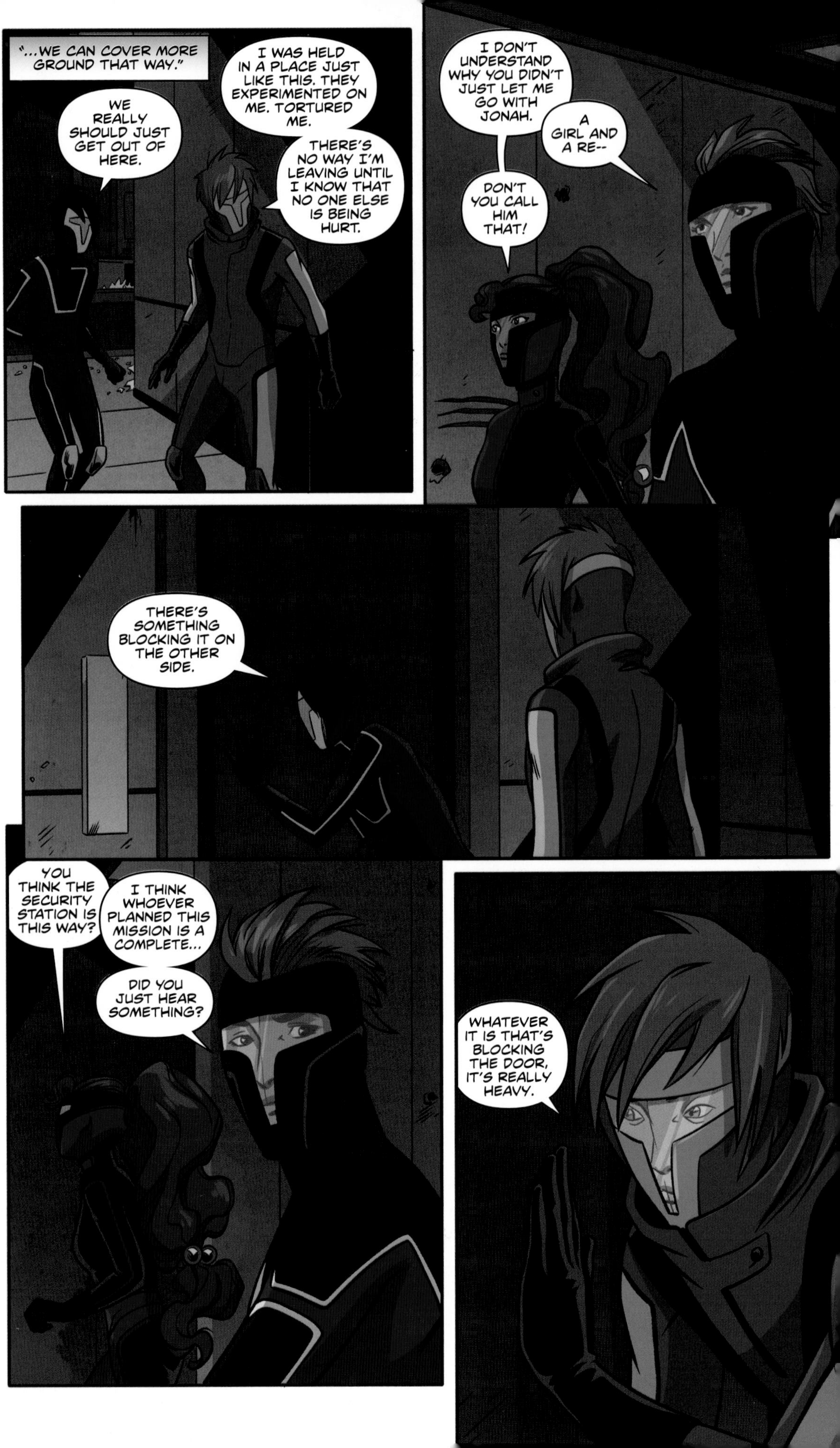
"...WE CAN COVER MORE GROUND THAT WAY."
WE REALLY SHOULD JUST GET OUT OF HERE.
I WAS HELD IN A PLACE JUST LIKE THIS. THEY EXPERIMENTED ON ME. TORTURED ME.
THERE'S NO WAY I'M LEAVING UNTIL I KNOW THAT NO ONE ELSE IS BEING HURT.
I DON'T UNDERSTAND WHY YOU DIDN'T JUST LET ME GO WITH JONAH.
A GIRL AND A RE--
DON'T YOU CALL HIM THAT!
THERE'S SOMETHING BLOCKING IT ON THE OTHER SIDE.
YOU THINK THE SECURITY STATION IS THIS WAY?
I THINK WHOEVER PLANNED THIS MISSION IS A COMPLETE...
DID YOU JUST HEAR SOMETHING?
WHATEVER IT IS THAT'S BLOCKING THE DOOR, IT'S REALLY HEAVY.

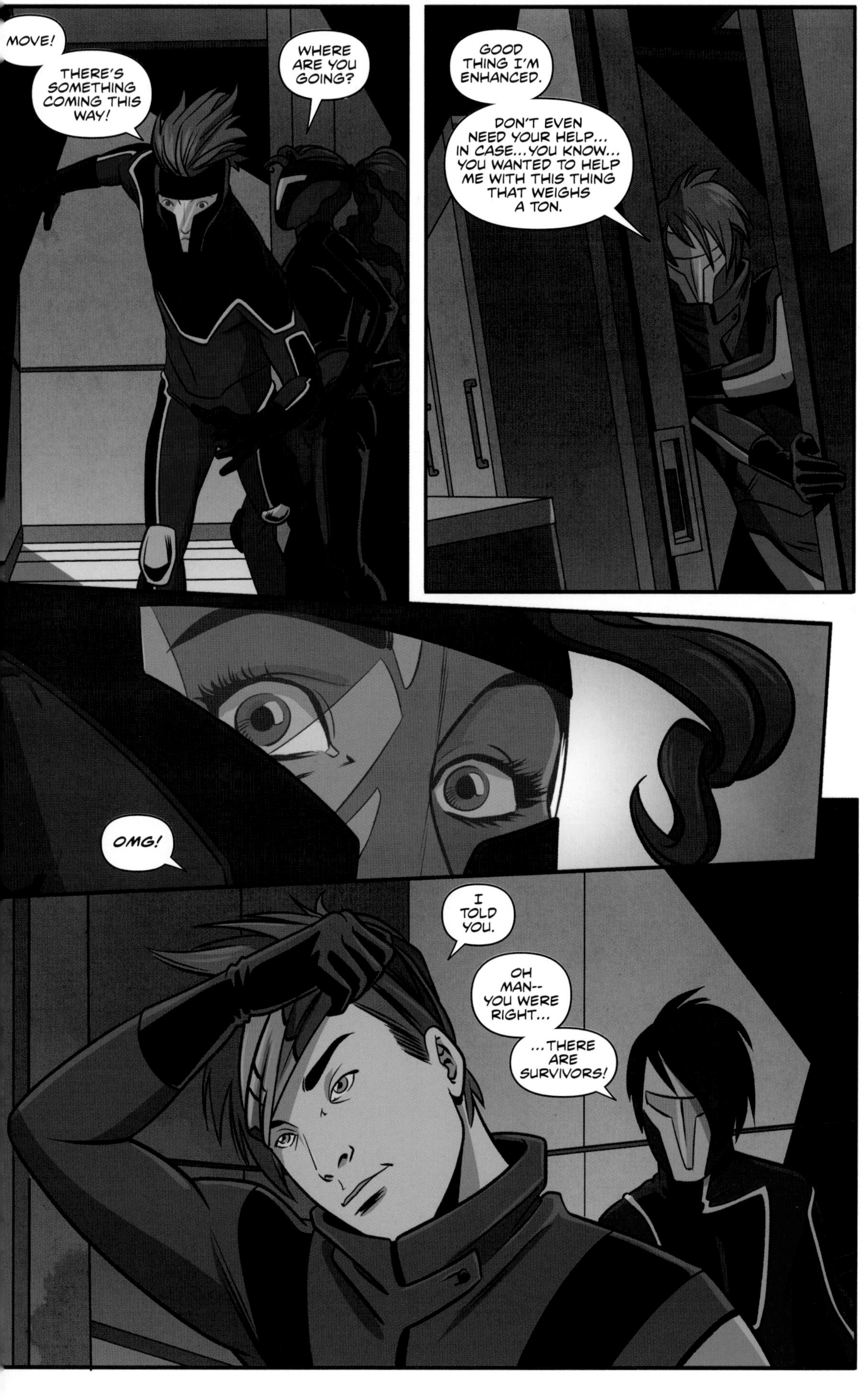
MOVE!
THERE'S SOMETHING COMING THIS WAY!
WHERE ARE YOU GOING?
GOOD THING I'M ENHANCED.
DON'T EVEN NEED YOUR HELP... IN CASE...YOU KNOW... YOU WANTED TO HELP ME WITH THIS THING THAT WEIGHS A TON.
OMG!
I TOLD YOU.
OH MAN-- YOU WERE RIGHT...
...THERE ARE SURVIVORS!

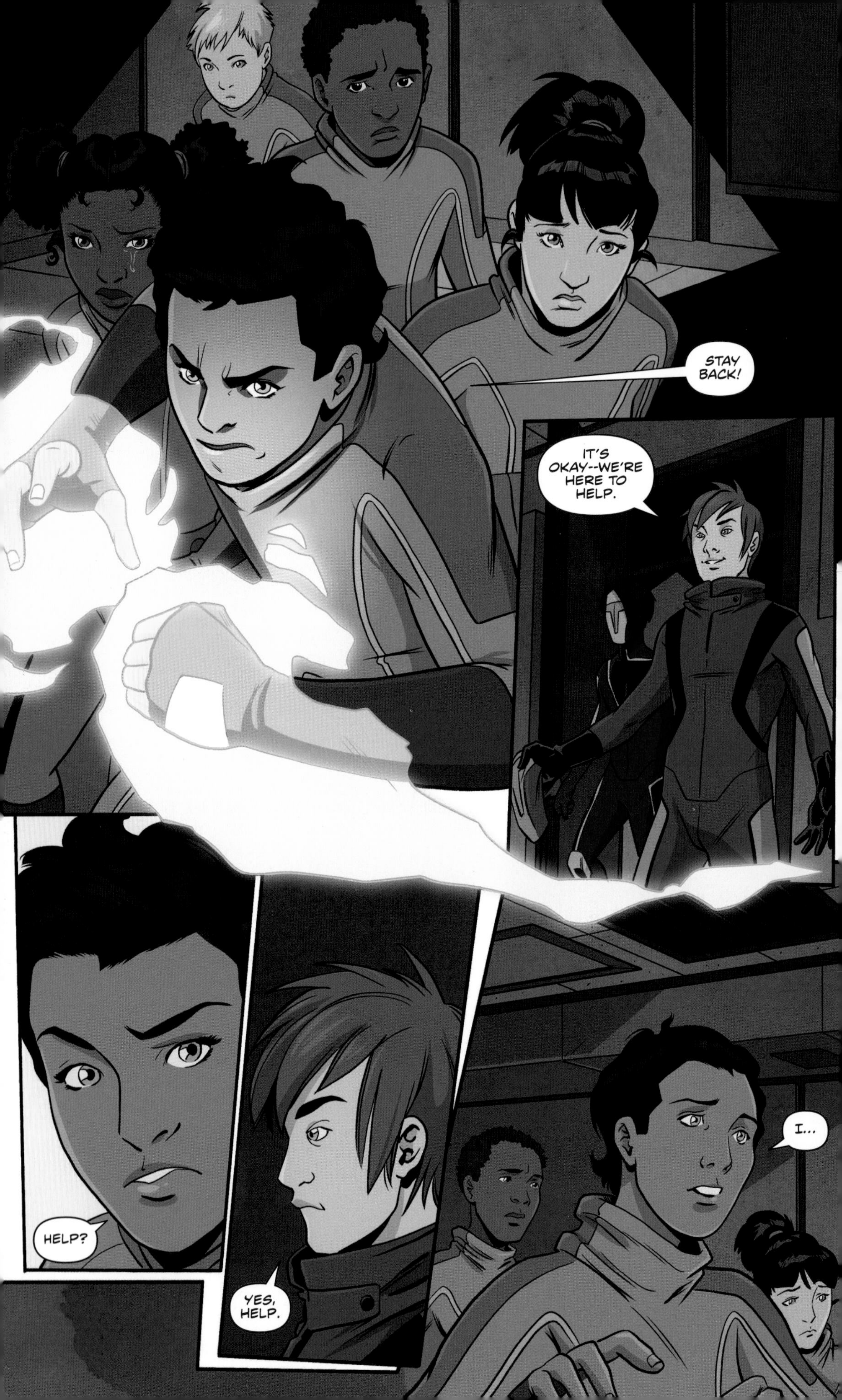
STAY BACK!
IT'S OKAY--WE'RE HERE TO HELP.
HELP?
YES, HELP.
I...

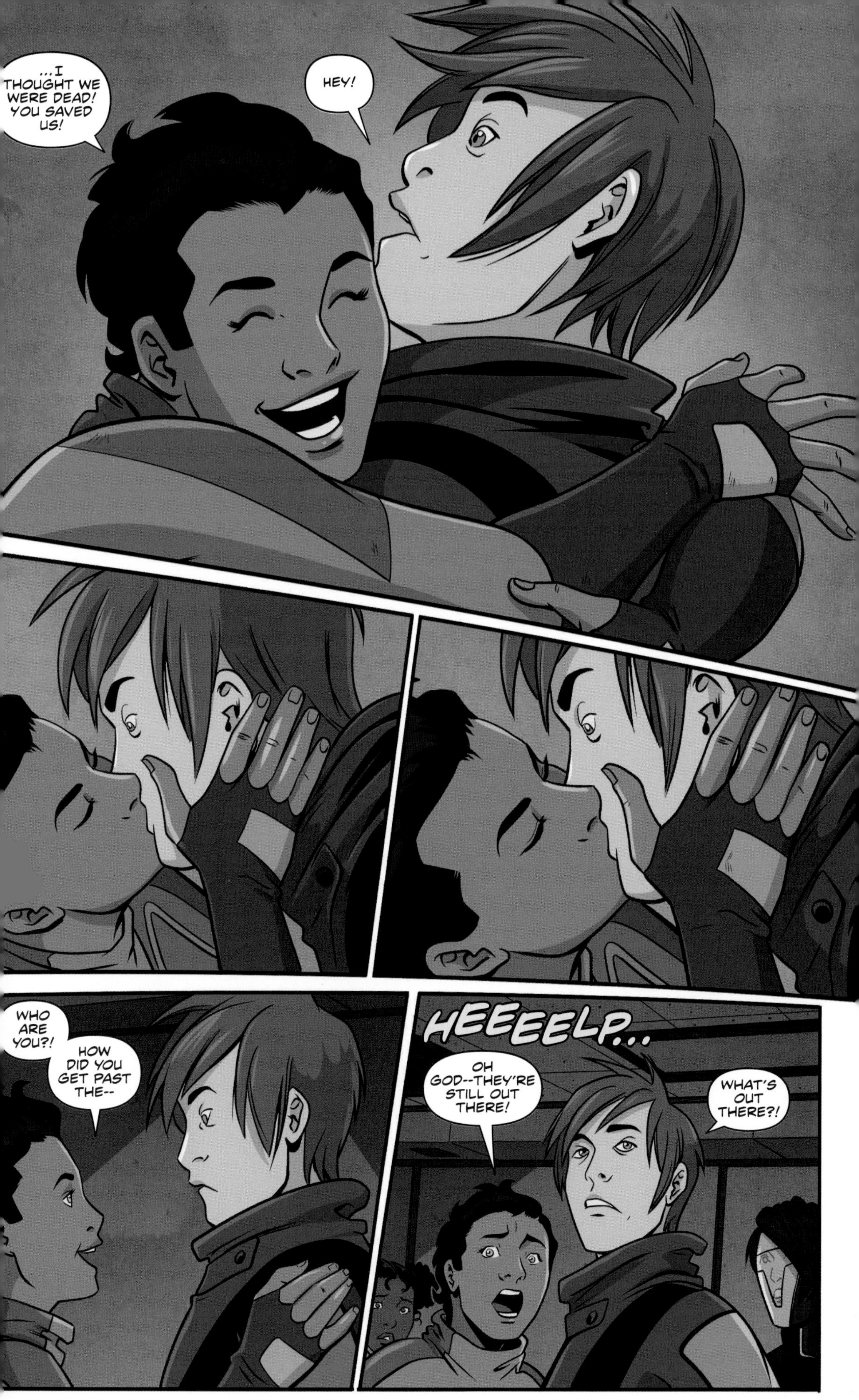
...I THOUGHT WE WERE DEAD! YOU SAVED US!
HEY!
WHO ARE YOU?!
HOW DID YOU GET PAST THE--
HEEEEELP...
OH GOD--THEY'RE STILL OUT THERE!
WHAT'S OUT THERE?!

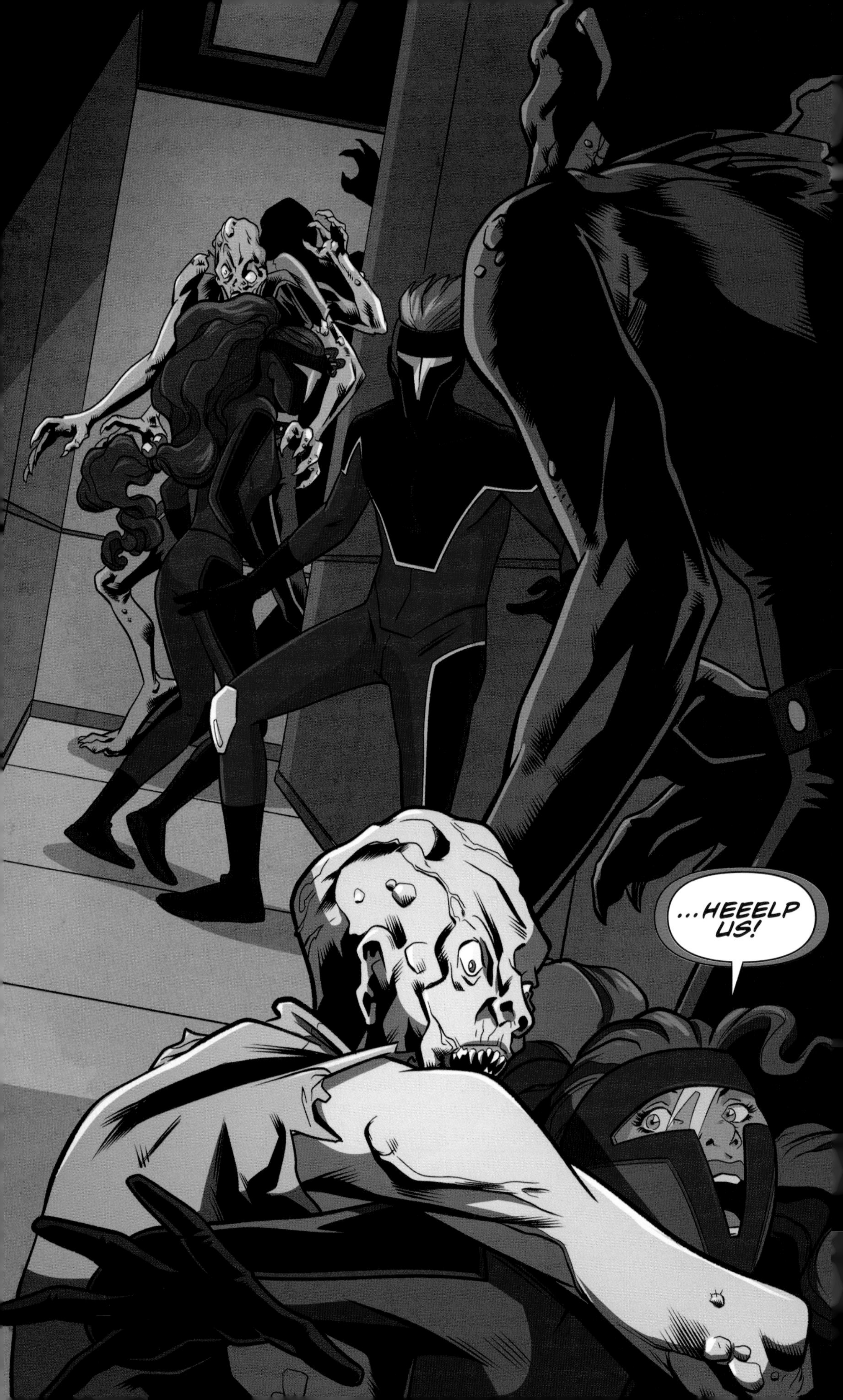
...HEEELP US!

CHAPTER TWO

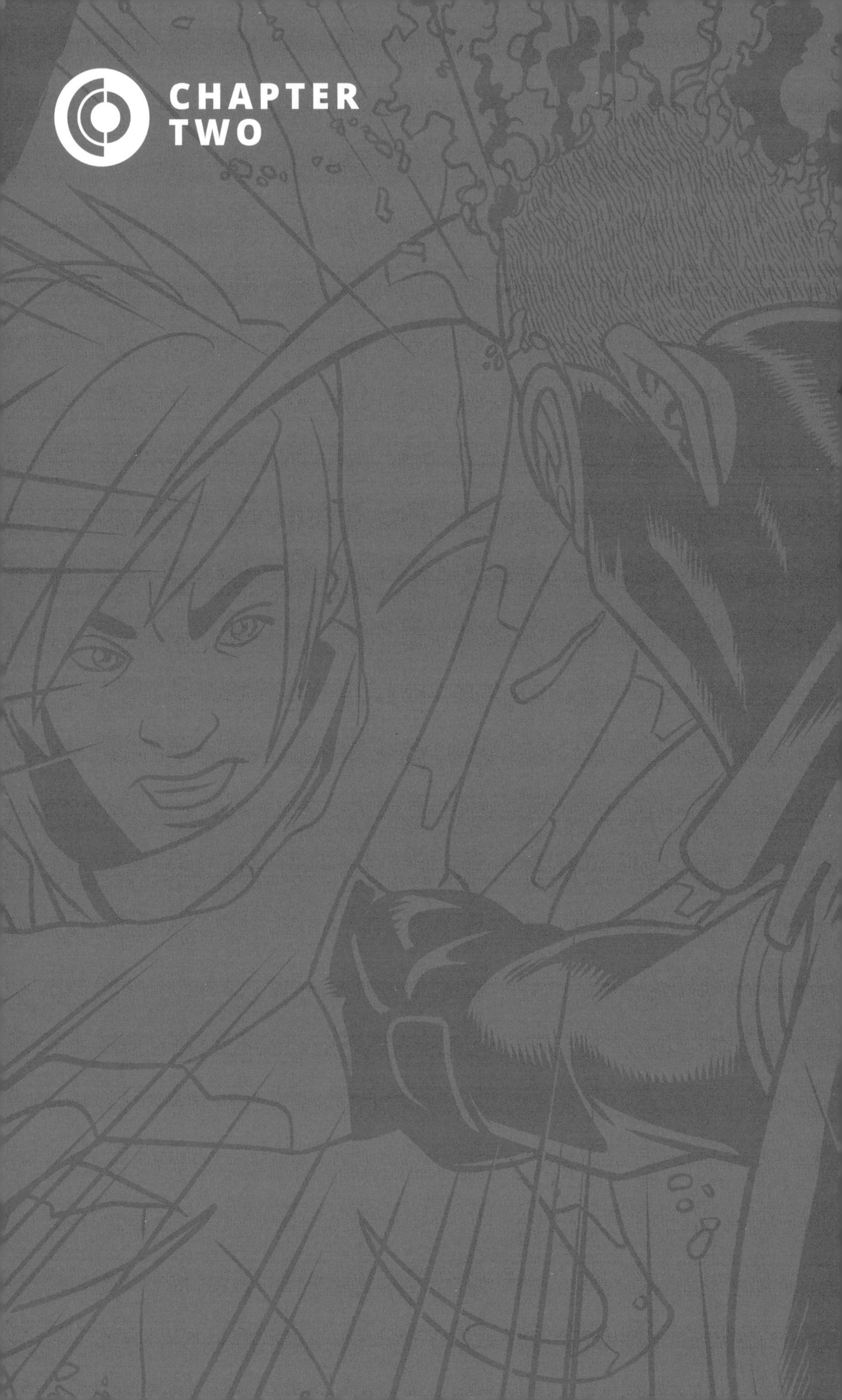

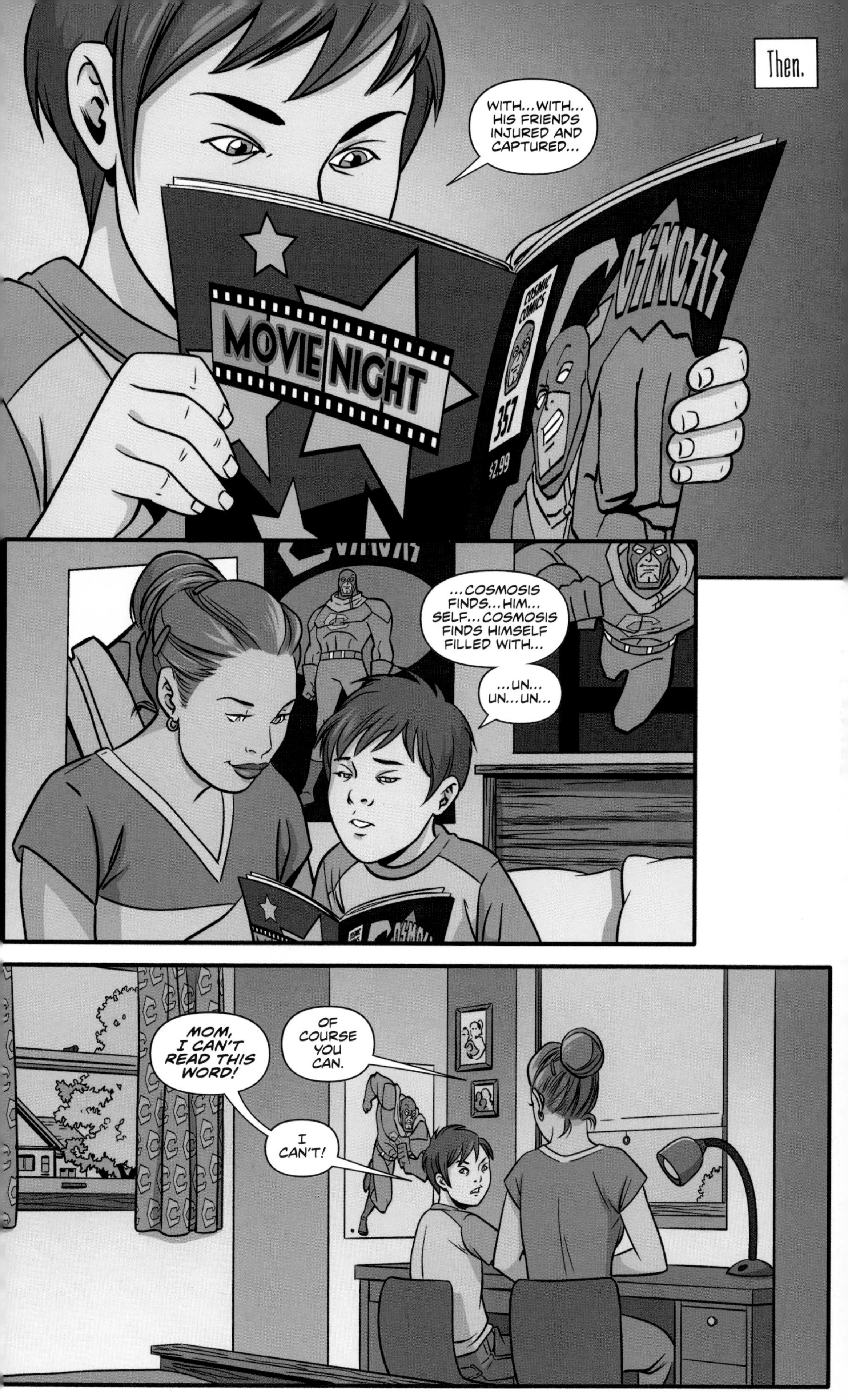
Then.
WITH...WITH... HIS FRIENDS INJURED AND CAPTURED...
MOVIE NIGHT
COSMIC COMICS
357
$2.99
COSMOSIS
...COSMOSIS FINDS...HIM... SELF...COSMOSIS FINDS HIMSELF FILLED WITH...
...UN... UN...UN...
MOM, I CAN'T READ THIS WORD!
OF COURSE YOU CAN.
I CAN'T!

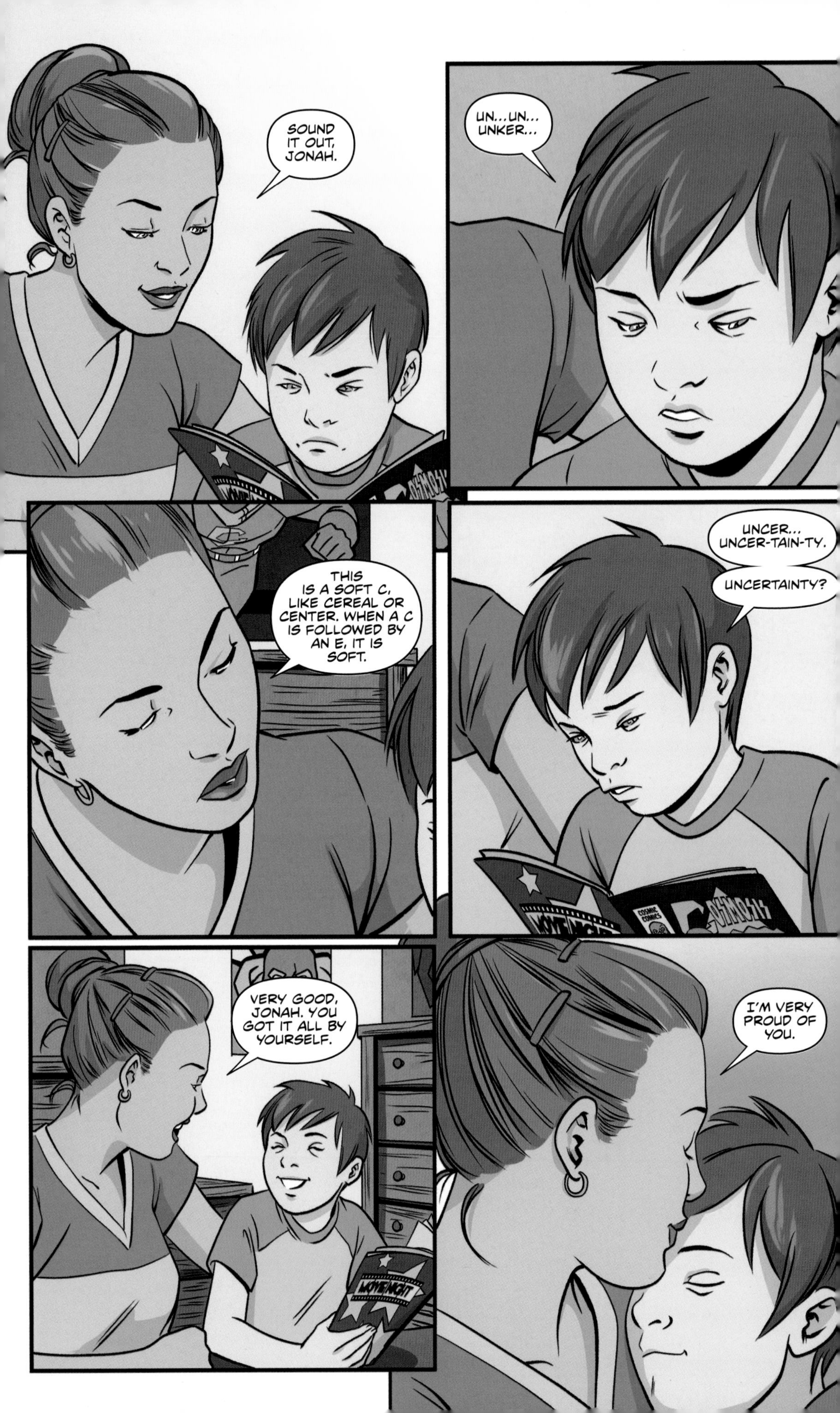

SOUND IT OUT, JONAH.
UN...UN... UNKER...
THIS IS A SOFT C, LIKE CEREAL OR CENTER. WHEN A C IS FOLLOWED BY AN E, IT IS SOFT.
UNCER... UNCER-TAIN-TY.
UNCERTAINTY?
VERY GOOD, JONAH. YOU GOT IT ALL BY YOURSELF.
I'M VERY PROUD OF YOU.

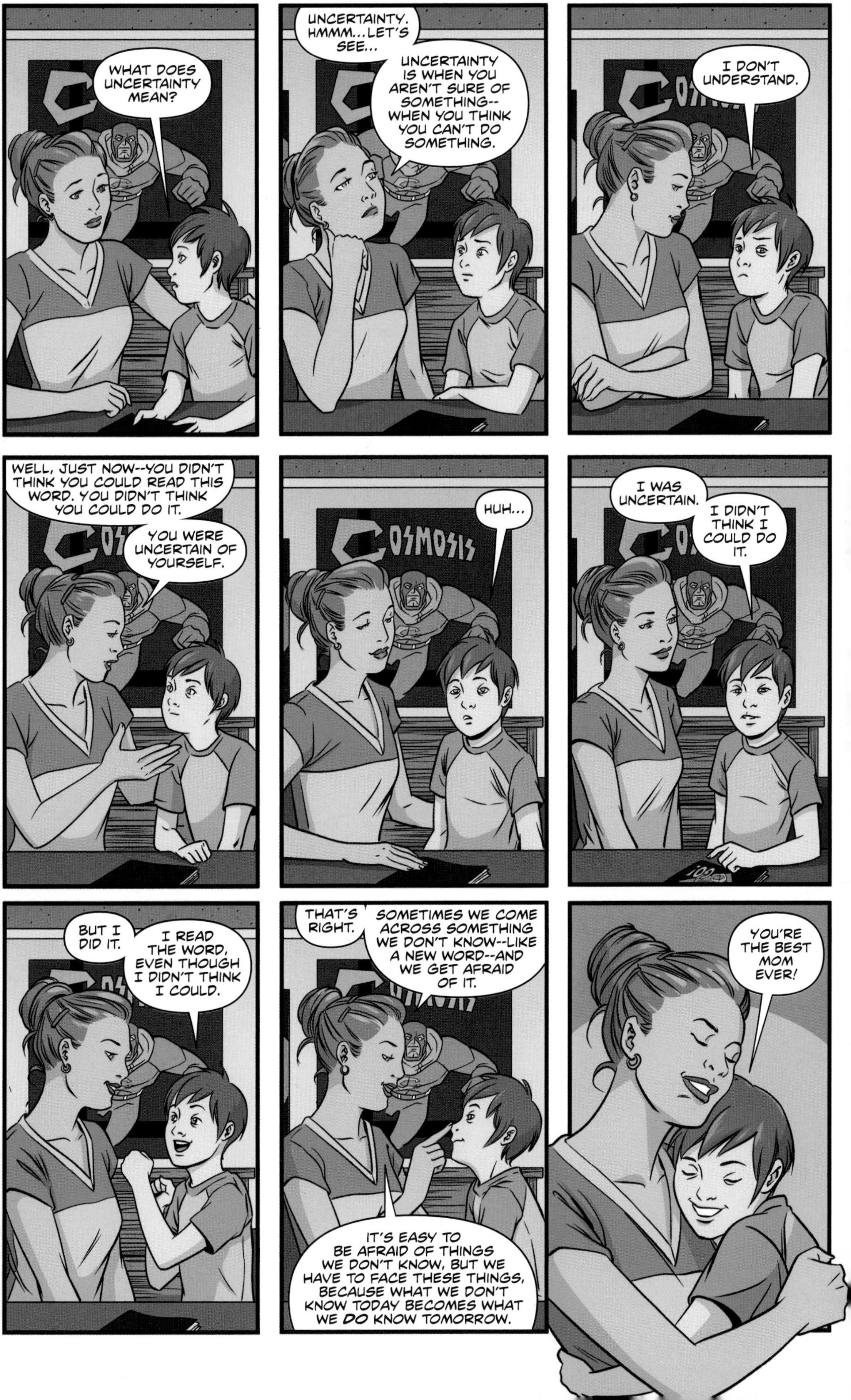
WHAT DOES UNCERTAINTY MEAN?
UNCERTAINTY. HMMM...LET'S SEE...
UNCERTAINTY IS WHEN YOU AREN'T SURE OF SOMETHING-- WHEN YOU THINK YOU CAN'T DO SOMETHING.
I DON'T UNDERSTAND.
WELL, JUST NOW--YOU DIDN'T THINK YOU COULD READ THIS WORD. YOU DIDN'T THINK YOU COULD DO IT.
YOU WERE UNCERTAIN OF YOURSELF.
COSMOSIS
HUH...
I WAS UNCERTAIN.
I DIDN'T THINK I COULD DO IT.
BUT I DID IT.
I READ THE WORD, EVEN THOUGH I DIDN'T THINK I COULD.
THAT'S RIGHT.
SOMETIMES WE COME ACROSS SOMETHING WE DON'T KNOW--LIKE A NEW WORD--AND WE GET AFRAID OF IT.
IT'S EASY TO BE AFRAID OF THINGS WE DON'T KNOW, BUT WE HAVE TO FACE THESE THINGS, BECAUSE WHAT WE DON'T KNOW TODAY BECOMES WHAT WE *DO* KNOW TOMORROW.
YOU'RE THE BEST MOM EVER!

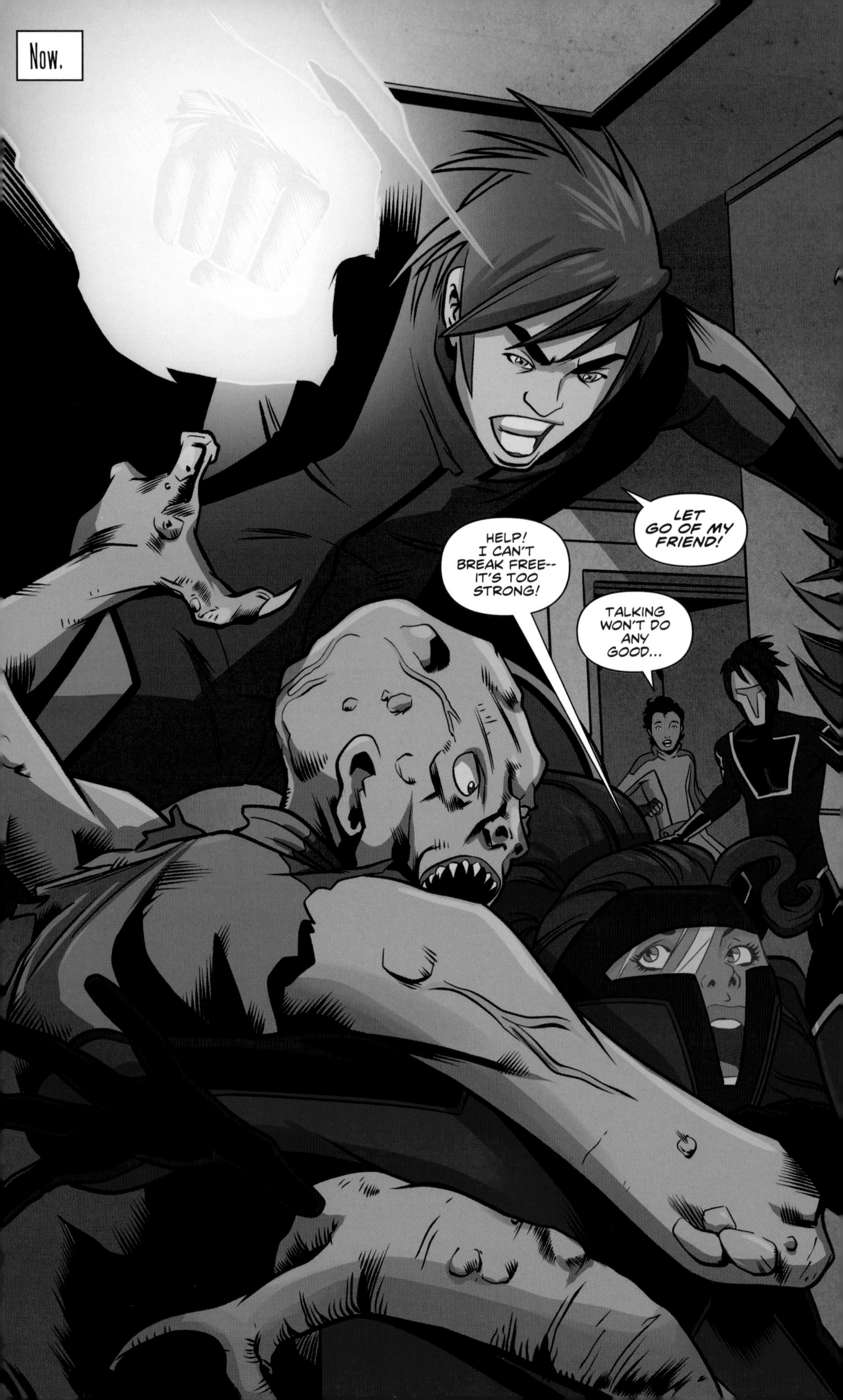
Now.
HELP! I CAN'T BREAK FREE-- IT'S TOO STRONG!
LET GO OF MY FRIEND!
TALKING WON'T DO ANY GOOD...

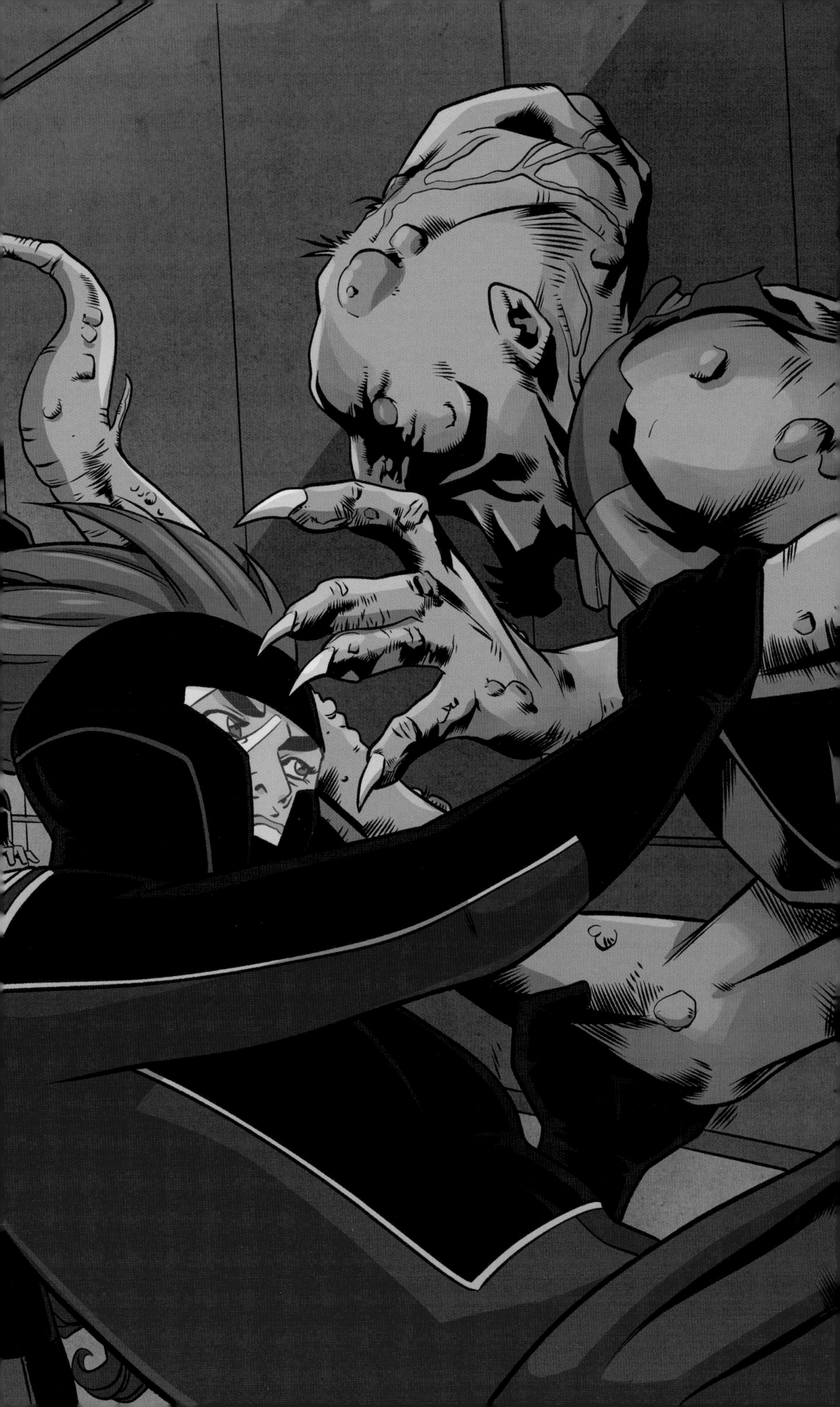

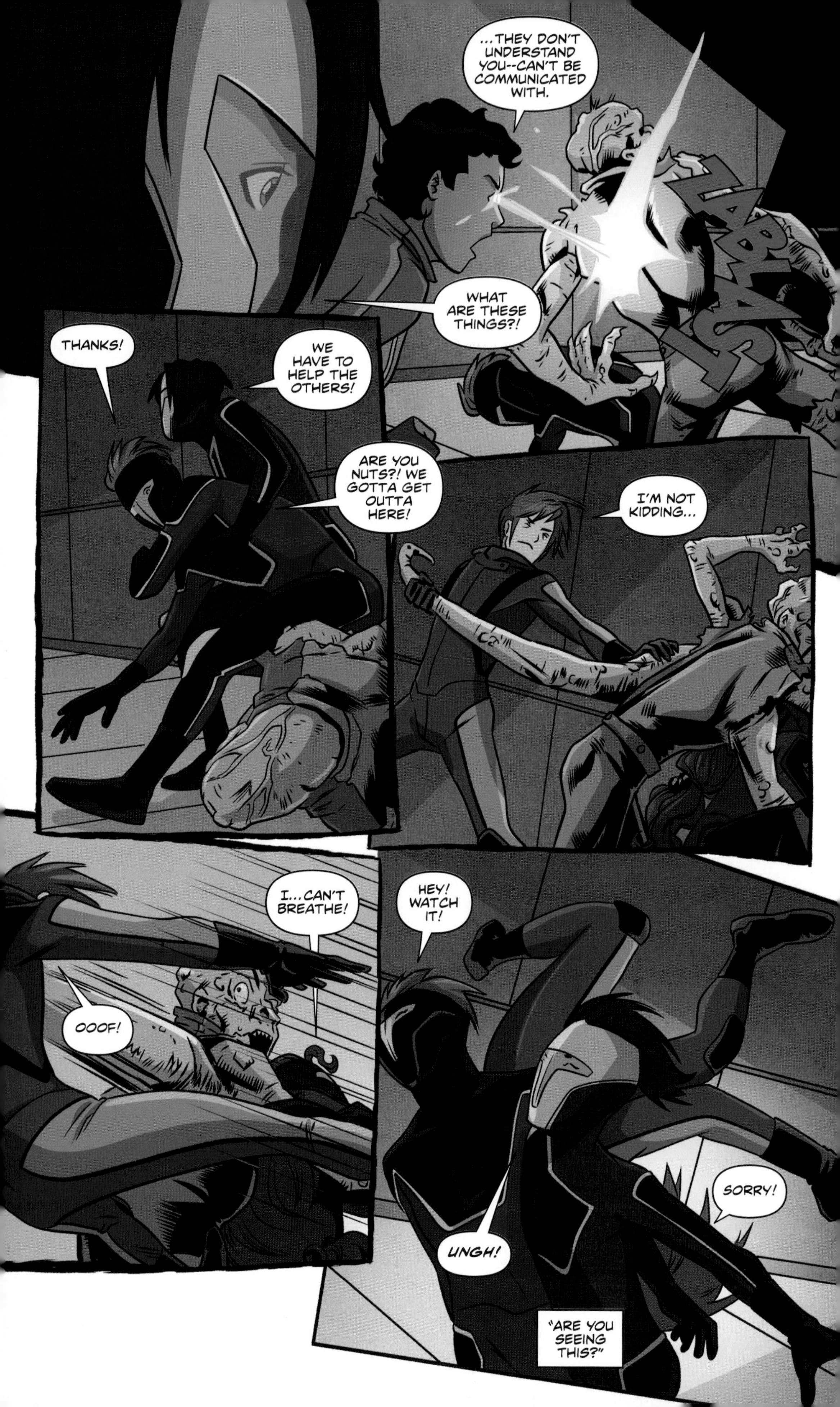
...THEY DON'T UNDERSTAND YOU--CAN'T BE COMMUNICATED WITH.
ZABLAST
WHAT ARE THESE THINGS?!
THANKS!
WE HAVE TO HELP THE OTHERS!
ARE YOU NUTS?! WE GOTTA GET OUTTA HERE!
I'M NOT KIDDING...
I...CAN'T BREATHE!
OOOF!
HEY! WATCH IT!
SORRY!
UNGH!
"ARE YOU SEEING THIS?"

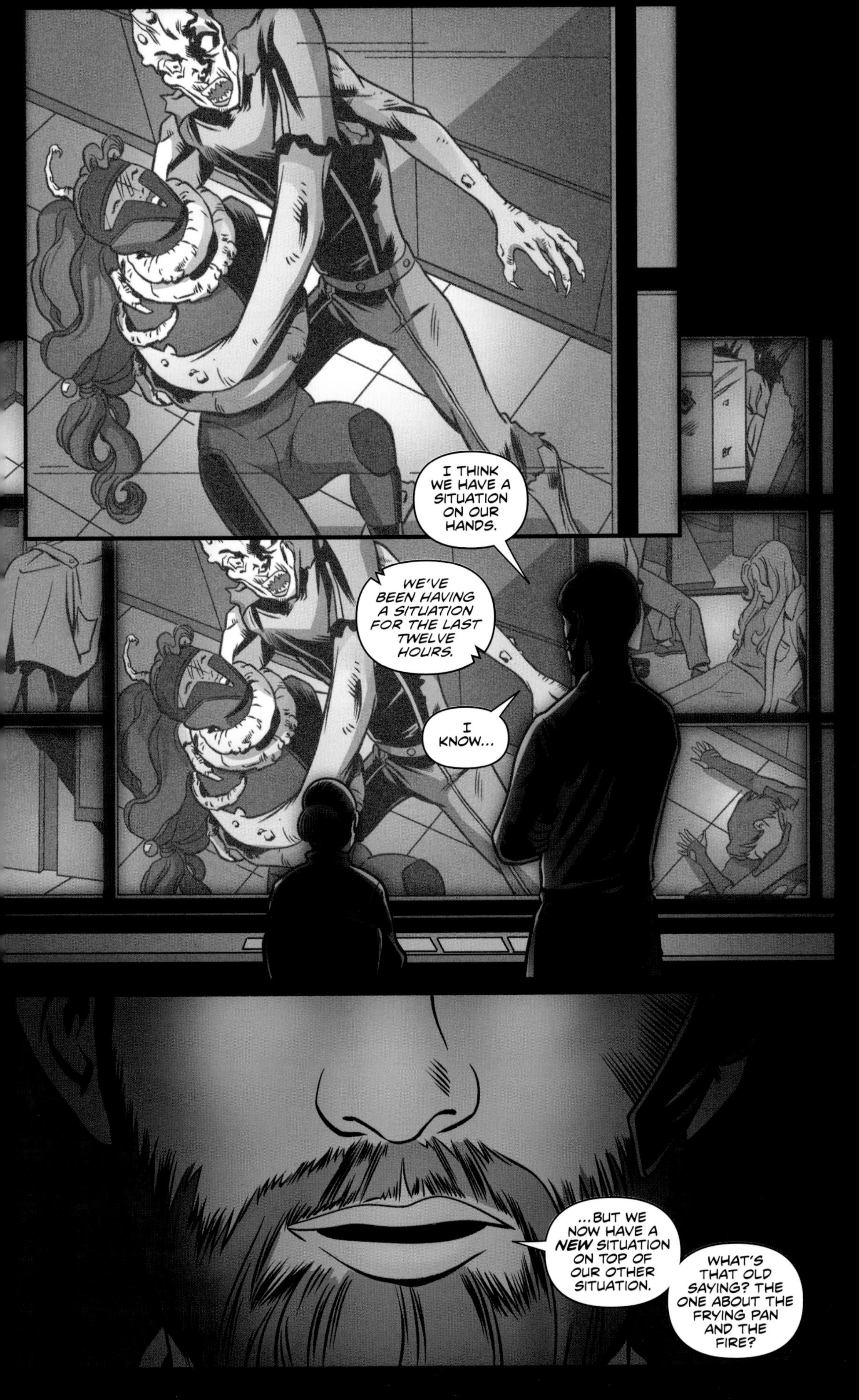
I THINK WE HAVE A SITUATION ON OUR HANDS.
WE'VE BEEN HAVING A SITUATION FOR THE LAST TWELVE HOURS.
I KNOW...
...BUT WE NOW HAVE A ***NEW*** SITUATION ON TOP OF OUR OTHER SITUATION.
WHAT'S THAT OLD SAYING? THE ONE ABOUT THE FRYING PAN AND THE FIRE?

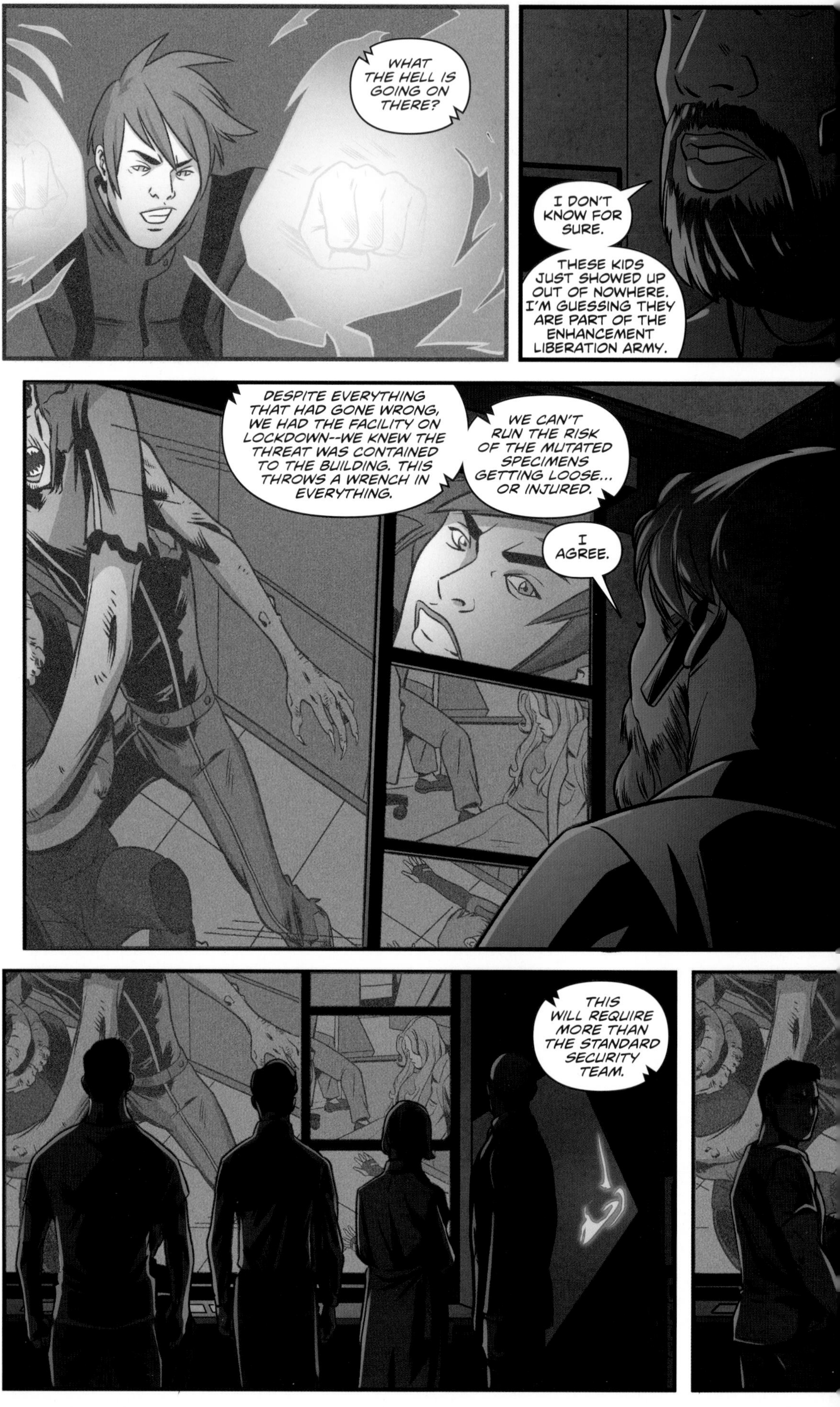
WHAT THE HELL IS GOING ON THERE?
I DON'T KNOW FOR SURE.
THESE KIDS JUST SHOWED UP OUT OF NOWHERE. I'M GUESSING THEY ARE PART OF THE ENHANCEMENT LIBERATION ARMY.
DESPITE EVERYTHING THAT HAD GONE WRONG, WE HAD THE FACILITY ON LOCKDOWN--WE KNEW THE THREAT WAS CONTAINED TO THE BUILDING. THIS THROWS A WRENCH IN EVERYTHING.
WE CAN'T RUN THE RISK OF THE MUTATED SPECIMENS GETTING LOOSE... OR INJURED.
I AGREE.
THIS WILL REQUIRE MORE THAN THE STANDARD SECURITY TEAM.

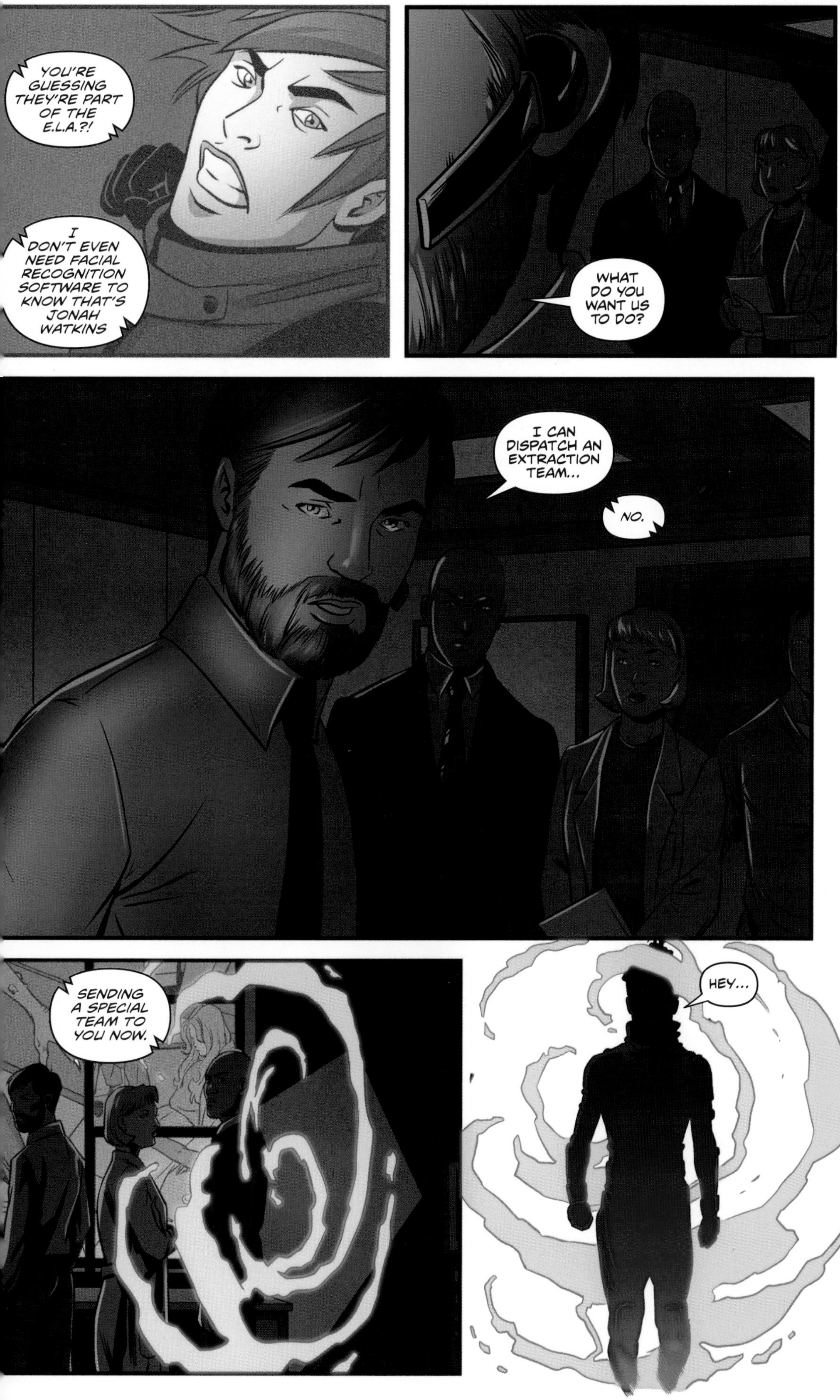
YOU'RE GUESSING THEY'RE PART OF THE E.L.A.?!
I DON'T EVEN NEED FACIAL RECOGNITION SOFTWARE TO KNOW THAT'S JONAH WATKINS
WHAT DO YOU WANT US TO DO?
I CAN DISPATCH AN EXTRACTION TEAM...
NO.
SENDING A SPECIAL TEAM TO YOU NOW.
HEY...

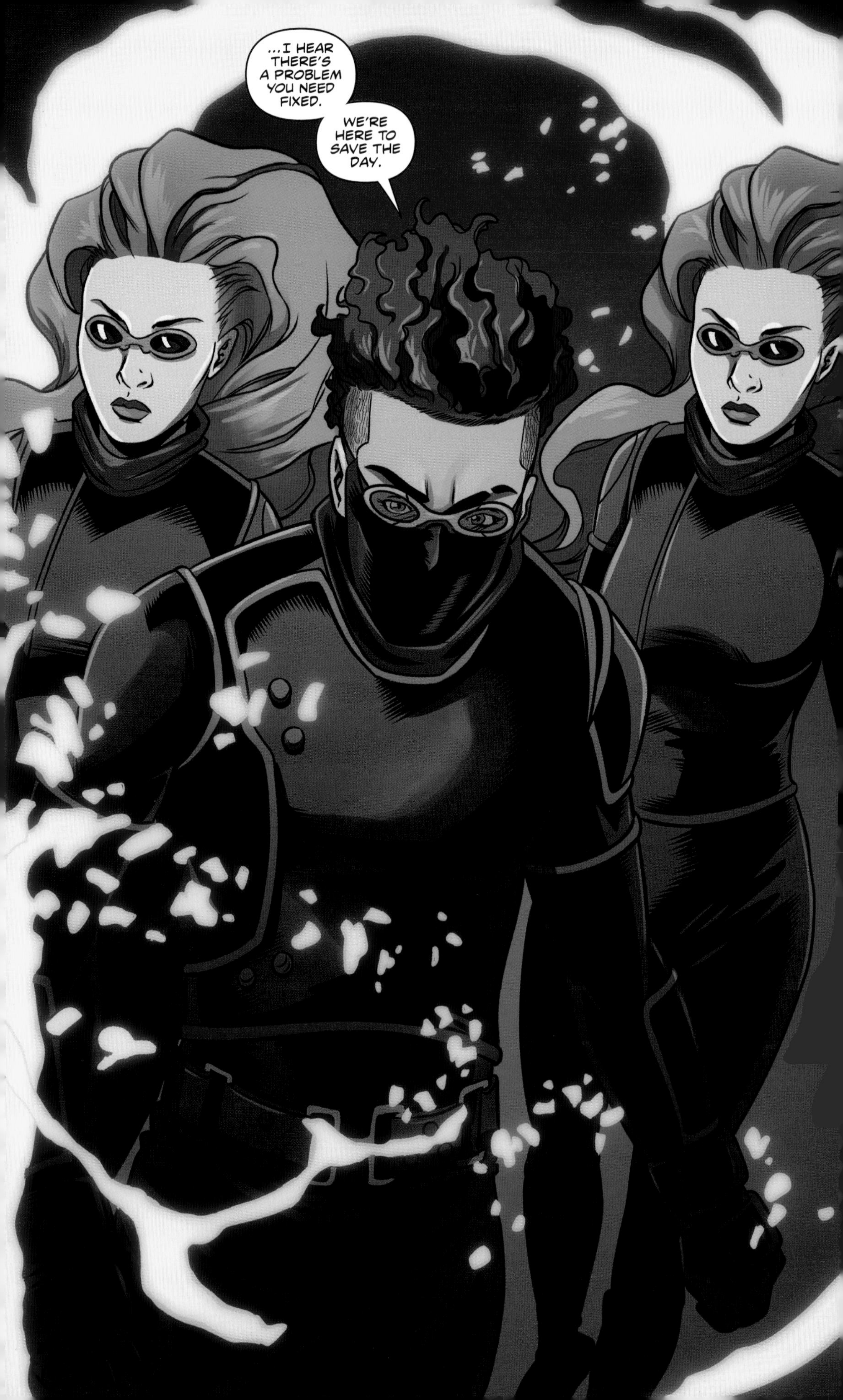
...I HEAR THERE'S A PROBLEM YOU NEED FIXED.
WE'RE HERE TO SAVE THE DAY.

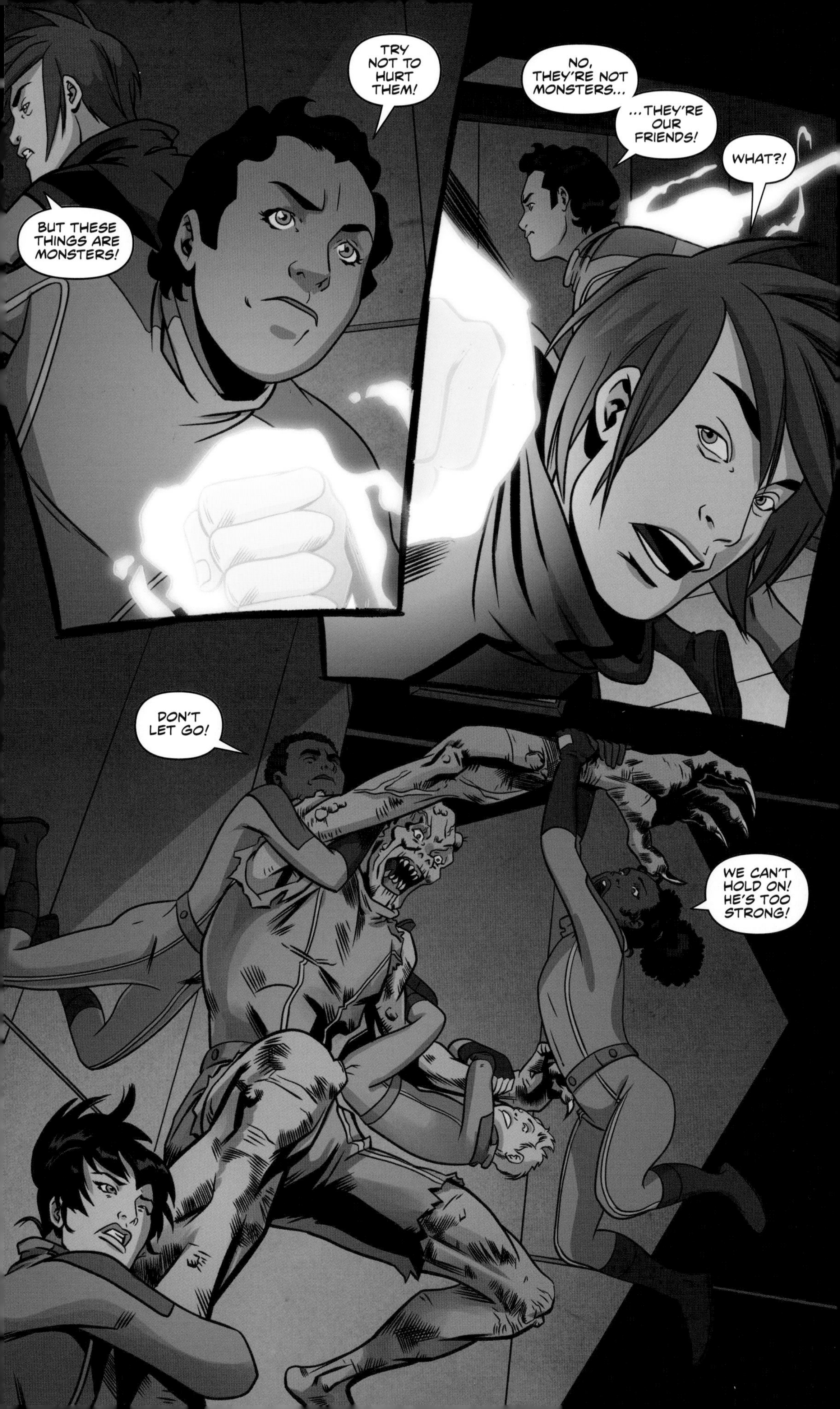
BUT THESE THINGS ARE MONSTERS!
TRY NOT TO HURT THEM!
NO, THEY'RE NOT MONSTERS...
...THEY'RE OUR FRIENDS!
WHAT?!
DON'T LET GO!
WE CAN'T HOLD ON! HE'S TOO STRONG!

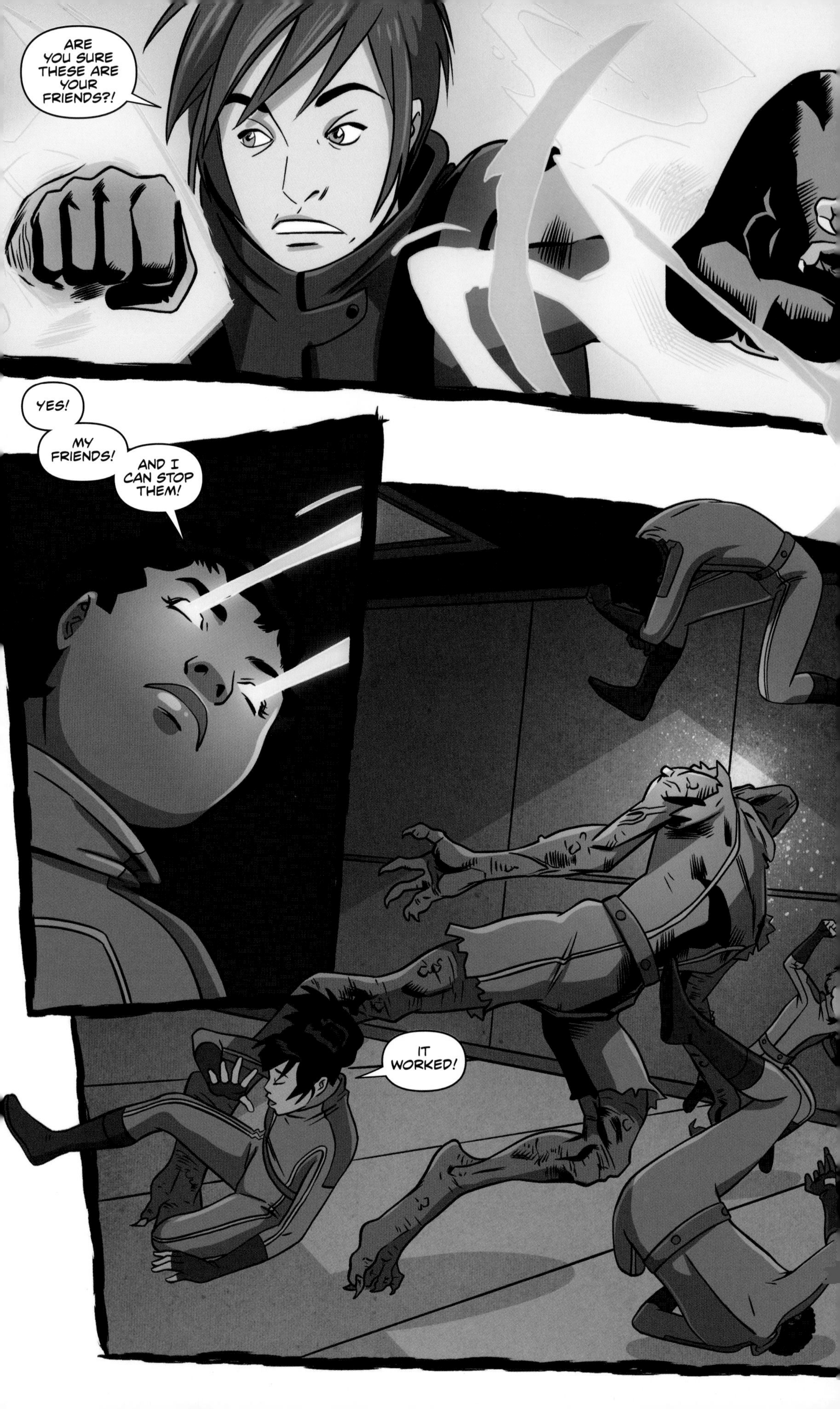
ARE YOU SURE THESE ARE YOUR FRIENDS?!
YES!
MY FRIENDS!
AND I CAN STOP THEM!
IT WORKED!

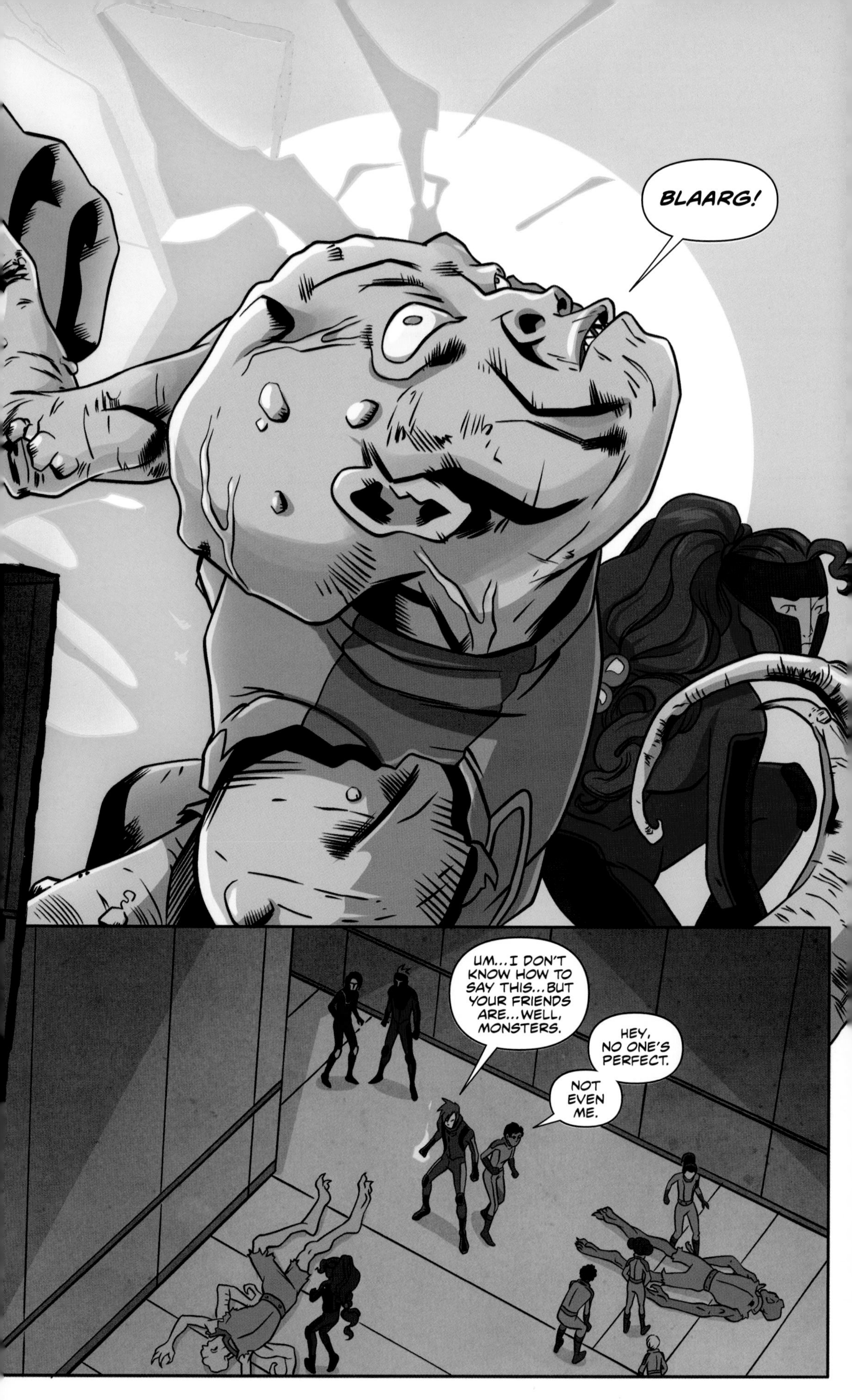
BLAARG!
UM...I DON'T KNOW HOW TO SAY THIS...BUT YOUR FRIENDS ARE...WELL, MONSTERS.
HEY, NO ONE'S PERFECT.
NOT EVEN ME.

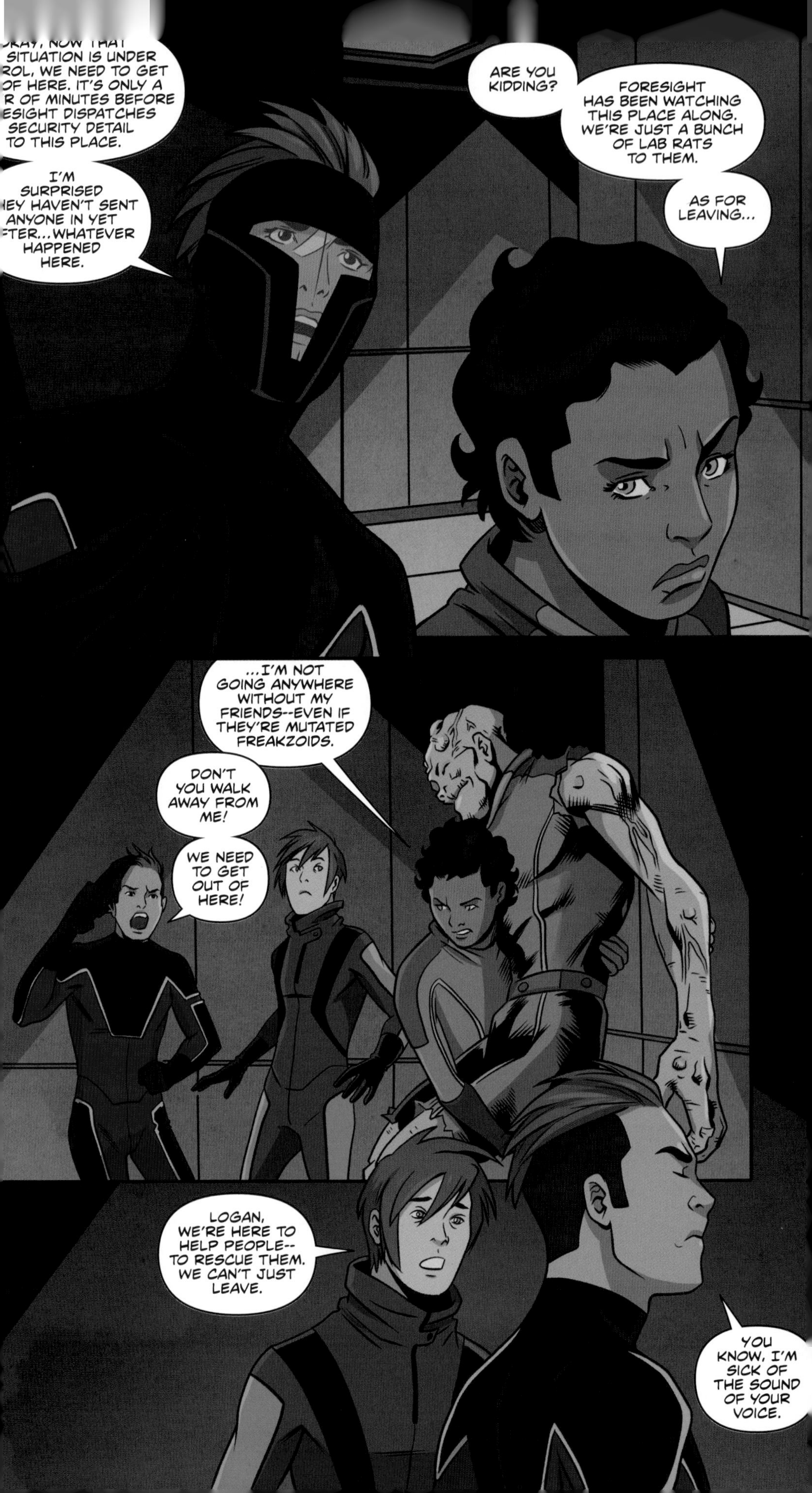

SITUATION IS UNDER
ROL, WE NEED TO GET
OF HERE. IT'S ONLY A
R OF MINUTES BEFORE
ESIGHT DISPATCHES
SECURITY DETAIL
TO THIS PLACE.
I'M SURPRISED
HEY HAVEN'T SENT ANYONE IN YET
FTER...WHATEVER HAPPENED HERE.
ARE YOU KIDDING?
FORESIGHT HAS BEEN WATCHING THIS PLACE ALONG. WE'RE JUST A BUNCH OF LAB RATS TO THEM.
AS FOR LEAVING...
...I'M NOT GOING ANYWHERE WITHOUT MY FRIENDS--EVEN IF THEY'RE MUTATED FREAKZOIDS.
DON'T YOU WALK AWAY FROM ME!
WE NEED TO GET OUT OF HERE!
LOGAN, WE'RE HERE TO HELP PEOPLE--TO RESCUE THEM. WE CAN'T JUST LEAVE.
YOU KNOW, I'M SICK OF THE SOUND OF YOUR VOICE.

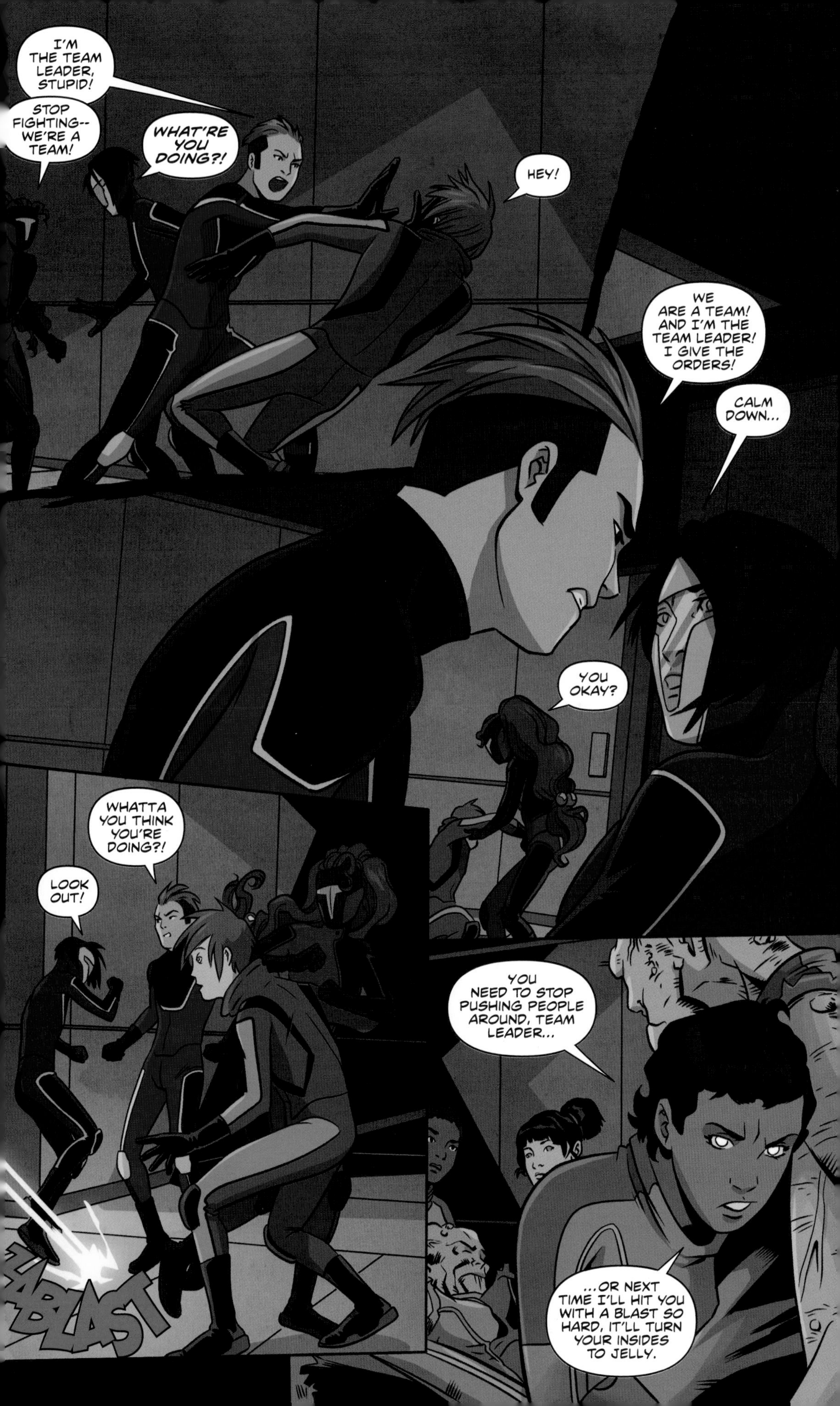

I'M THE TEAM LEADER, STUPID!
STOP FIGHTING-- WE'RE A TEAM!
WHAT'RE YOU DOING?!
HEY!
WE ARE A TEAM! AND I'M THE TEAM LEADER! I GIVE THE ORDERS!
CALM DOWN...
YOU OKAY?
WHATTA YOU THINK YOU'RE DOING?!
LOOK OUT!
ZABLAST
YOU NEED TO STOP PUSHING PEOPLE AROUND, TEAM LEADER...
...OR NEXT TIME I'LL HIT YOU WITH A BLAST SO HARD, IT'LL TURN YOUR INSIDES TO JELLY.

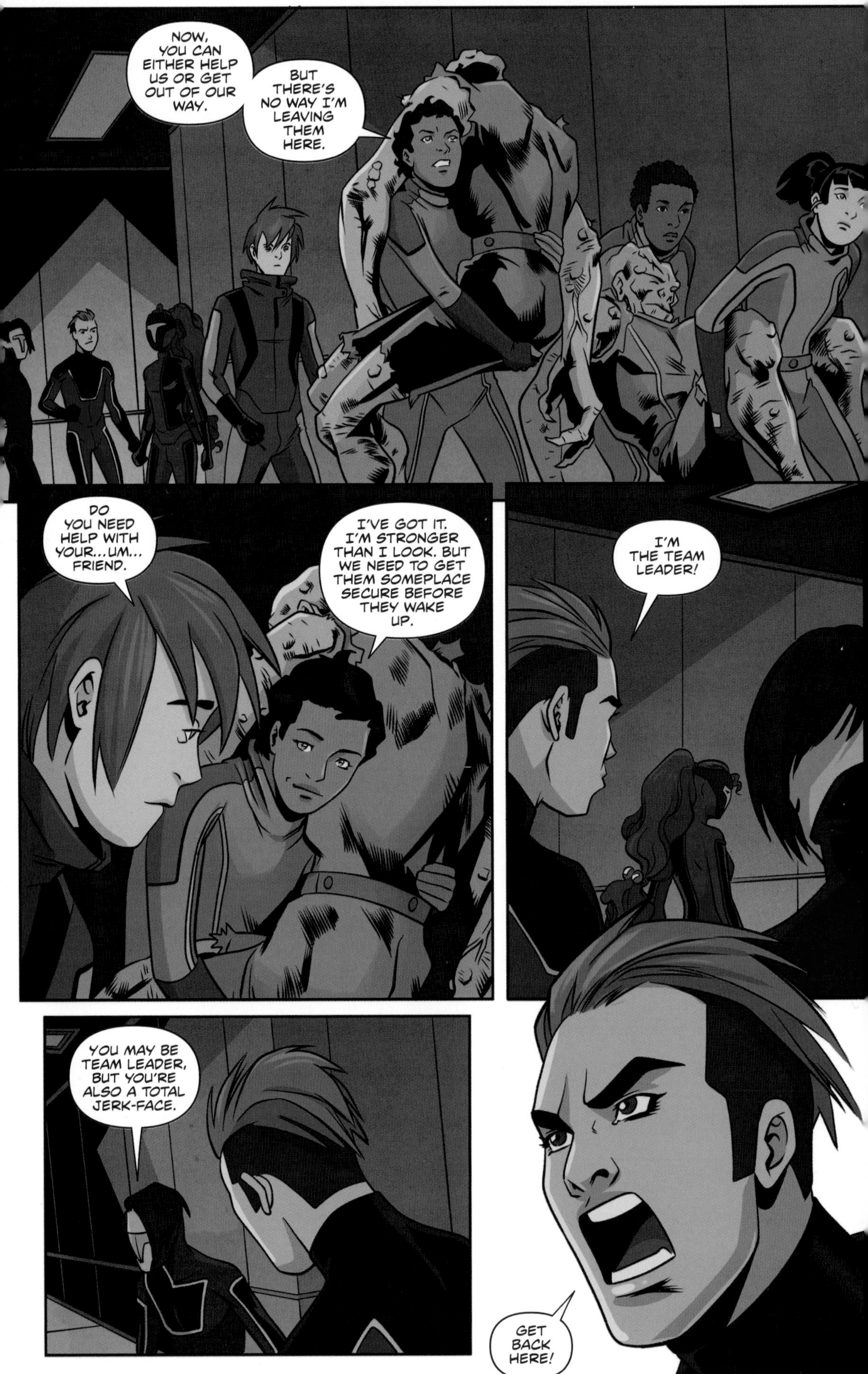
NOW, YOU CAN EITHER HELP US OR GET OUT OF OUR WAY.
BUT THERE'S NO WAY I'M LEAVING THEM HERE.
DO YOU NEED HELP WITH YOUR...UM... FRIEND.
I'VE GOT IT. I'M STRONGER THAN I LOOK. BUT WE NEED TO GET THEM SOMEPLACE SECURE BEFORE THEY WAKE UP.
I'M THE TEAM LEADER!
YOU MAY BE TEAM LEADER, BUT YOU'RE ALSO A TOTAL JERK-FACE.
GET BACK HERE!

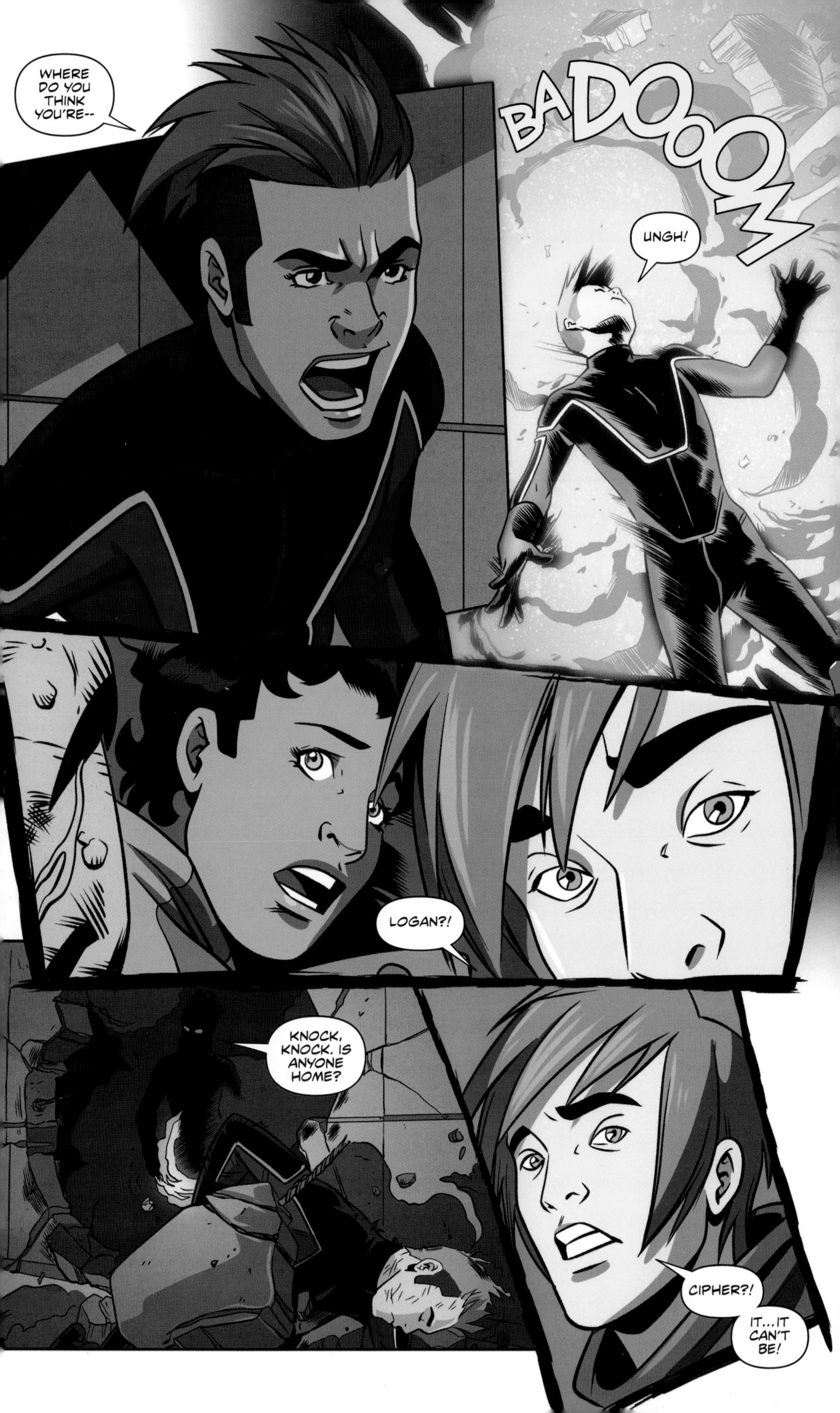
WHERE DO YOU THINK YOU'RE--
BADOOOOM
UNGH!
LOGAN?!
KNOCK, KNOCK. IS ANYONE HOME?
CIPHER?!
IT...IT CAN'T BE!

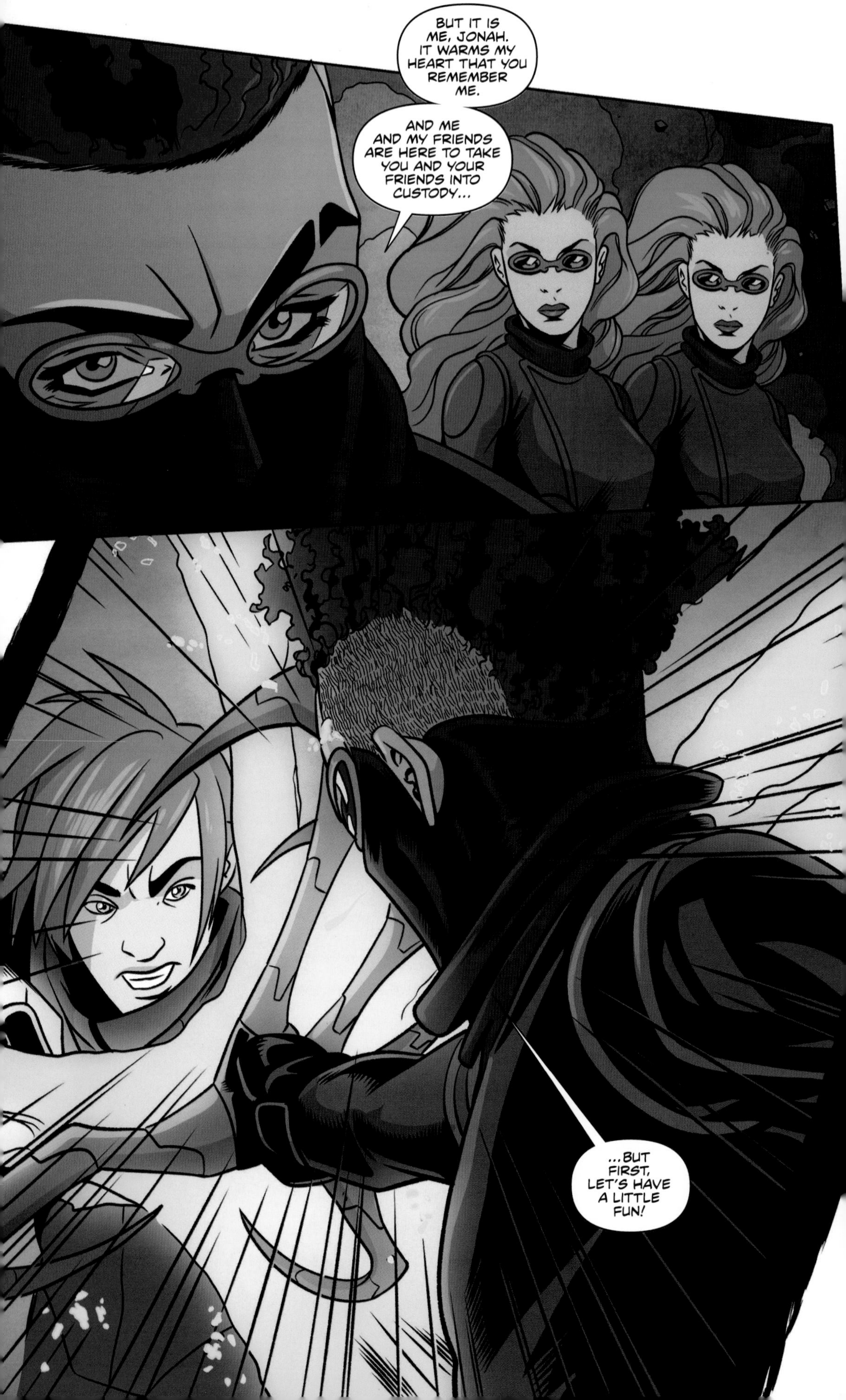
BUT IT IS ME, JONAH. IT WARMS MY HEART THAT YOU REMEMBER ME.
AND ME AND MY FRIENDS ARE HERE TO TAKE YOU AND YOUR FRIENDS INTO CUSTODY...
...BUT FIRST, LET'S HAVE A LITTLE FUN!

CHAPTER THREE

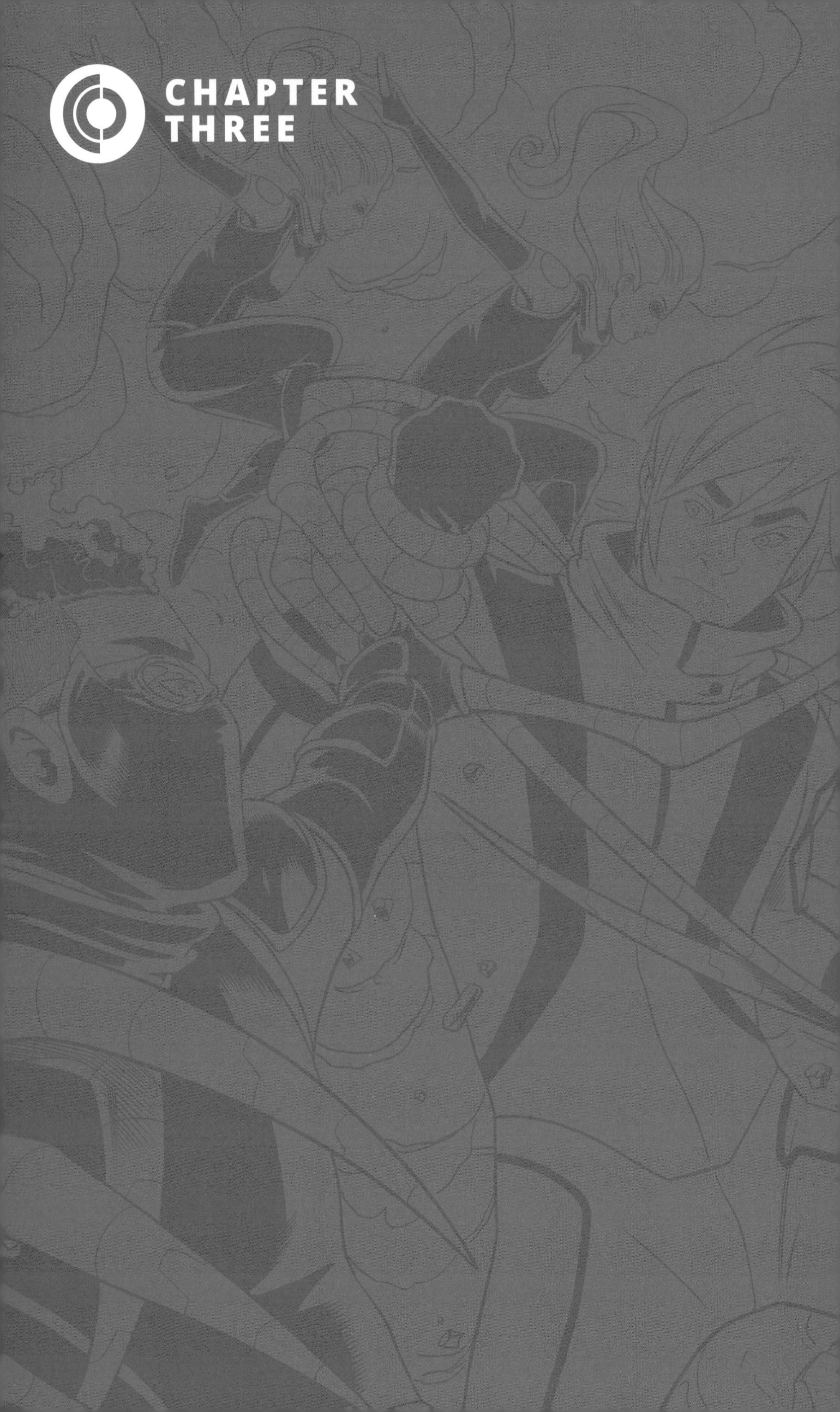

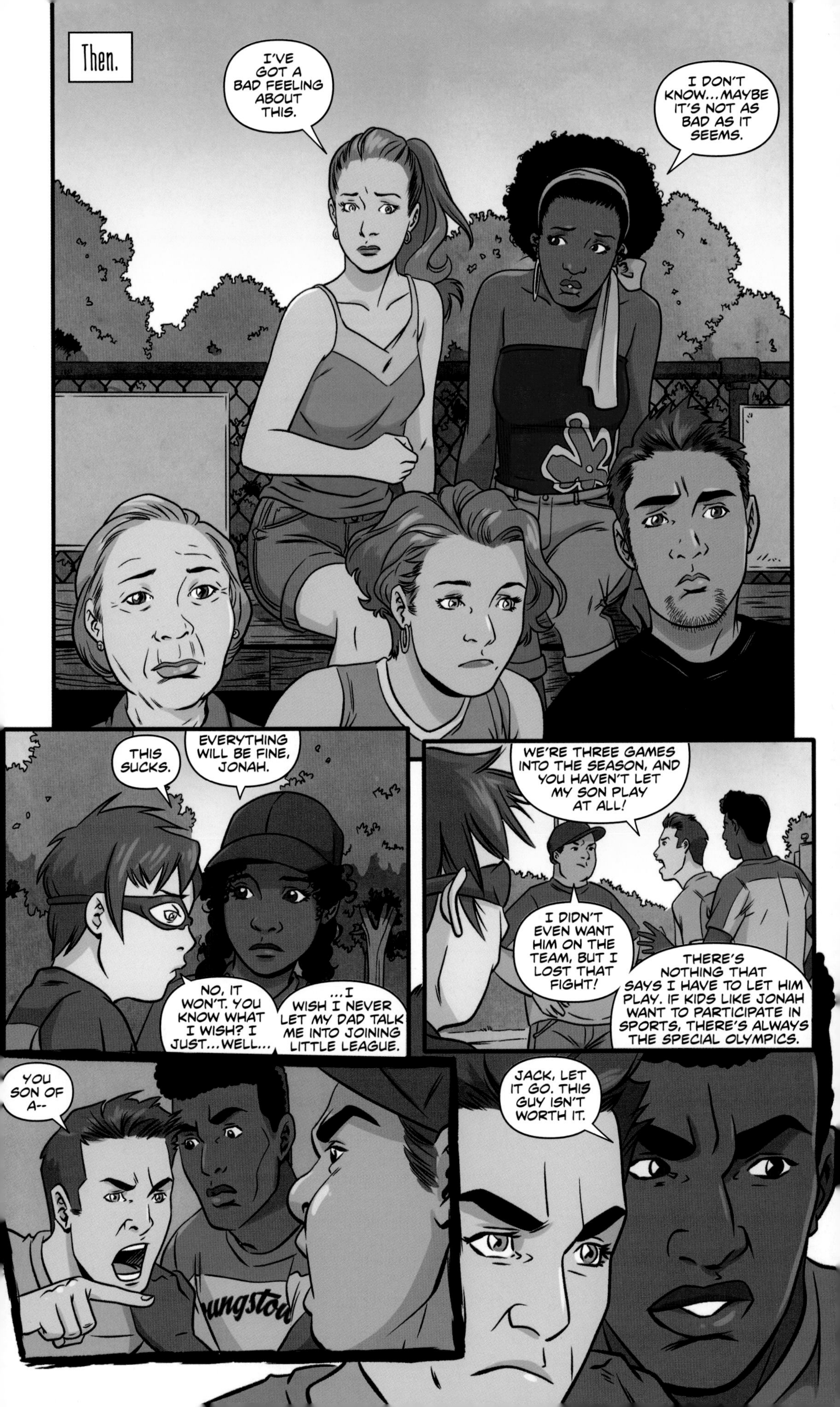
Then.
I'VE GOT A BAD FEELING ABOUT THIS.
I DON'T KNOW...MAYBE IT'S NOT AS BAD AS IT SEEMS.
THIS SUCKS.
EVERYTHING WILL BE FINE, JONAH.
NO, IT WON'T. YOU KNOW WHAT I WISH? I JUST...WELL...
...I WISH I NEVER LET MY DAD TALK ME INTO JOINING LITTLE LEAGUE.
WE'RE THREE GAMES INTO THE SEASON, AND YOU HAVEN'T LET MY SON PLAY AT ALL!
I DIDN'T EVEN WANT HIM ON THE TEAM, BUT I LOST THAT FIGHT!
THERE'S NOTHING THAT SAYS I HAVE TO LET HIM PLAY. IF KIDS LIKE JONAH WANT TO PARTICIPATE IN SPORTS, THERE'S ALWAYS THE SPECIAL OLYMPICS.
YOU SON OF A--
JACK, LET IT GO. THIS GUY ISN'T WORTH IT.

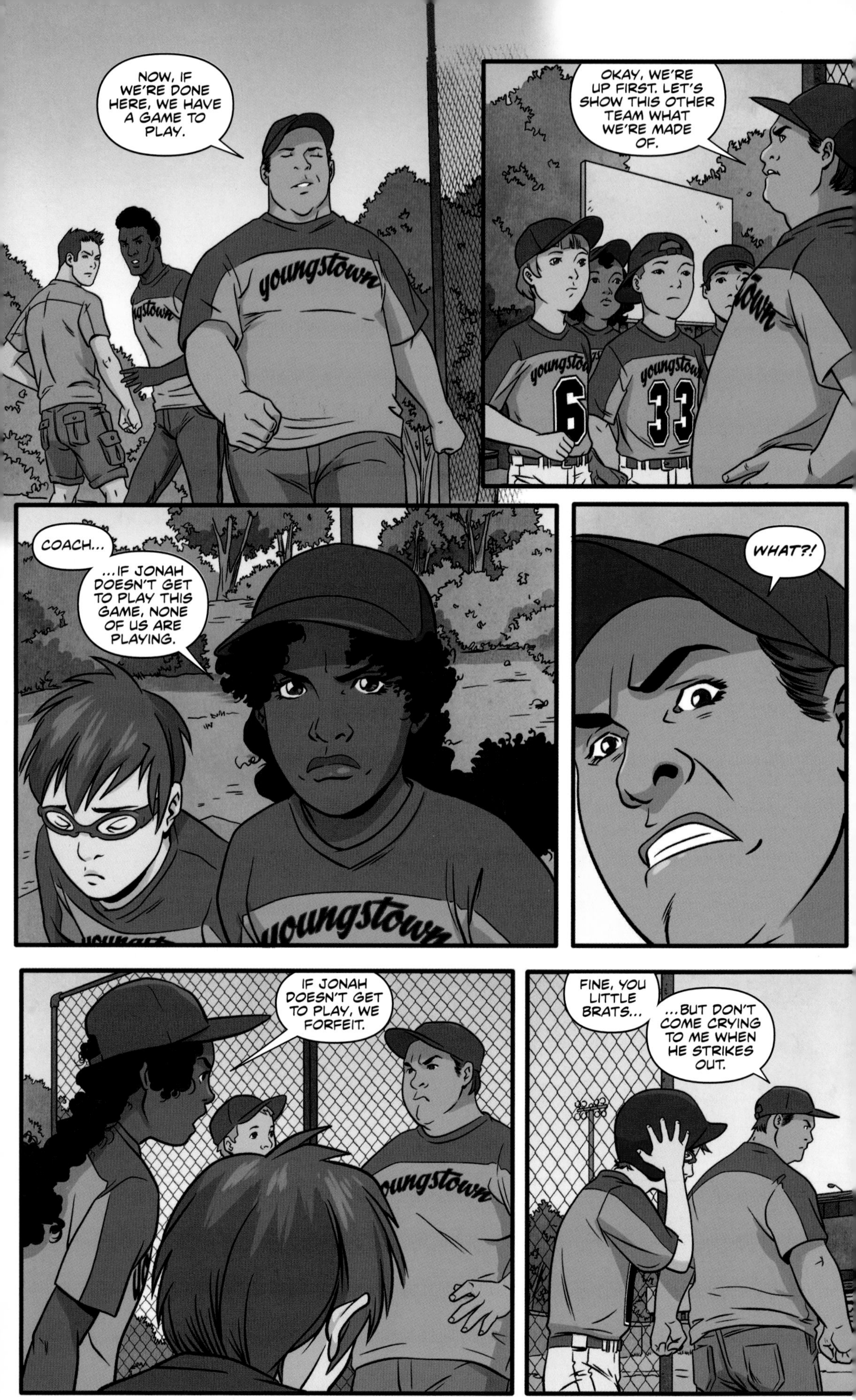
NOW, IF WE'RE DONE HERE, WE HAVE A GAME TO PLAY.
OKAY, WE'RE UP FIRST. LET'S SHOW THIS OTHER TEAM WHAT WE'RE MADE OF.
COACH...
...IF JONAH DOESN'T GET TO PLAY THIS GAME, NONE OF US ARE PLAYING.
WHAT?!
IF JONAH DOESN'T GET TO PLAY, WE FORFEIT.
FINE, YOU LITTLE BRATS...
...BUT DON'T COME CRYING TO ME WHEN HE STRIKES OUT.

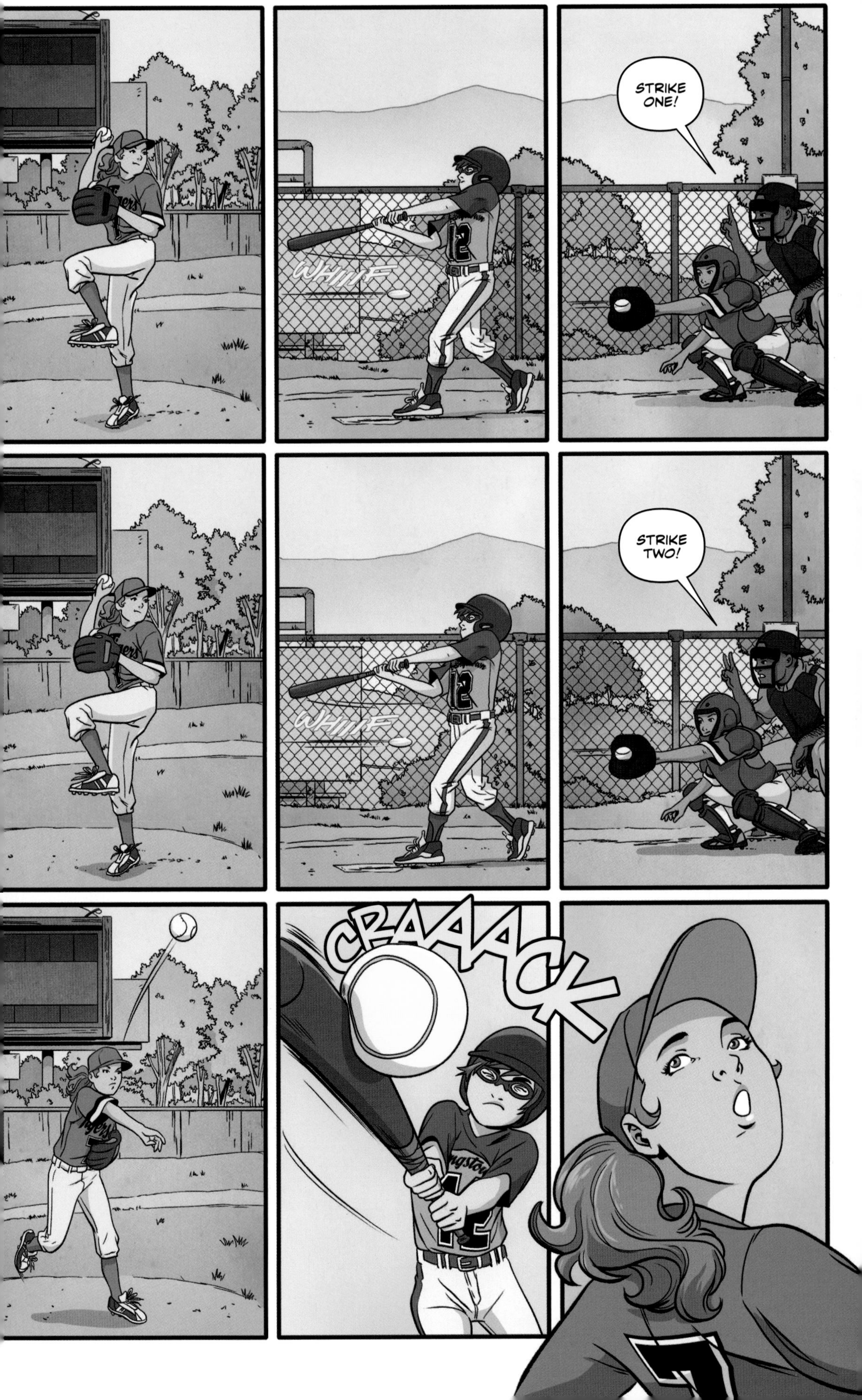
WHIIIF
STRIKE ONE!
WHIIIF
STRIKE TWO!
CRAAACK

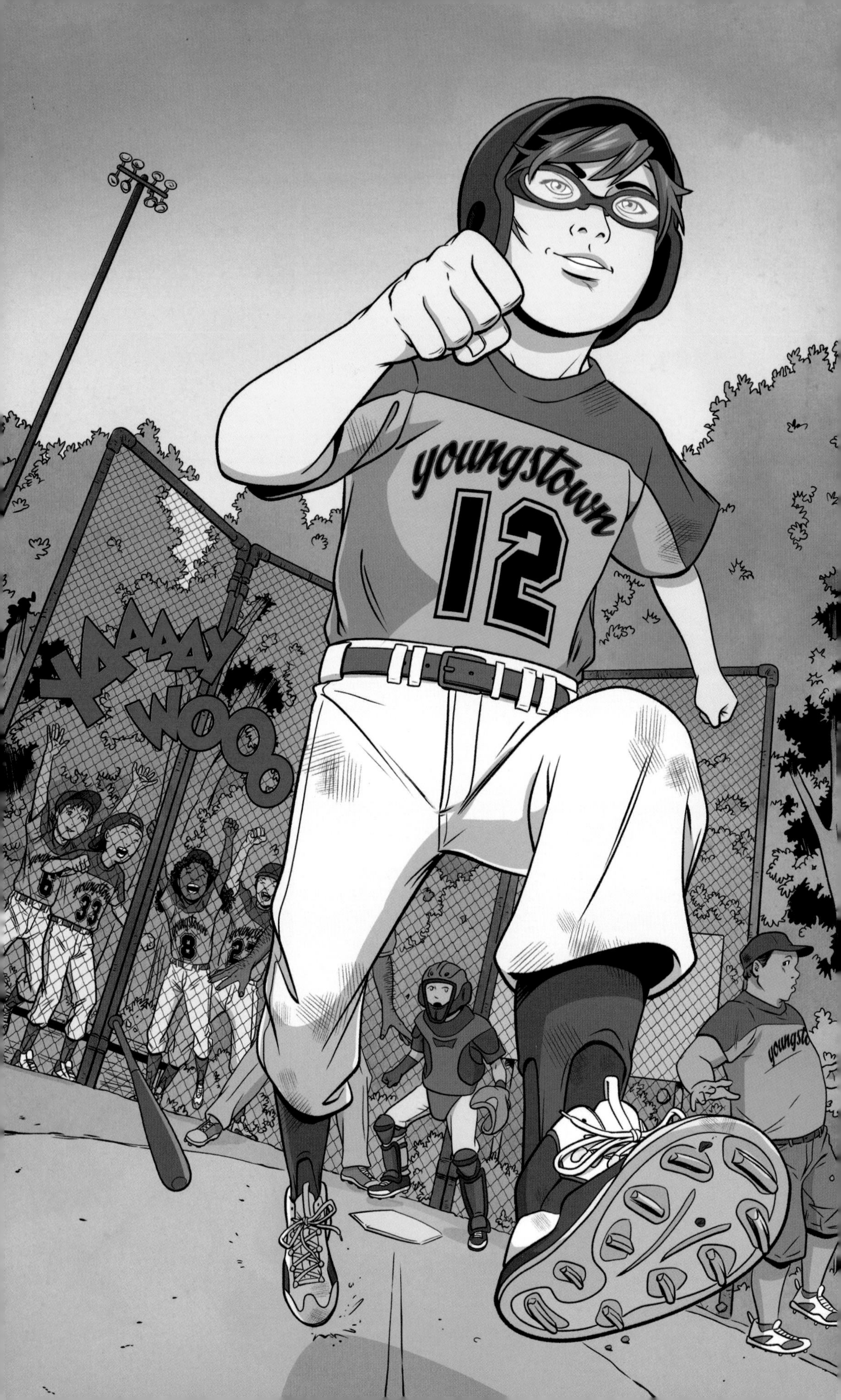
YAAAAY
WOOO
youngstown
12

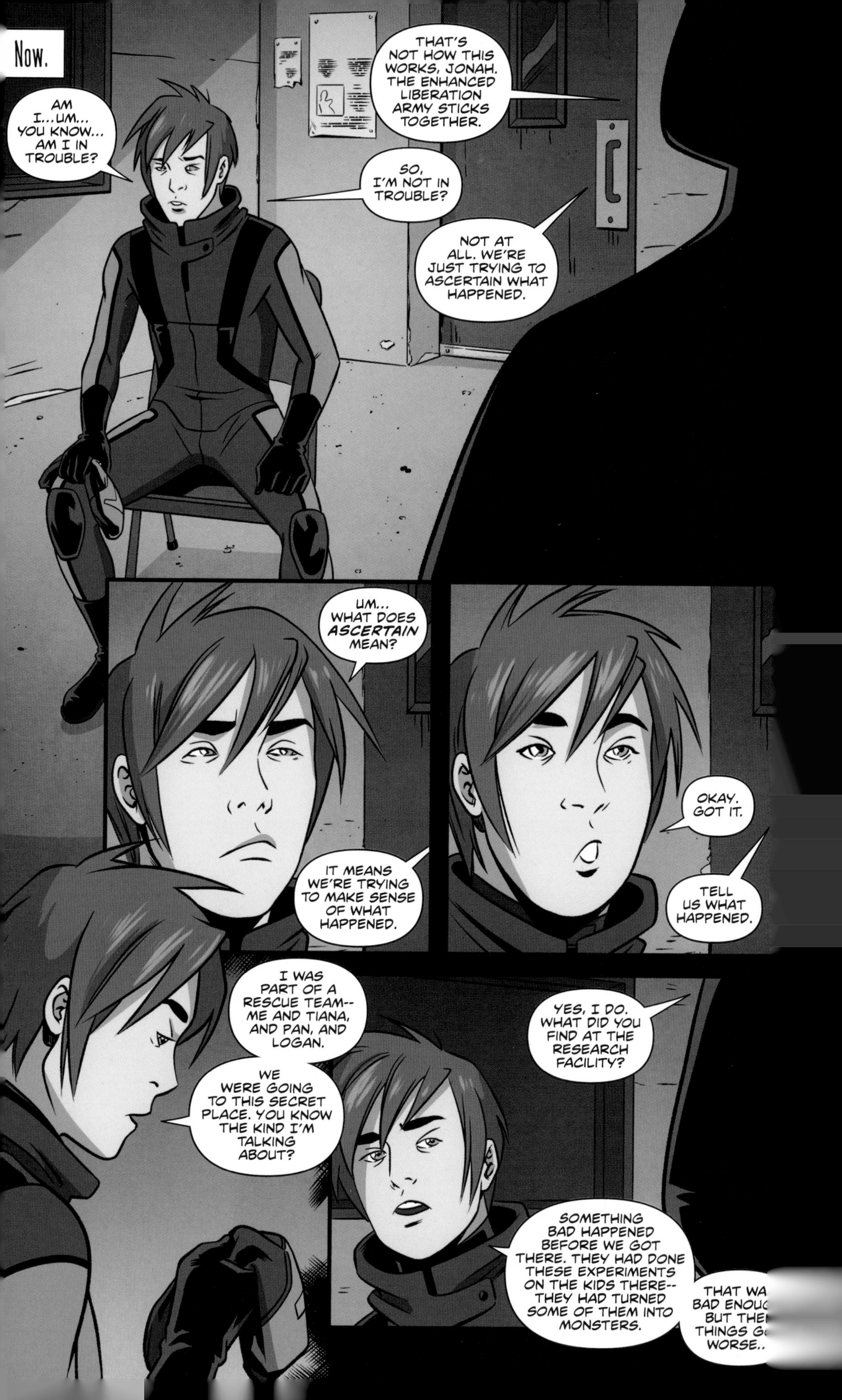
Now.
AM I...UM... YOU KNOW... AM I IN TROUBLE?
THAT'S NOT HOW THIS WORKS, JONAH. THE ENHANCED LIBERATION ARMY STICKS TOGETHER.
SO, I'M NOT IN TROUBLE?
NOT AT ALL. WE'RE JUST TRYING TO ASCERTAIN WHAT HAPPENED.
UM... WHAT DOES *ASCERTAIN* MEAN?
IT MEANS WE'RE TRYING TO MAKE SENSE OF WHAT HAPPENED.
OKAY. GOT IT.
TELL US WHAT HAPPENED.
I WAS PART OF A RESCUE TEAM-- ME AND TIANA, AND PAN, AND LOGAN.
WE WERE GOING TO THIS SECRET PLACE. YOU KNOW THE KIND I'M TALKING ABOUT?
YES, I DO. WHAT DID YOU FIND AT THE RESEARCH FACILITY?
SOMETHING BAD HAPPENED BEFORE WE GOT THERE. THEY HAD DONE THESE EXPERIMENTS ON THE KIDS THERE-- THEY HAD TURNED SOME OF THEM INTO MONSTERS.

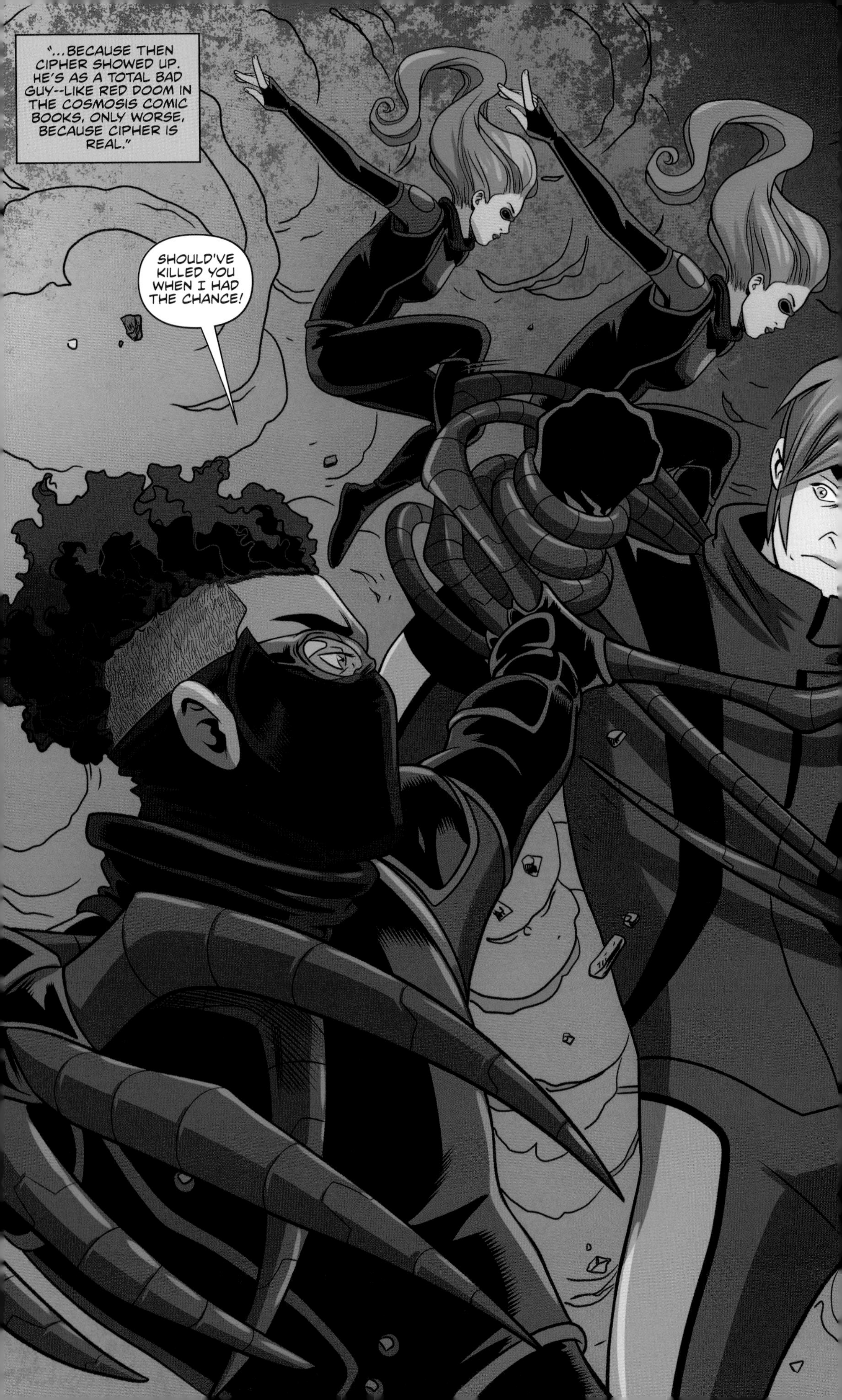
"...BECAUSE THEN CIPHER SHOWED UP. HE'S AS A TOTAL BAD GUY--LIKE RED DOOM IN THE COSMOSIS COMIC BOOKS, ONLY WORSE, BECAUSE CIPHER IS REAL."
SHOULD'VE KILLED YOU WHEN I HAD THE CHANCE!

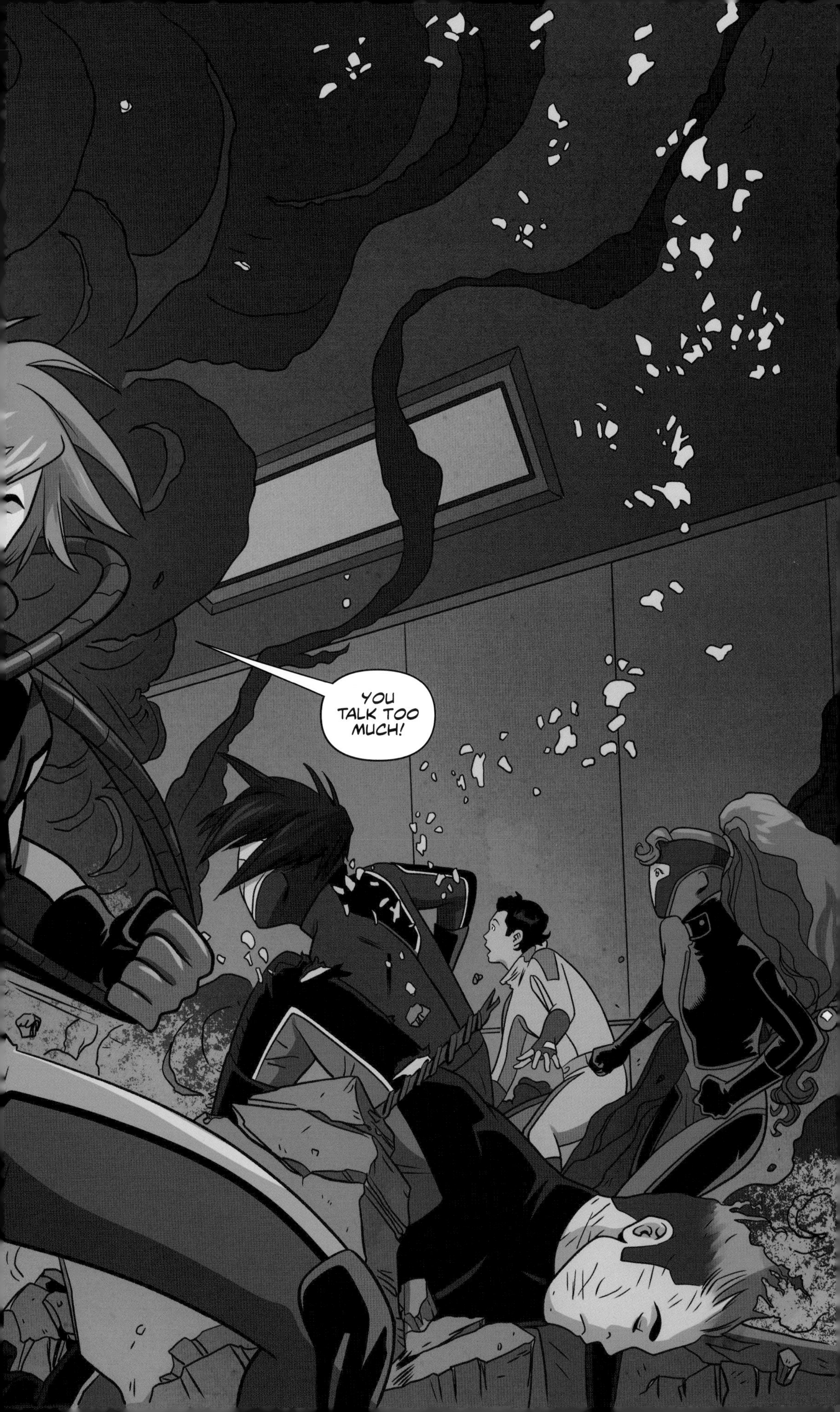
YOU TALK TOO MUCH!

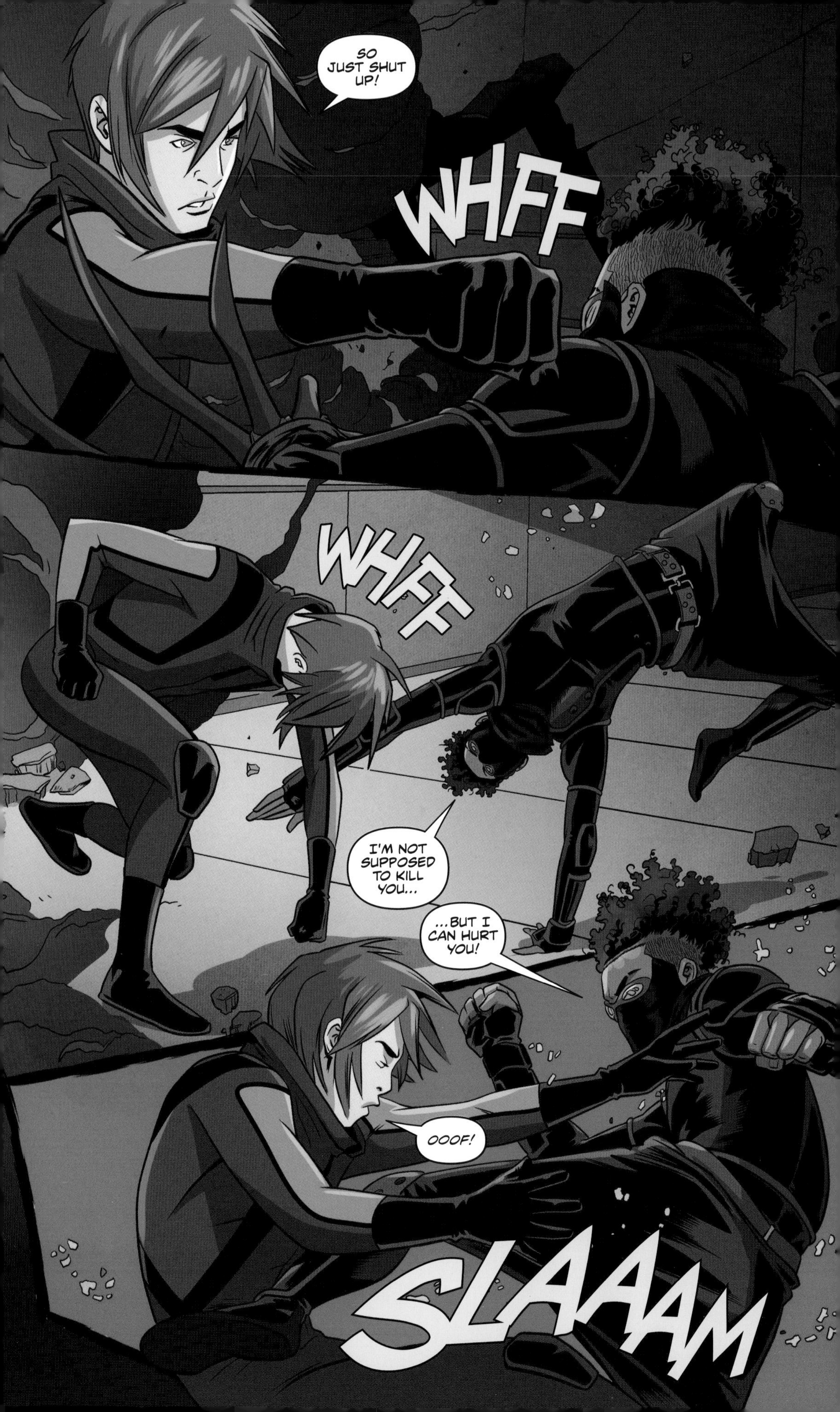
SO JUST SHUT UP!
WHFF
WHFF
I'M NOT SUPPOSED TO KILL YOU...
...BUT I CAN HURT YOU!
OOOF!
SLAAAM

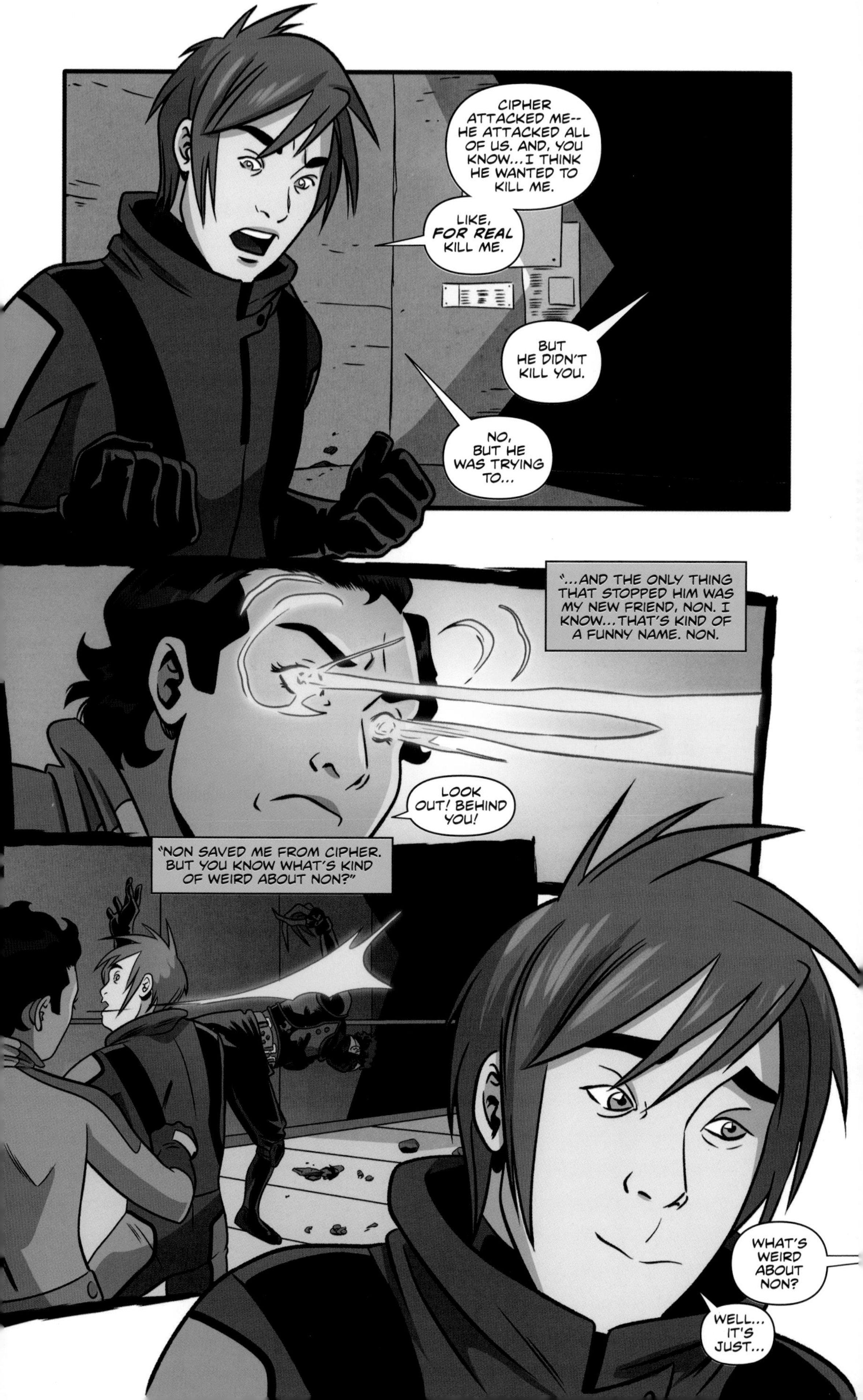
CIPHER ATTACKED ME-- HE ATTACKED ALL OF US. AND, YOU KNOW...I THINK HE WANTED TO KILL ME.
LIKE, FOR REAL KILL ME.
BUT HE DIDN'T KILL YOU.
NO, BUT HE WAS TRYING TO...
"...AND THE ONLY THING THAT STOPPED HIM WAS MY NEW FRIEND, NON. I KNOW...THAT'S KIND OF A FUNNY NAME. NON.
LOOK OUT! BEHIND YOU!
"NON SAVED ME FROM CIPHER. BUT YOU KNOW WHAT'S KIND OF WEIRD ABOUT NON?"
WHAT'S WEIRD ABOUT NON?
WELL... IT'S JUST...

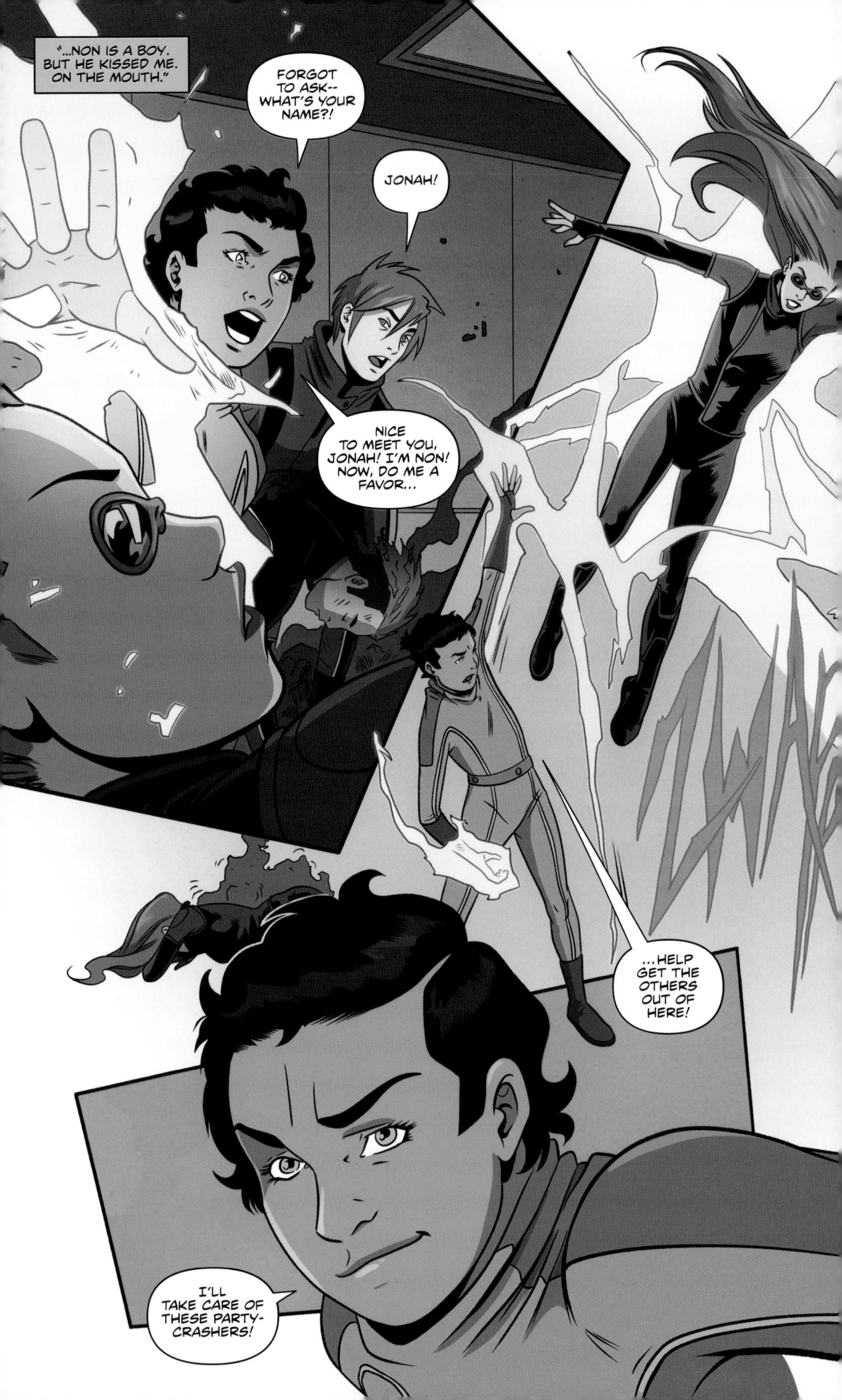
"...NON IS A BOY. BUT HE KISSED ME. ON THE MOUTH."
FORGOT TO ASK-- WHAT'S YOUR NAME?!
JONAH!
NICE TO MEET YOU, JONAH! I'M NON! NOW, DO ME A FAVOR...
...HELP GET THE OTHERS OUT OF HERE!
I'LL TAKE CARE OF THESE PARTY-CRASHERS!

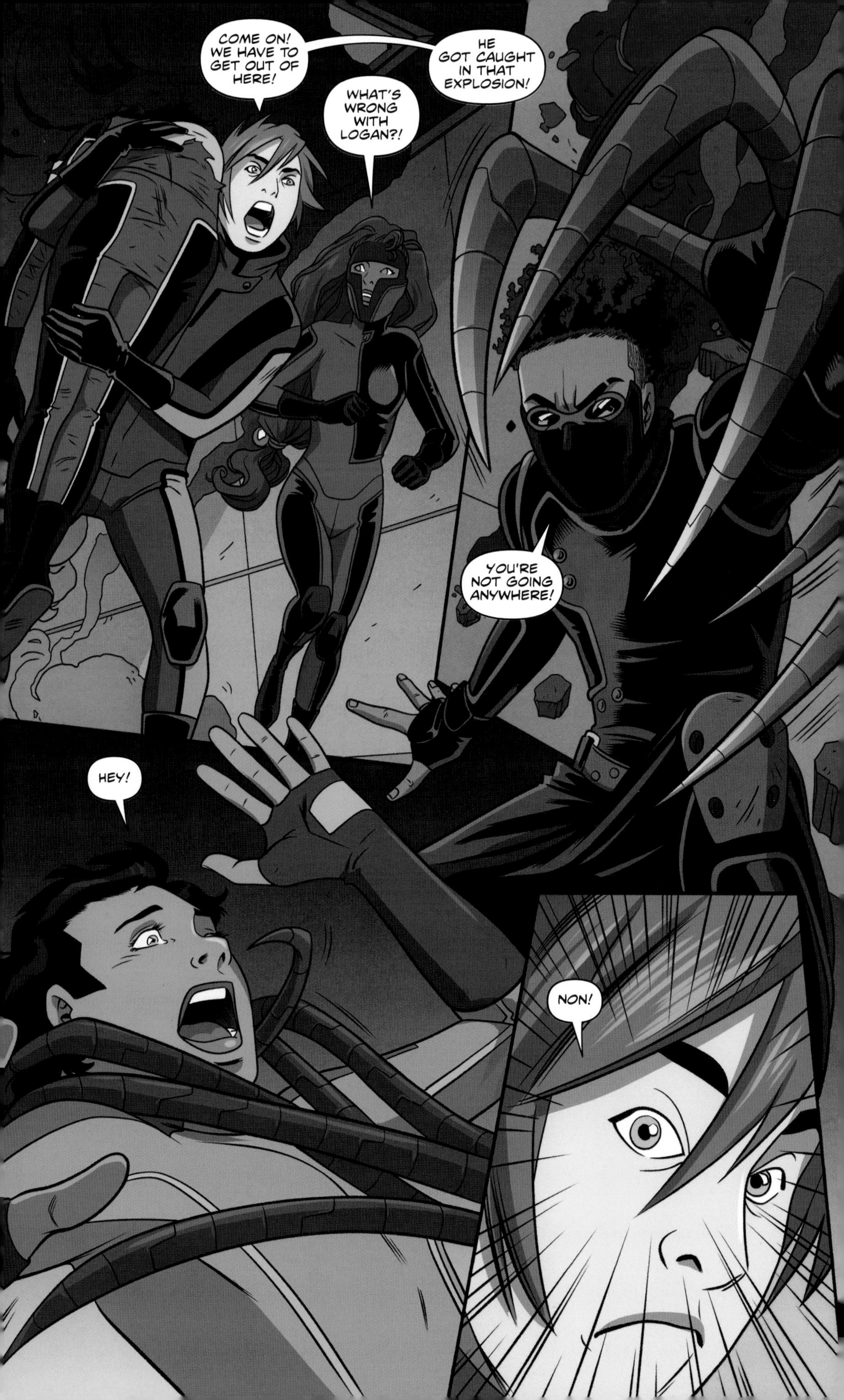
COME ON! WE HAVE TO GET OUT OF HERE!
HE GOT CAUGHT IN THAT EXPLOSION!
WHAT'S WRONG WITH LOGAN?!
YOU'RE NOT GOING ANYWHERE!
HEY!
NON!

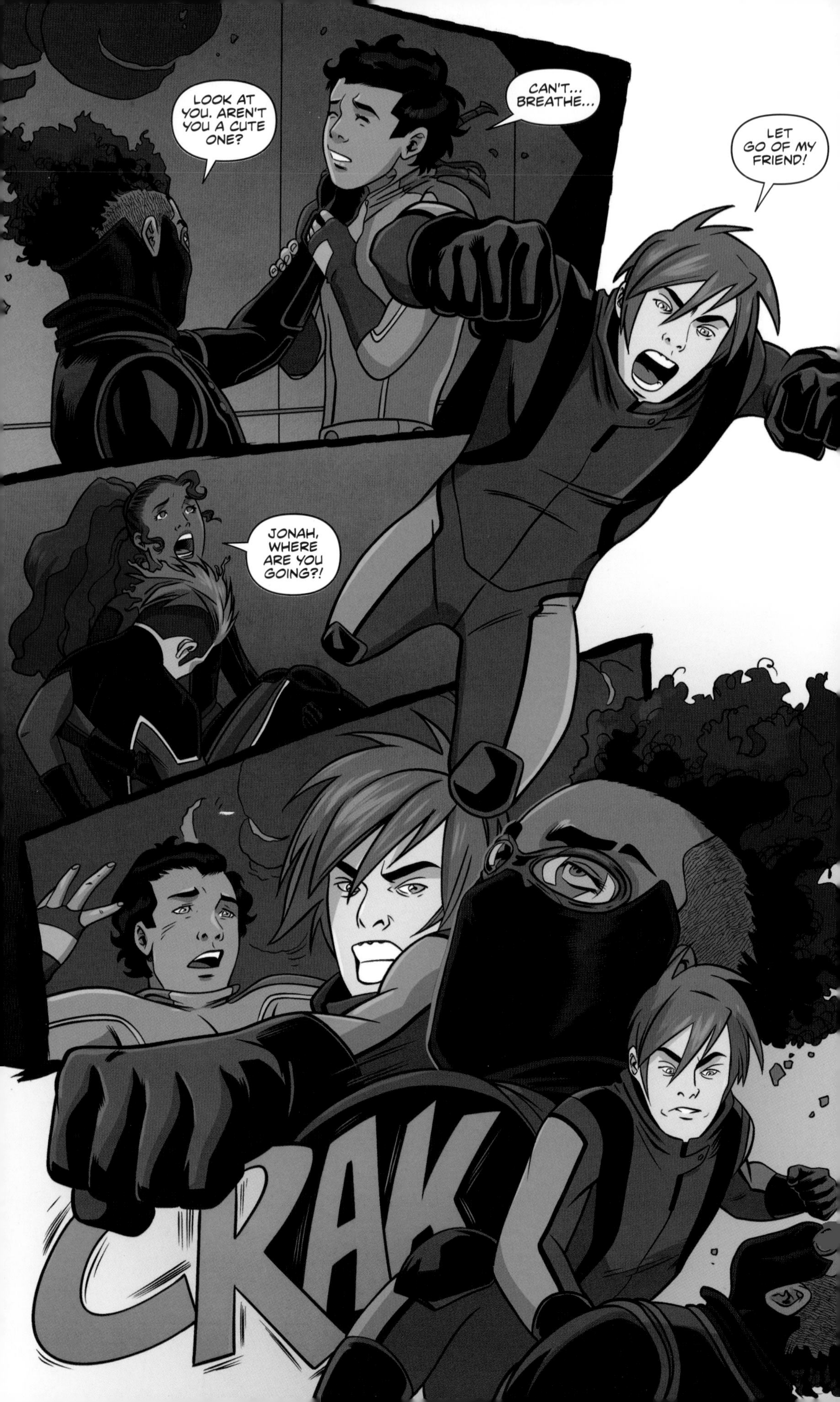
LOOK AT YOU. AREN'T YOU A CUTE ONE?
CAN'T... BREATHE...
LET GO OF MY FRIEND!
JONAH, WHERE ARE YOU GOING?!
CRAK!

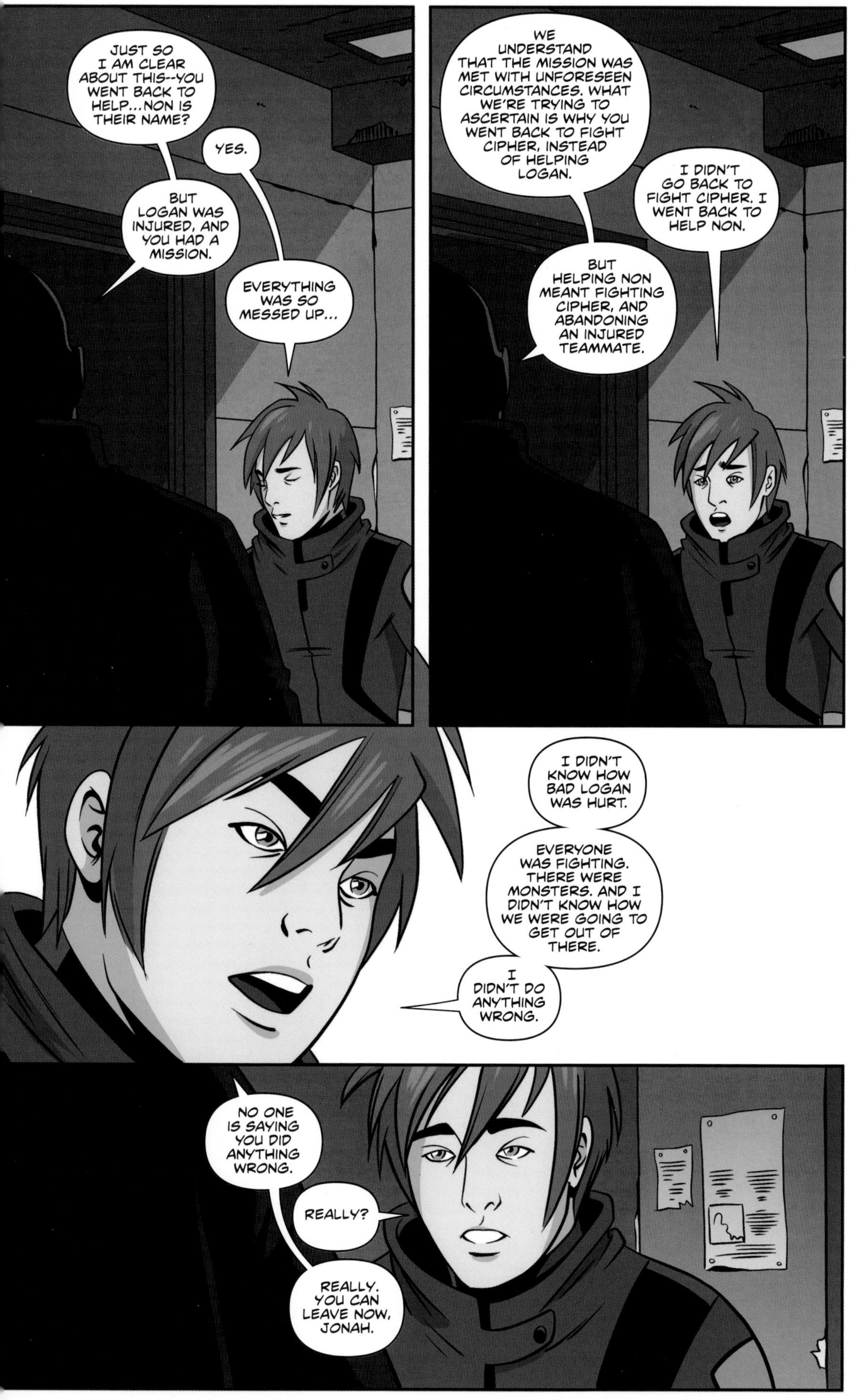
JUST SO I AM CLEAR ABOUT THIS--YOU WENT BACK TO HELP...NON IS THEIR NAME?
YES.
BUT LOGAN WAS INJURED, AND YOU HAD A MISSION.
EVERYTHING WAS SO MESSED UP...
WE UNDERSTAND THAT THE MISSION WAS MET WITH UNFORESEEN CIRCUMSTANCES. WHAT WE'RE TRYING TO ASCERTAIN IS WHY YOU WENT BACK TO FIGHT CIPHER, INSTEAD OF HELPING LOGAN.
I DIDN'T GO BACK TO FIGHT CIPHER. I WENT BACK TO HELP NON.
BUT HELPING NON MEANT FIGHTING CIPHER, AND ABANDONING AN INJURED TEAMMATE.
I DIDN'T KNOW HOW BAD LOGAN WAS HURT.
EVERYONE WAS FIGHTING. THERE WERE MONSTERS. AND I DIDN'T KNOW HOW WE WERE GOING TO GET OUT OF THERE.
I DIDN'T DO ANYTHING WRONG.
NO ONE IS SAYING YOU DID ANYTHING WRONG.
REALLY?
REALLY. YOU CAN LEAVE NOW, JONAH.

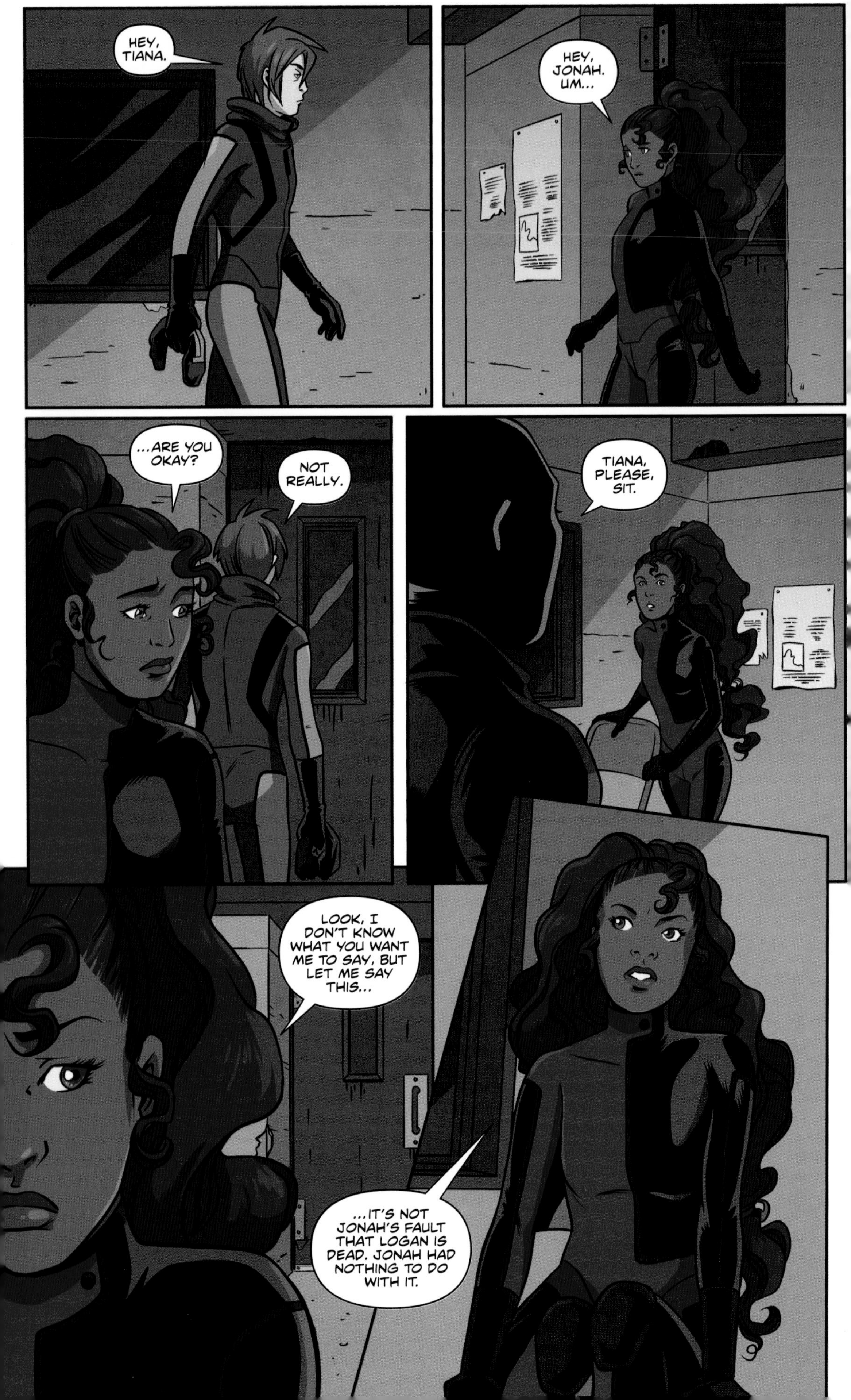
HEY, TIANA.
HEY, JONAH. UM...
...ARE YOU OKAY?
NOT REALLY.
TIANA, PLEASE, SIT.
LOOK, I DON'T KNOW WHAT YOU WANT ME TO SAY, BUT LET ME SAY THIS...
...IT'S NOT JONAH'S FAULT THAT LOGAN IS DEAD. JONAH HAD NOTHING TO DO WITH IT.

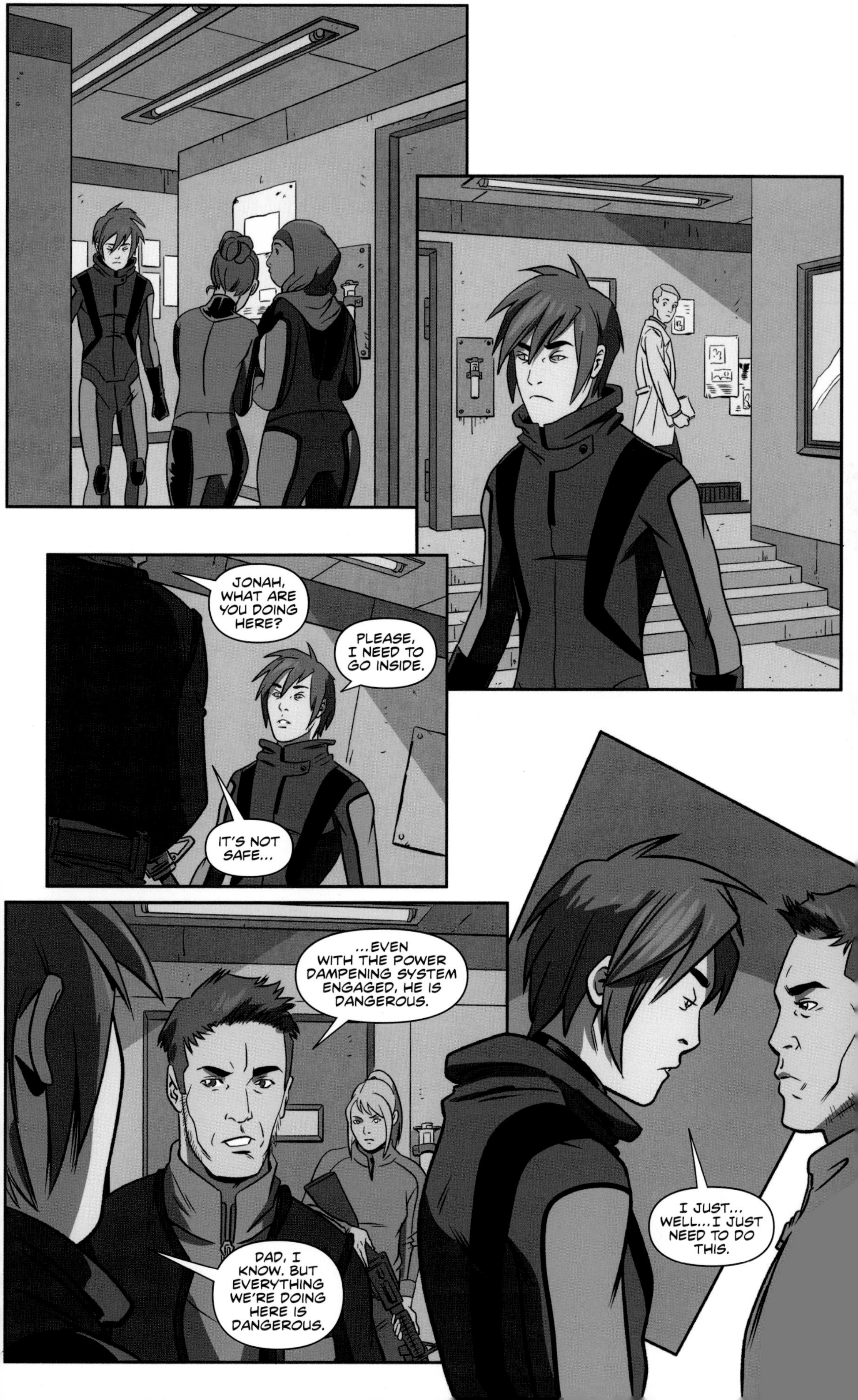
JONAH, WHAT ARE YOU DOING HERE?
PLEASE, I NEED TO GO INSIDE.
IT'S NOT SAFE...
...EVEN WITH THE POWER DAMPENING SYSTEM ENGAGED, HE IS DANGEROUS.
DAD, I KNOW. BUT EVERYTHING WE'RE DOING HERE IS DANGEROUS.
I JUST... WELL... I JUST NEED TO DO THIS.

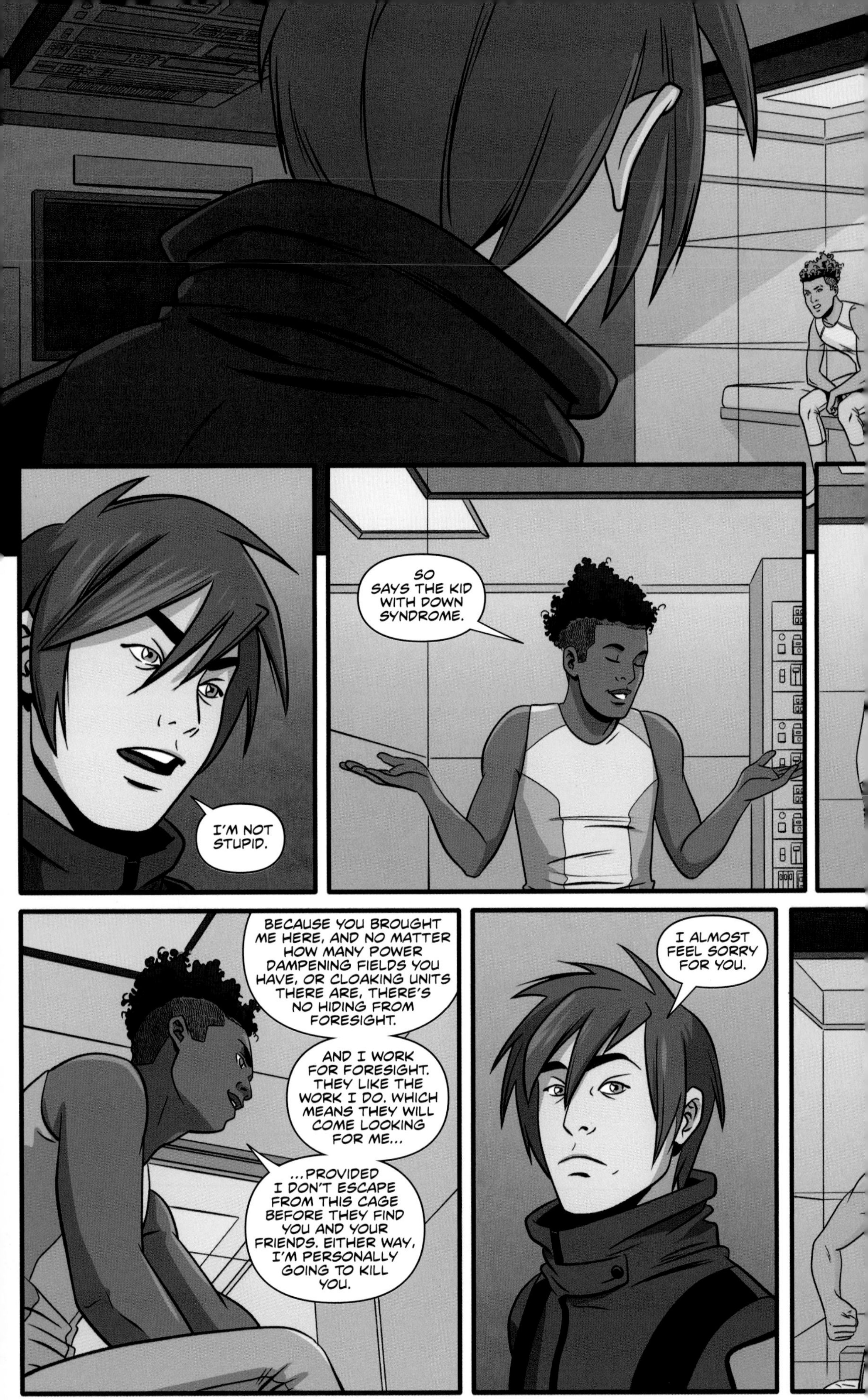
I'M NOT STUPID.
SO SAYS THE KID WITH DOWN SYNDROME.
BECAUSE YOU BROUGHT ME HERE, AND NO MATTER HOW MANY POWER DAMPENING FIELDS YOU HAVE, OR CLOAKING UNITS THERE ARE, THERE'S NO HIDING FROM FORESIGHT.
AND I WORK FOR FORESIGHT. THEY LIKE THE WORK I DO. WHICH MEANS THEY WILL COME LOOKING FOR ME...
...PROVIDED I DON'T ESCAPE FROM THIS CAGE BEFORE THEY FIND YOU AND YOUR FRIENDS. EITHER WAY, I'M PERSONALLY GOING TO KILL YOU.
I ALMOST FEEL SORRY FOR YOU.

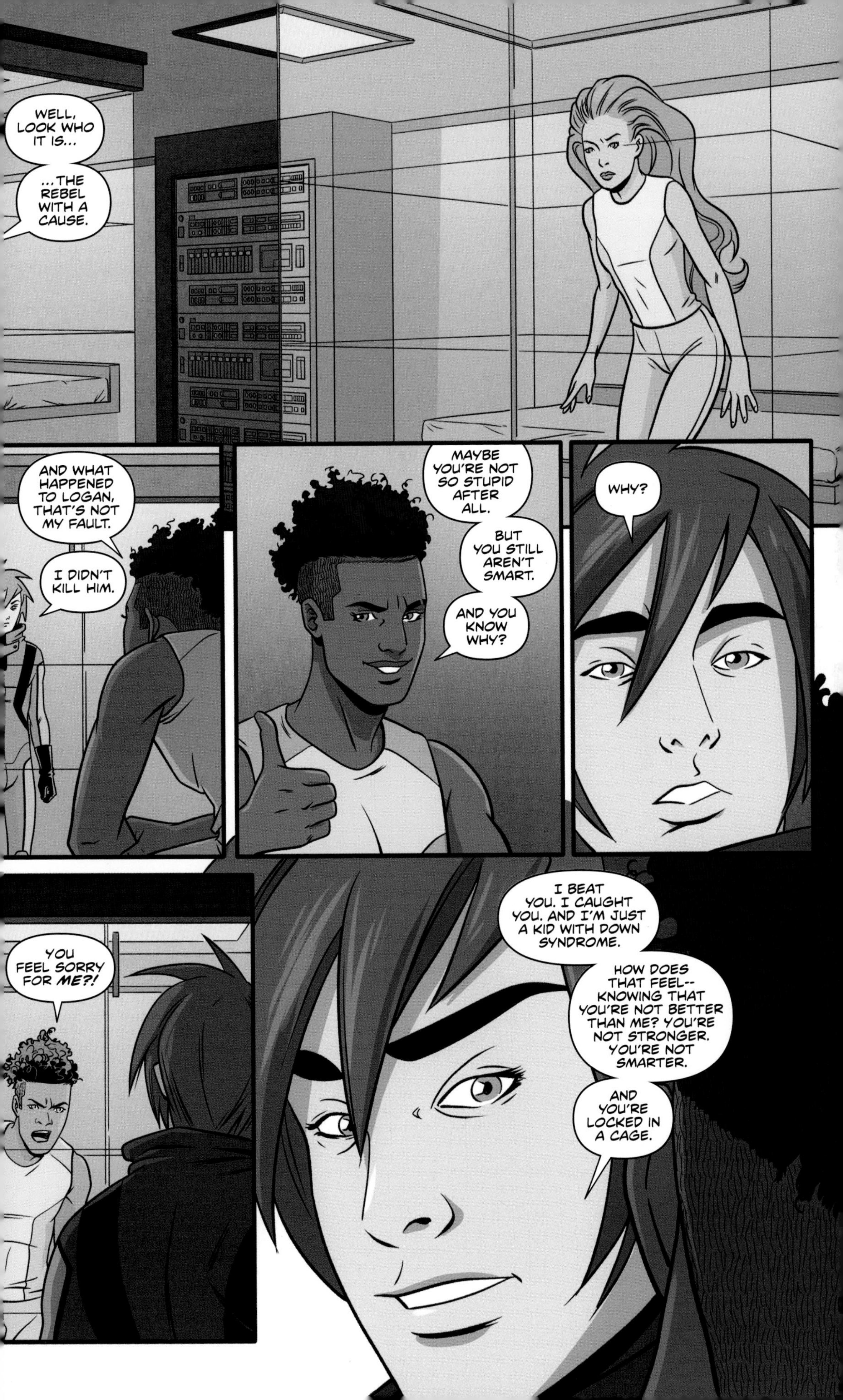
WELL, LOOK WHO IT IS...
...THE REBEL WITH A CAUSE.
AND WHAT HAPPENED TO LOGAN, THAT'S NOT MY FAULT.
I DIDN'T KILL HIM.
MAYBE YOU'RE NOT SO STUPID AFTER ALL.
BUT YOU STILL AREN'T SMART.
AND YOU KNOW WHY?
WHY?
YOU FEEL SORRY FOR *ME?!*
I BEAT YOU. I CAUGHT YOU. AND I'M JUST A KID WITH DOWN SYNDROME.
HOW DOES THAT FEEL-- KNOWING THAT YOU'RE NOT BETTER THAN ME? YOU'RE NOT STRONGER. YOU'RE NOT SMARTER.
AND YOU'RE LOCKED IN A CAGE.

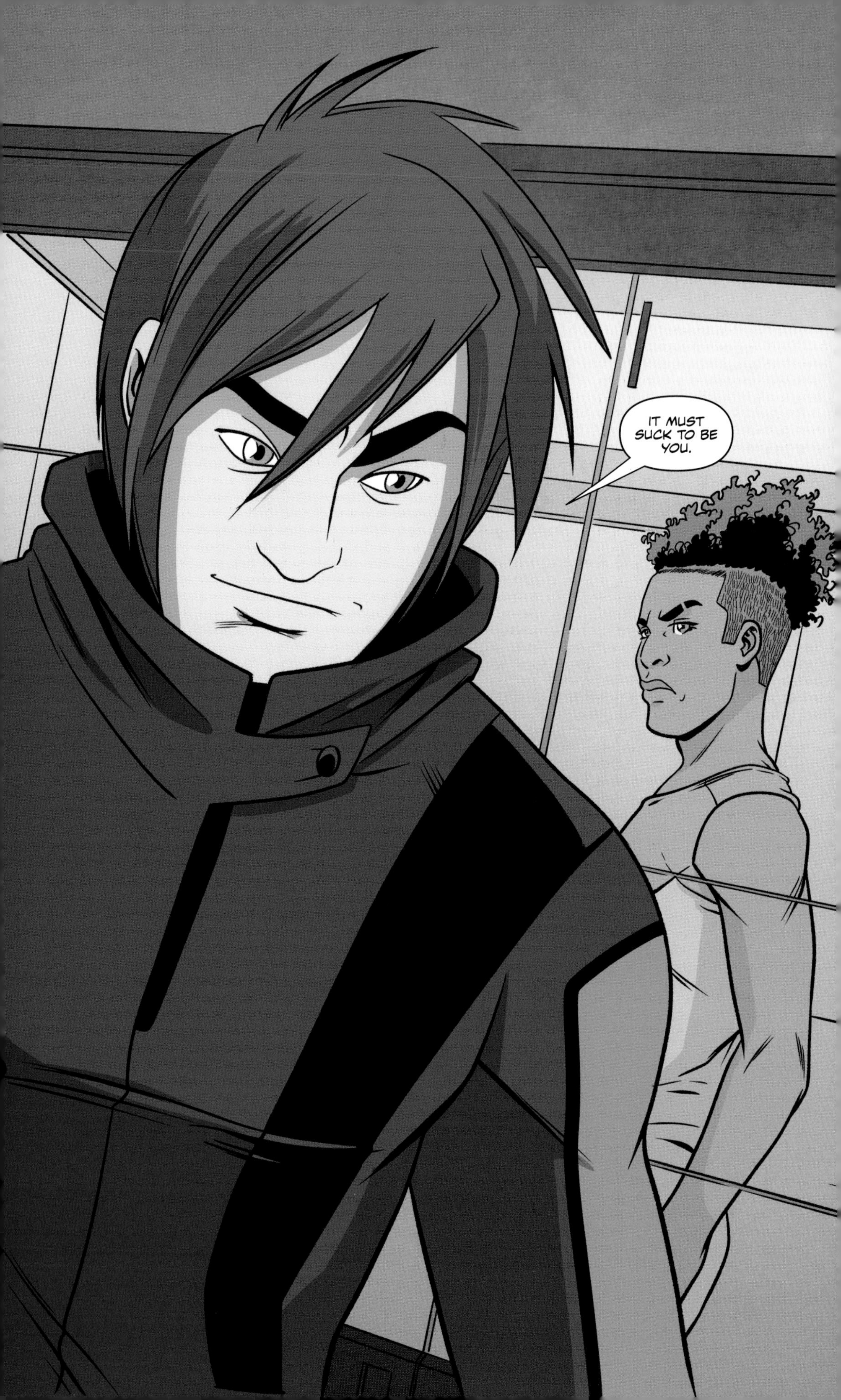
IT MUST SUCK TO BE YOU.

youngstown
12

CHAPTER FOUR

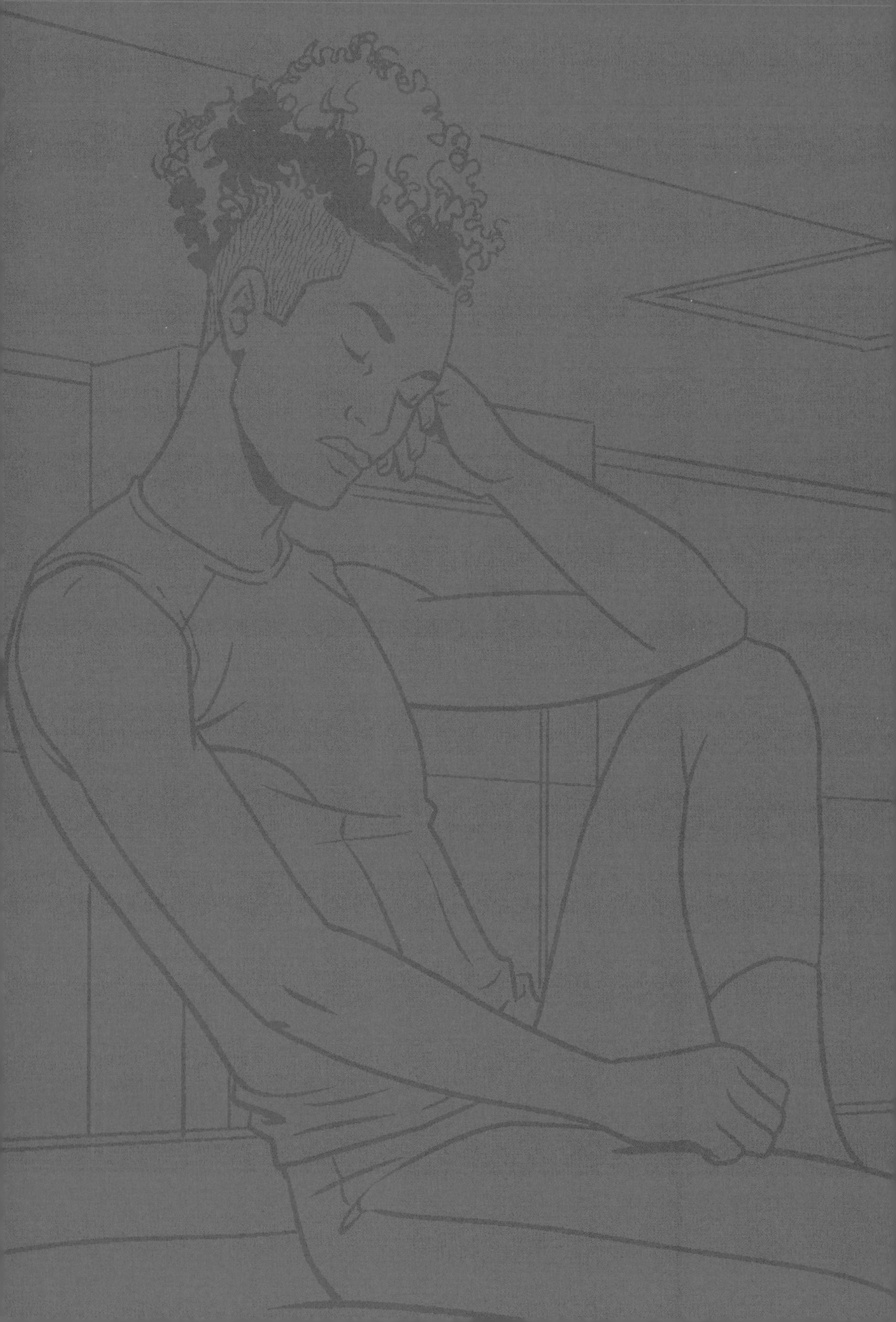

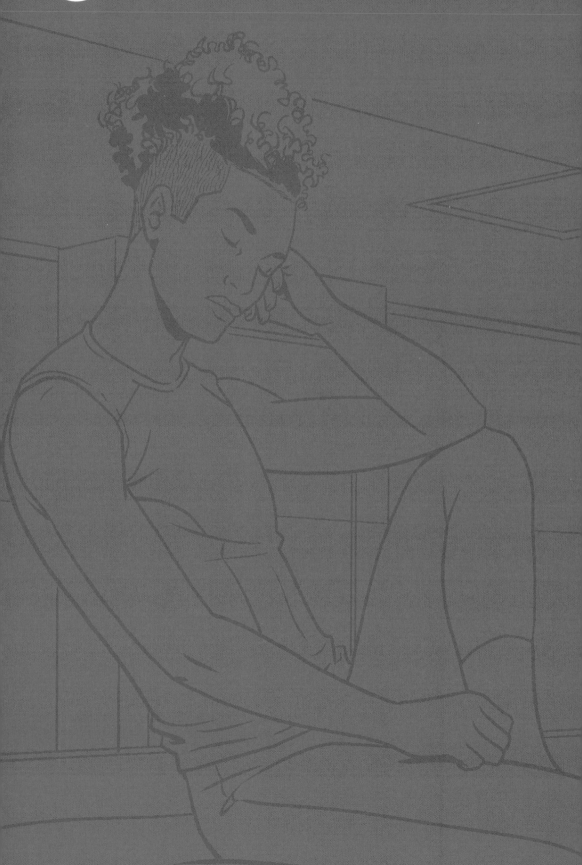

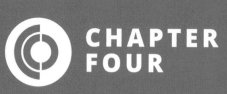

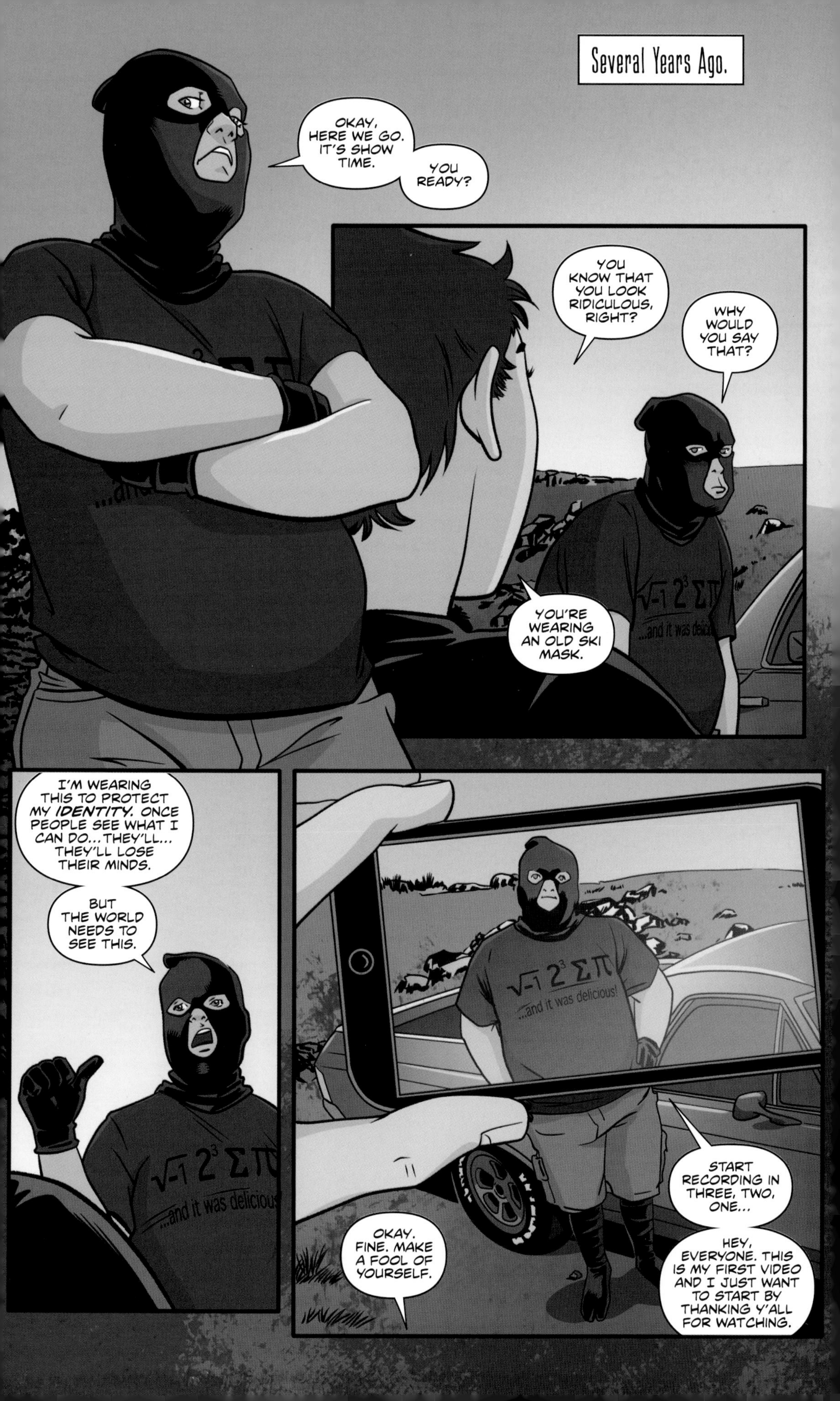
Several Years Ago.
OKAY, HERE WE GO. IT'S SHOW TIME.
YOU READY?
YOU KNOW THAT YOU LOOK RIDICULOUS, RIGHT?
WHY WOULD YOU SAY THAT?
YOU'RE WEARING AN OLD SKI MASK.
I'M WEARING THIS TO PROTECT MY IDENTITY. ONCE PEOPLE SEE WHAT I CAN DO...THEY'LL... THEY'LL LOSE THEIR MINDS.
BUT THE WORLD NEEDS TO SEE THIS.
START RECORDING IN THREE, TWO, ONE...
OKAY. FINE. MAKE A FOOL OF YOURSELF.
HEY, EVERYONE. THIS IS MY FIRST VIDEO AND I JUST WANT TO START BY THANKING Y'ALL FOR WATCHING.

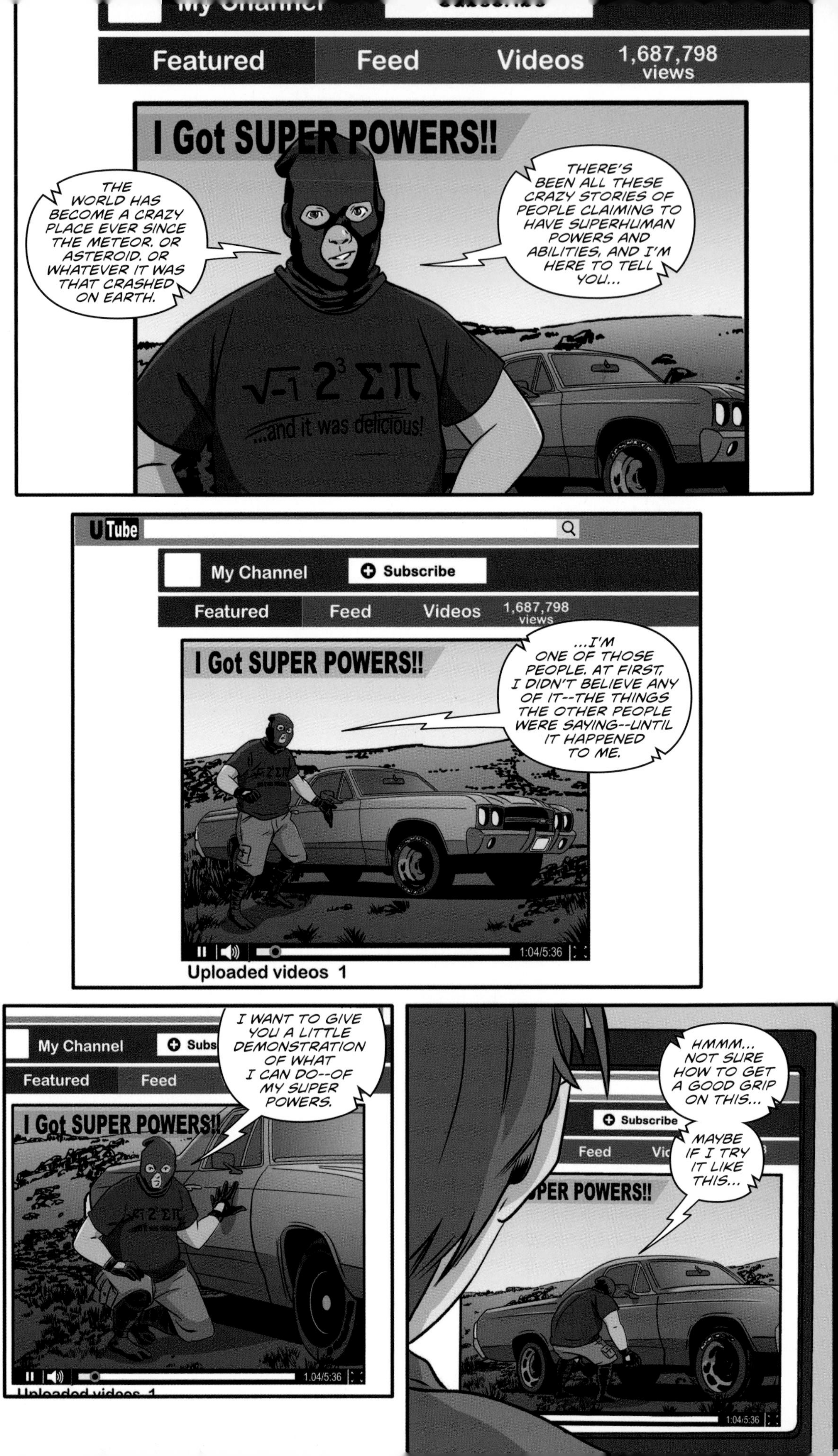

My Channel
Featured
Feed
Videos
1,687,798 views
I Got SUPER POWERS!!
THE WORLD HAS BECOME A CRAZY PLACE EVER SINCE THE METEOR. OR ASTEROID. OR WHATEVER IT WAS THAT CRASHED ON EARTH.
THERE'S BEEN ALL THESE CRAZY STORIES OF PEOPLE CLAIMING TO HAVE SUPERHUMAN POWERS AND ABILITIES, AND I'M HERE TO TELL YOU...
...and it was delicious!
UTube
My Channel
Subscribe
Featured
Feed
Videos
1,687,798 views
I Got SUPER POWERS!!
...I'M ONE OF THOSE PEOPLE. AT FIRST, I DIDN'T BELIEVE ANY OF IT--THE THINGS THE OTHER PEOPLE WERE SAYING--UNTIL IT HAPPENED TO ME.
1:04/5:36
Uploaded videos 1
My Channel
Featured
Feed
I Got SUPER POWERS!!
I WANT TO GIVE YOU A LITTLE DEMONSTRATION OF WHAT I CAN DO--OF MY SUPER POWERS.
1:04/5:36
HMMM... NOT SURE HOW TO GET A GOOD GRIP ON THIS...
Subscribe
Feed
MAYBE IF I TRY IT LIKE THIS...
1:04/5:36

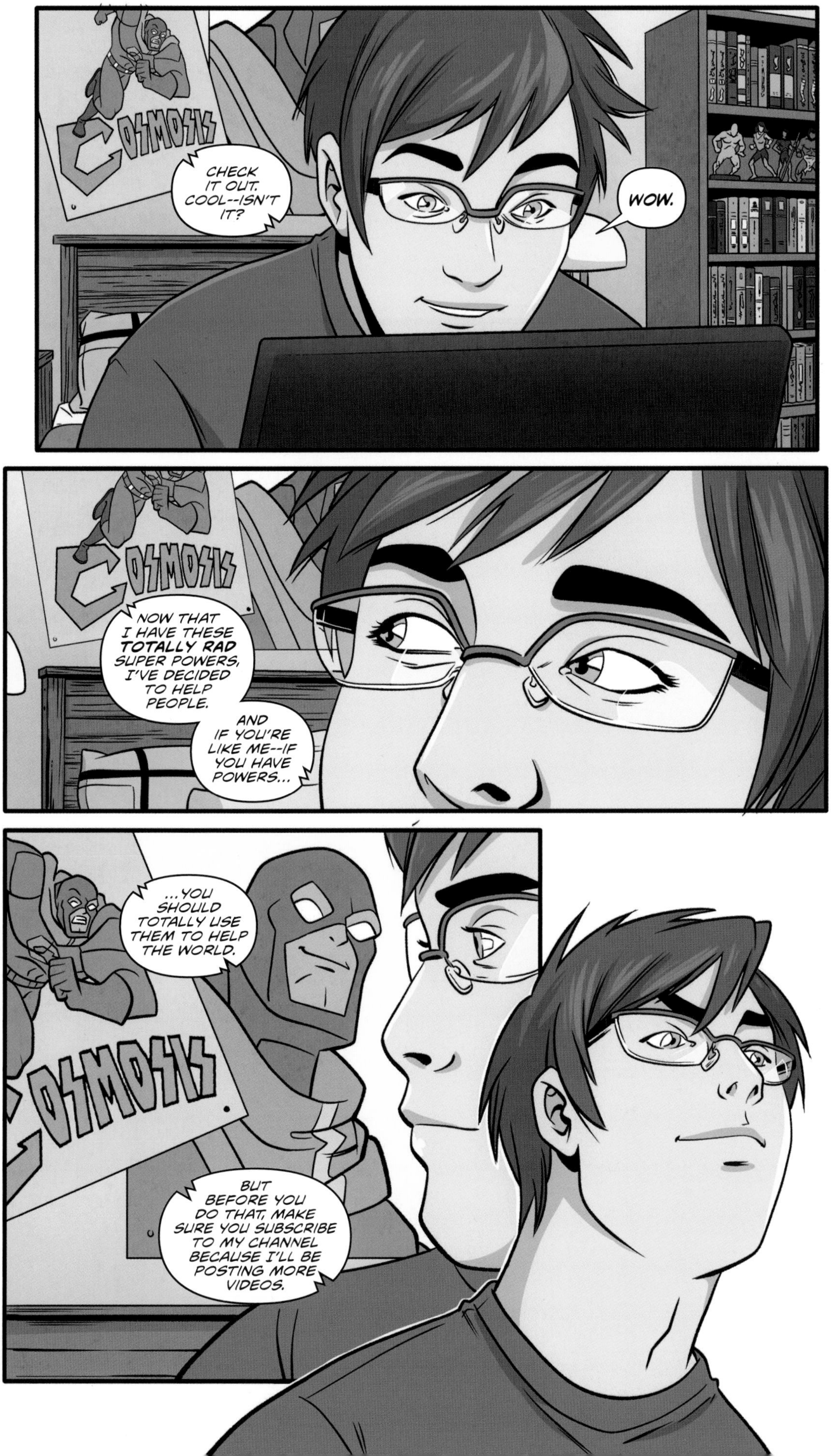
COSMOSIS
CHECK IT OUT. COOL--ISN'T IT?
WOW.
COSMOSIS
NOW THAT I HAVE THESE **TOTALLY RAD** SUPER POWERS, I'VE DECIDED TO HELP PEOPLE.
AND IF YOU'RE LIKE ME--IF YOU HAVE POWERS...
...YOU SHOULD TOTALLY USE THEM TO HELP THE WORLD.
COSMOSIS
BUT BEFORE YOU DO THAT, MAKE SURE YOU SUBSCRIBE TO MY CHANNEL BECAUSE I'LL BE POSTING MORE VIDEOS.

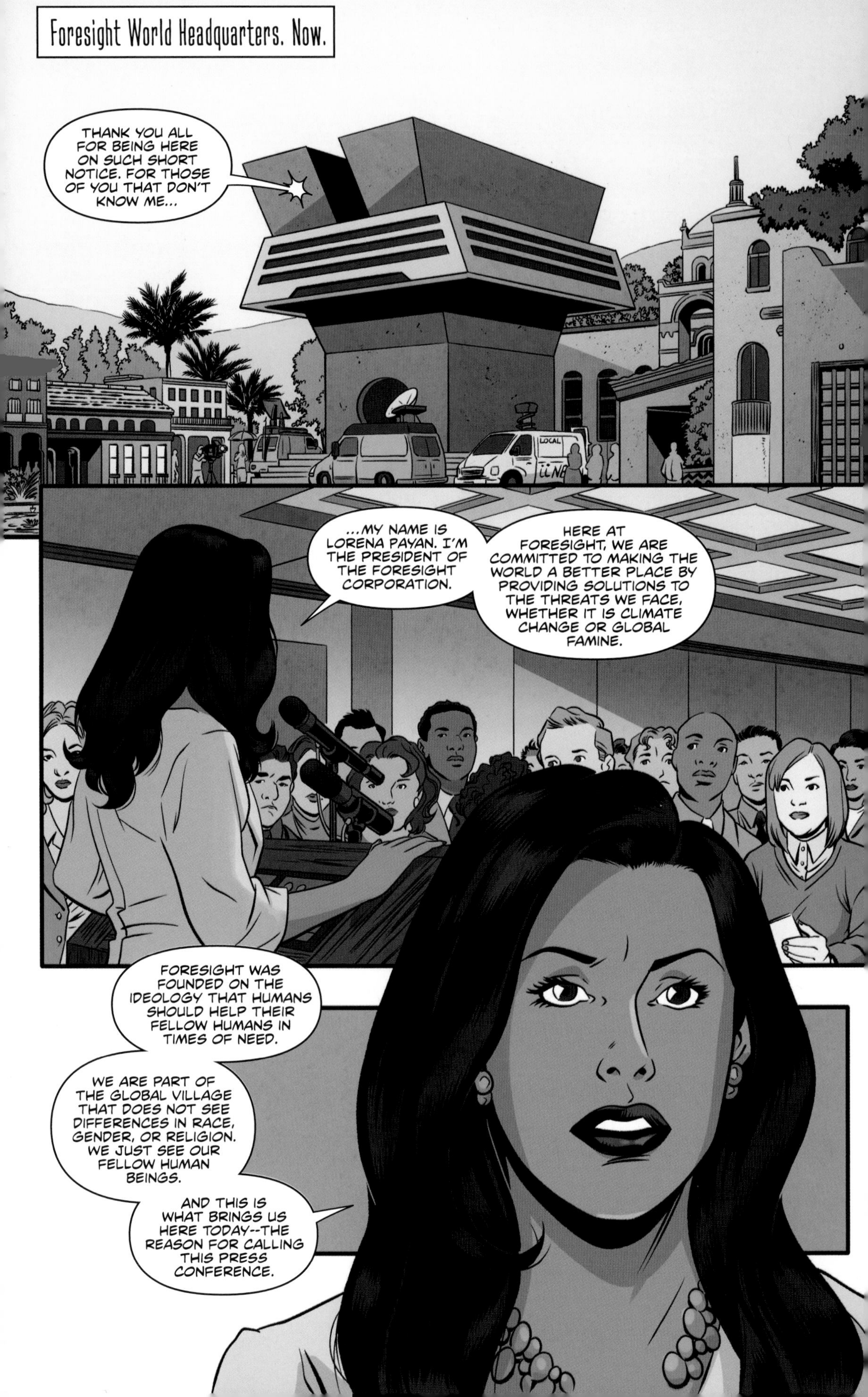

Foresight World Headquarters. Now.
THANK YOU ALL FOR BEING HERE ON SUCH SHORT NOTICE. FOR THOSE OF YOU THAT DON'T KNOW ME...
LOCAL
...MY NAME IS LORENA PAYAN. I'M THE PRESIDENT OF THE FORESIGHT CORPORATION.
HERE AT FORESIGHT, WE ARE COMMITTED TO MAKING THE WORLD A BETTER PLACE BY PROVIDING SOLUTIONS TO THE THREATS WE FACE, WHETHER IT IS CLIMATE CHANGE OR GLOBAL FAMINE.
FORESIGHT WAS FOUNDED ON THE IDEOLOGY THAT HUMANS SHOULD HELP THEIR FELLOW HUMANS IN TIMES OF NEED.
WE ARE PART OF THE GLOBAL VILLAGE THAT DOES NOT SEE DIFFERENCES IN RACE, GENDER, OR RELIGION. WE JUST SEE OUR FELLOW HUMAN BEINGS.
AND THIS IS WHAT BRINGS US HERE TODAY--THE REASON FOR CALLING THIS PRESS CONFERENCE.

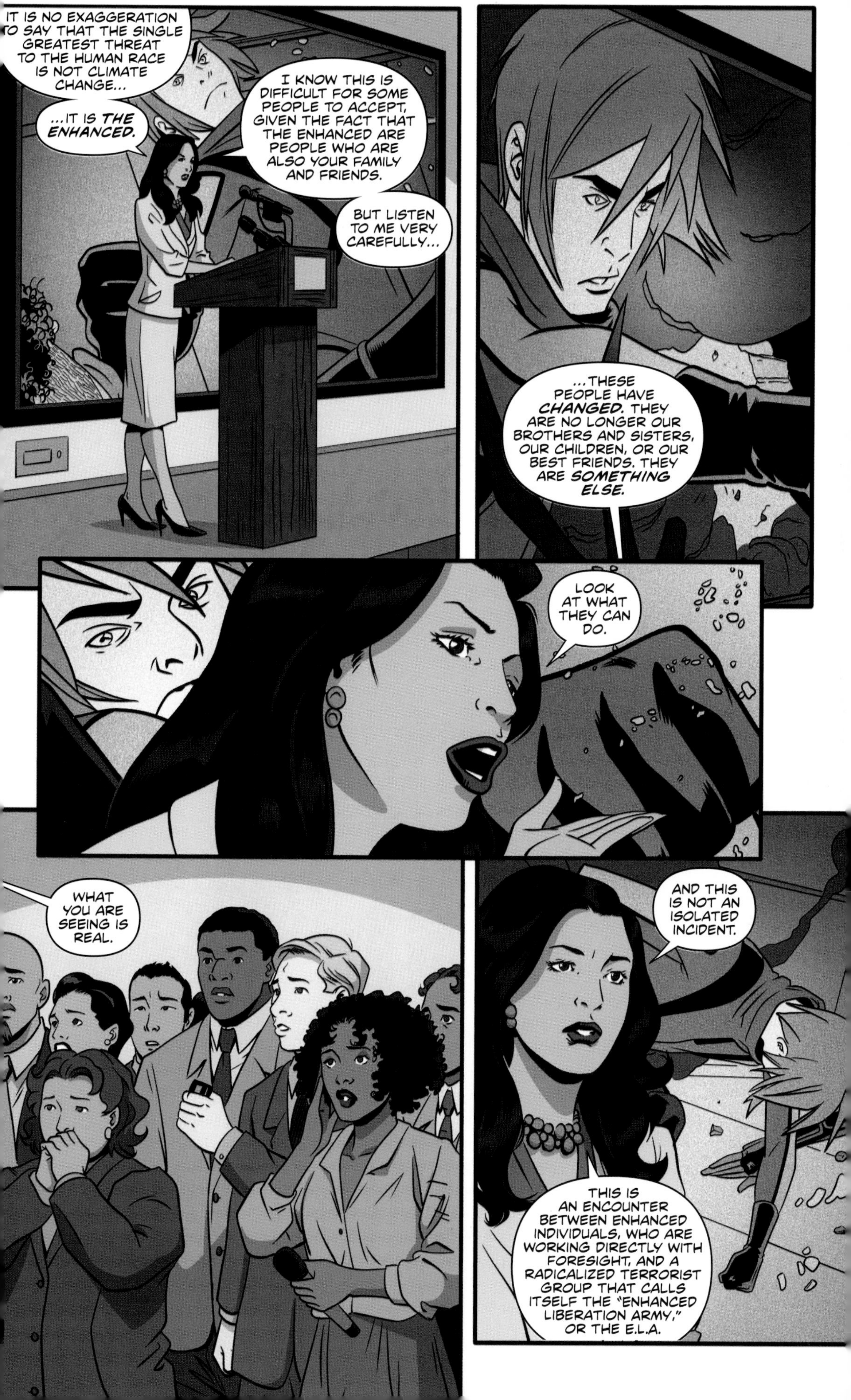
IT IS NO EXAGGERATION TO SAY THAT THE SINGLE GREATEST THREAT TO THE HUMAN RACE IS NOT CLIMATE CHANGE...
...IT IS *THE ENHANCED.*
I KNOW THIS IS DIFFICULT FOR SOME PEOPLE TO ACCEPT, GIVEN THE FACT THAT THE ENHANCED ARE PEOPLE WHO ARE ALSO YOUR FAMILY AND FRIENDS.
BUT LISTEN TO ME VERY CAREFULLY...
...THESE PEOPLE HAVE *CHANGED.* THEY ARE NO LONGER OUR BROTHERS AND SISTERS, OUR CHILDREN, OR OUR BEST FRIENDS. THEY ARE *SOMETHING ELSE.*
LOOK AT WHAT THEY CAN DO.
WHAT YOU ARE SEEING IS REAL.
AND THIS IS NOT AN ISOLATED INCIDENT.
THIS IS AN ENCOUNTER BETWEEN ENHANCED INDIVIDUALS, WHO ARE WORKING DIRECTLY WITH FORESIGHT, AND A RADICALIZED TERRORIST GROUP THAT CALLS ITSELF THE "ENHANCED LIBERATION ARMY," OR THE E.L.A.

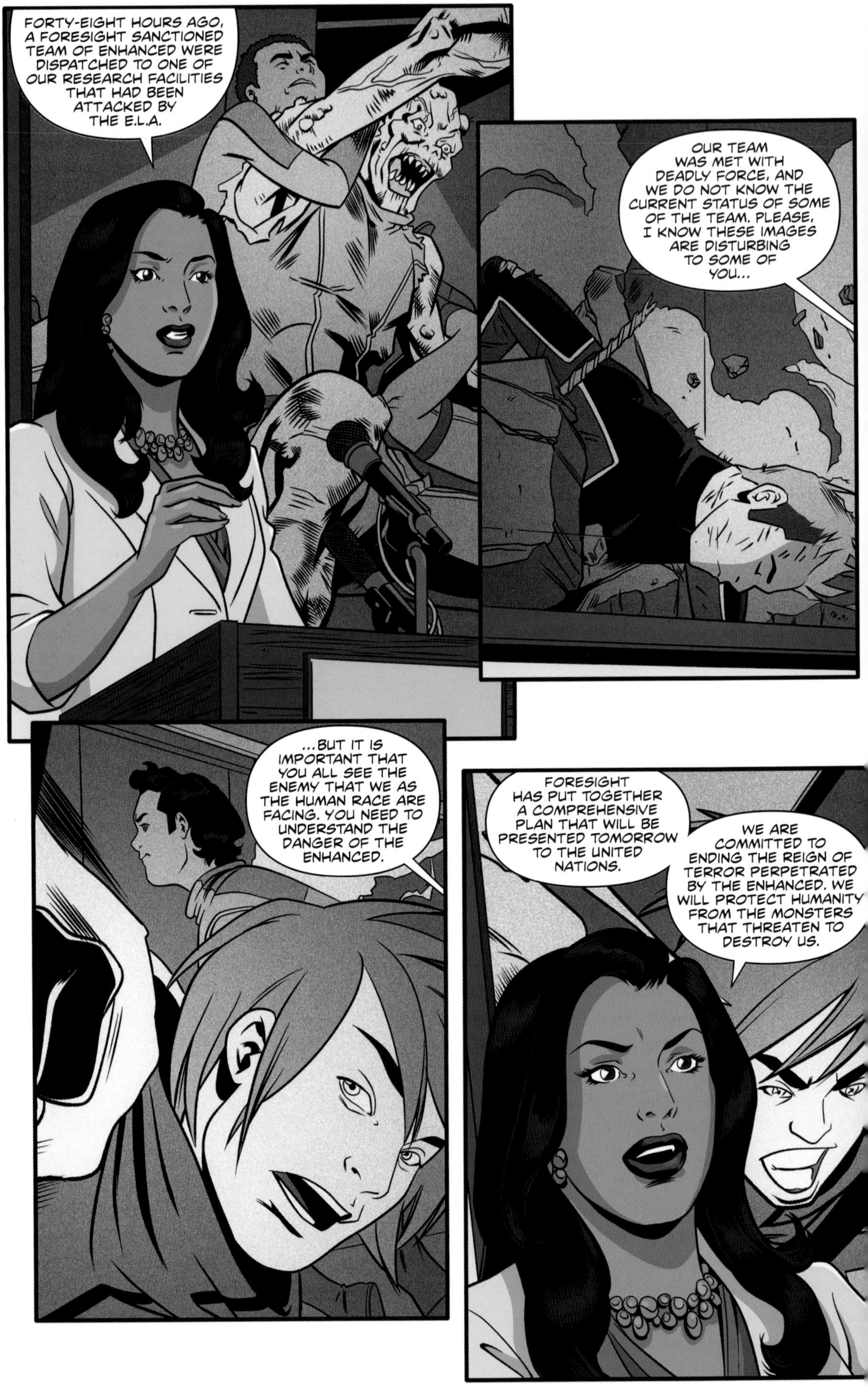

FORTY-EIGHT HOURS AGO, A FORESIGHT SANCTIONED TEAM OF ENHANCED WERE DISPATCHED TO ONE OF OUR RESEARCH FACILITIES THAT HAD BEEN ATTACKED BY THE E.L.A.
OUR TEAM WAS MET WITH DEADLY FORCE, AND WE DO NOT KNOW THE CURRENT STATUS OF SOME OF THE TEAM. PLEASE, I KNOW THESE IMAGES ARE DISTURBING TO SOME OF YOU...
...BUT IT IS IMPORTANT THAT YOU ALL SEE THE ENEMY THAT WE AS THE HUMAN RACE ARE FACING. YOU NEED TO UNDERSTAND THE DANGER OF THE ENHANCED.
FORESIGHT HAS PUT TOGETHER A COMPREHENSIVE PLAN THAT WILL BE PRESENTED TOMORROW TO THE UNITED NATIONS.
WE ARE COMMITTED TO ENDING THE REIGN OF TERROR PERPETRATED BY THE ENHANCED. WE WILL PROTECT HUMANITY FROM THE MONSTERS THAT THREATEN TO DESTROY US.

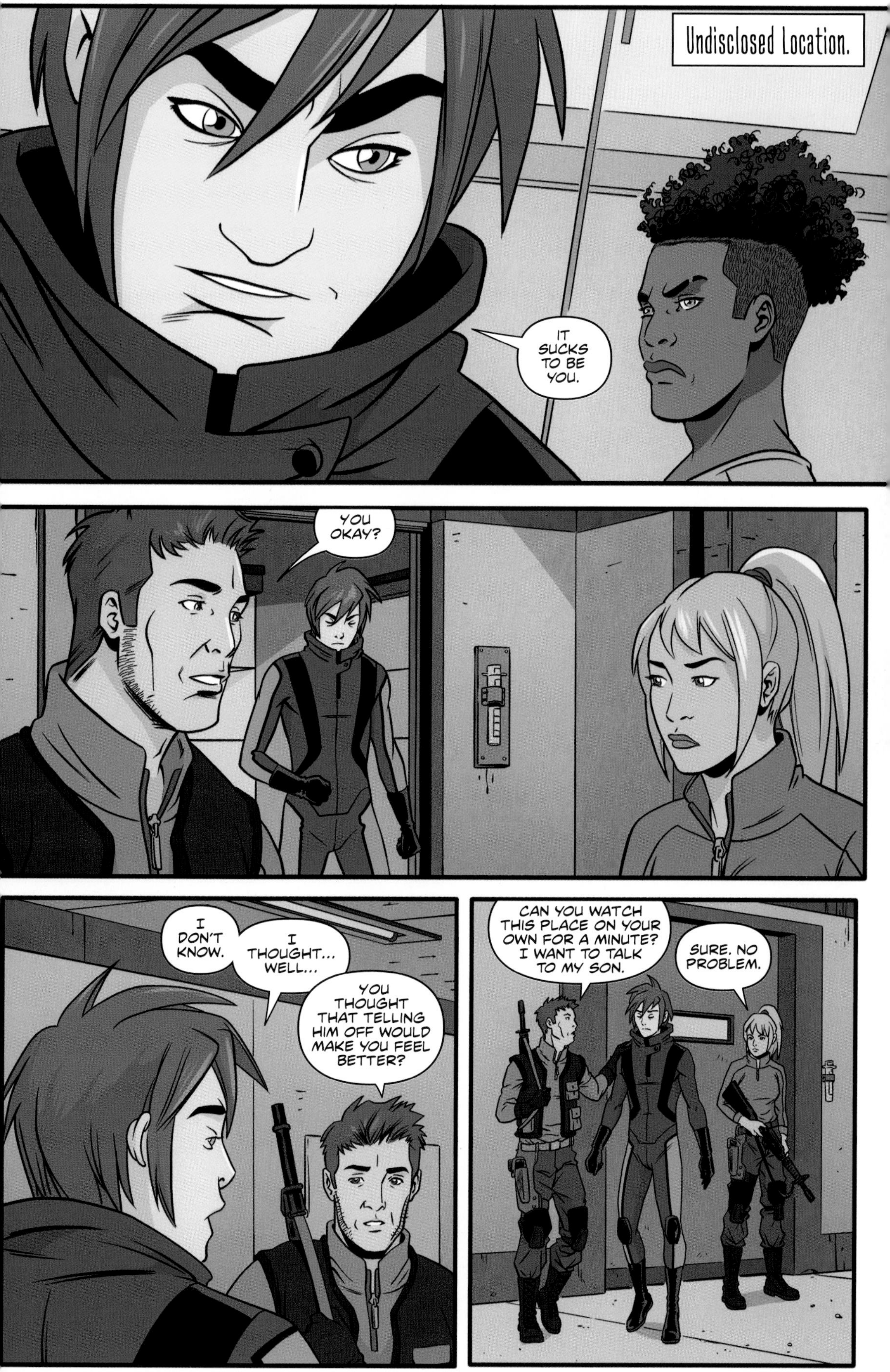

Undisclosed Location.
IT SUCKS TO BE YOU.
YOU OKAY?
I DON'T KNOW.
I THOUGHT... WELL...
YOU THOUGHT THAT TELLING HIM OFF WOULD MAKE YOU FEEL BETTER?
CAN YOU WATCH THIS PLACE ON YOUR OWN FOR A MINUTE? I WANT TO TALK TO MY SON.
SURE. NO PROBLEM.

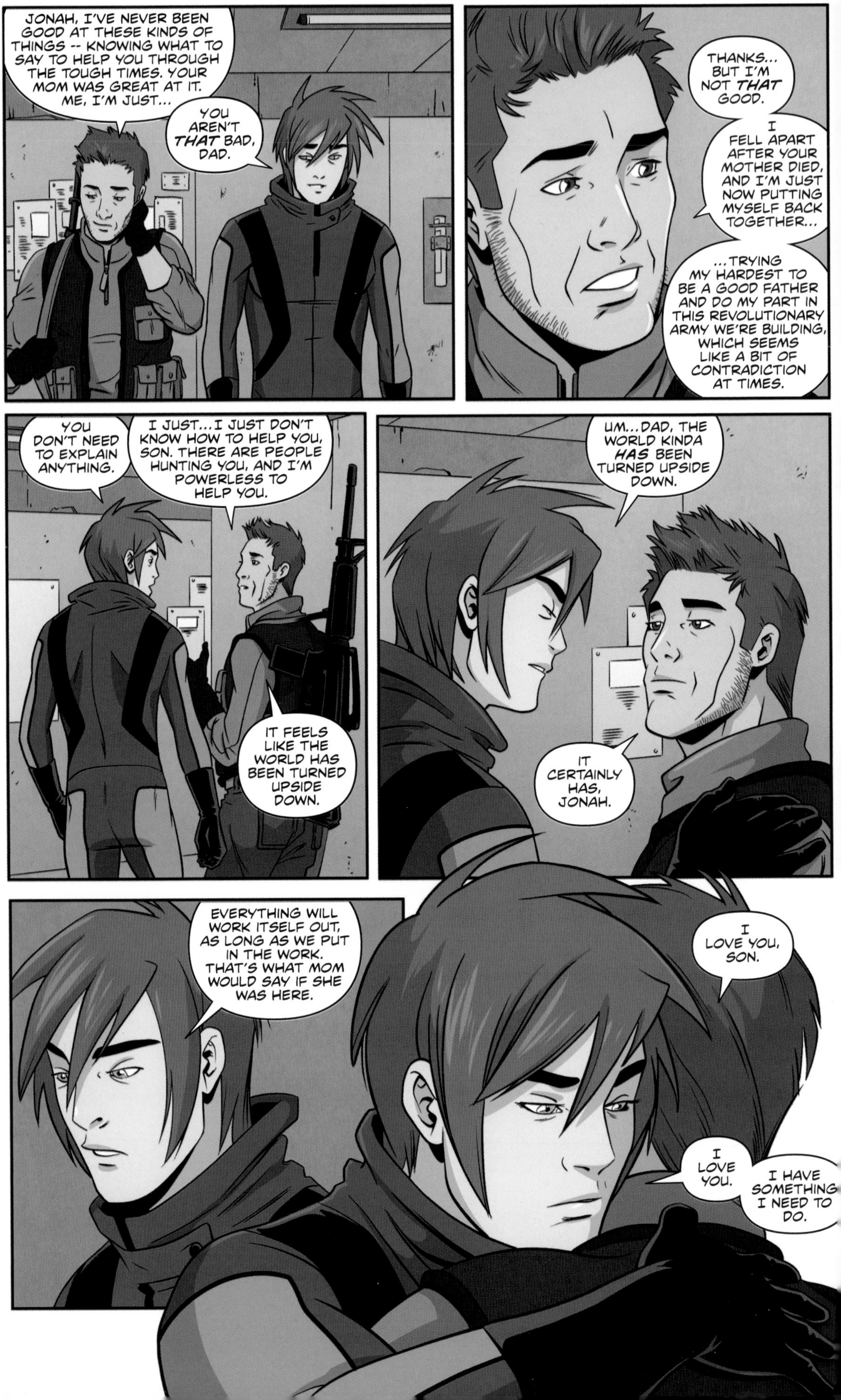
JONAH, I'VE NEVER BEEN GOOD AT THESE KINDS OF THINGS -- KNOWING WHAT TO SAY TO HELP YOU THROUGH THE TOUGH TIMES. YOUR MOM WAS GREAT AT IT. ME, I'M JUST...
YOU AREN'T THAT BAD, DAD.
THANKS... BUT I'M NOT THAT GOOD.
I FELL APART AFTER YOUR MOTHER DIED, AND I'M JUST NOW PUTTING MYSELF BACK TOGETHER...
...TRYING MY HARDEST TO BE A GOOD FATHER AND DO MY PART IN THIS REVOLUTIONARY ARMY WE'RE BUILDING, WHICH SEEMS LIKE A BIT OF CONTRADICTION AT TIMES.
YOU DON'T NEED TO EXPLAIN ANYTHING.
I JUST...I JUST DON'T KNOW HOW TO HELP YOU, SON. THERE ARE PEOPLE HUNTING YOU, AND I'M POWERLESS TO HELP YOU.
IT FEELS LIKE THE WORLD HAS BEEN TURNED UPSIDE DOWN.
UM...DAD, THE WORLD KINDA HAS BEEN TURNED UPSIDE DOWN.
IT CERTAINLY HAS, JONAH.
EVERYTHING WILL WORK ITSELF OUT, AS LONG AS WE PUT IN THE WORK. THAT'S WHAT MOM WOULD SAY IF SHE WAS HERE.
I LOVE YOU, SON.
I LOVE YOU.
I HAVE SOMETHING I NEED TO DO.

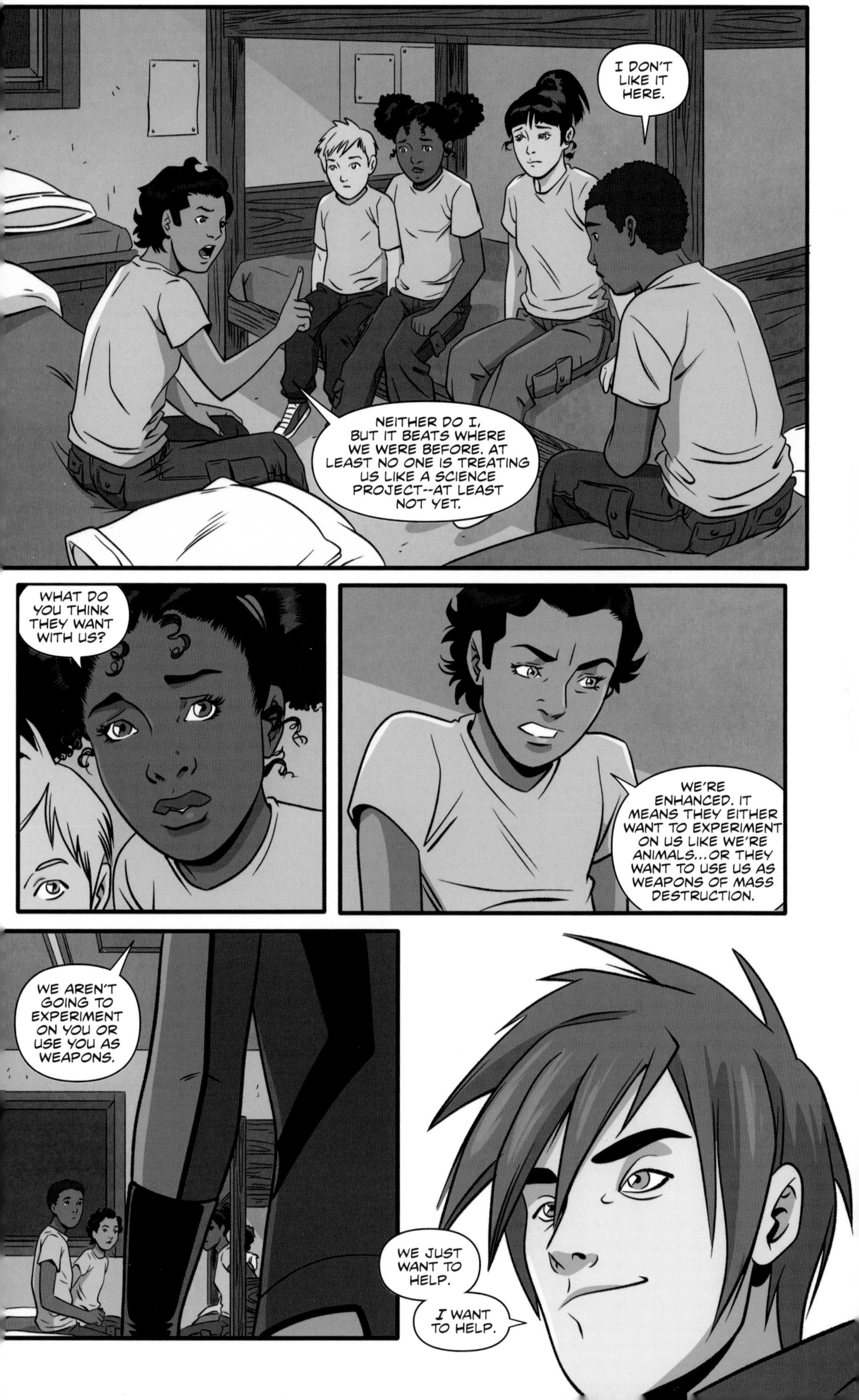
I DON'T LIKE IT HERE.
NEITHER DO I, BUT IT BEATS WHERE WE WERE BEFORE. AT LEAST NO ONE IS TREATING US LIKE A SCIENCE PROJECT--AT LEAST NOT YET.
WHAT DO YOU THINK THEY WANT WITH US?
WE'RE ENHANCED. IT MEANS THEY EITHER WANT TO EXPERIMENT ON US LIKE WE'RE ANIMALS...OR THEY WANT TO USE US AS WEAPONS OF MASS DESTRUCTION.
WE AREN'T GOING TO EXPERIMENT ON YOU OR USE YOU AS WEAPONS.
WE JUST WANT TO HELP.
I WANT TO HELP.

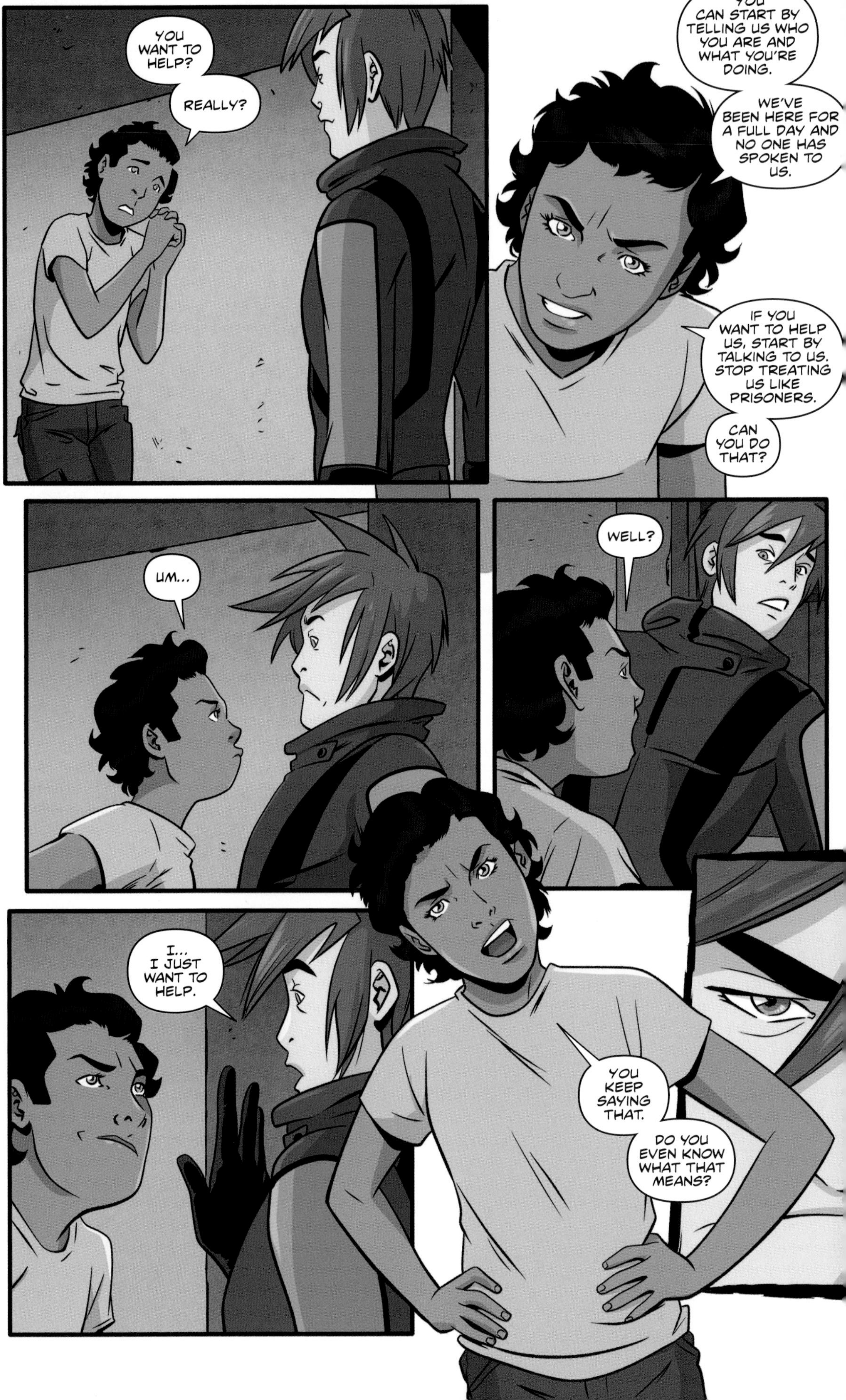
YOU WANT TO HELP?
REALLY?
YOU CAN START BY TELLING US WHO YOU ARE AND WHAT YOU'RE DOING.
WE'VE BEEN HERE FOR A FULL DAY AND NO ONE HAS SPOKEN TO US.
IF YOU WANT TO HELP US, START BY TALKING TO US. STOP TREATING US LIKE PRISONERS.
CAN YOU DO THAT?
UM...
WELL?
I... I JUST WANT TO HELP.
YOU KEEP SAYING THAT.
DO YOU EVEN KNOW WHAT THAT MEANS?

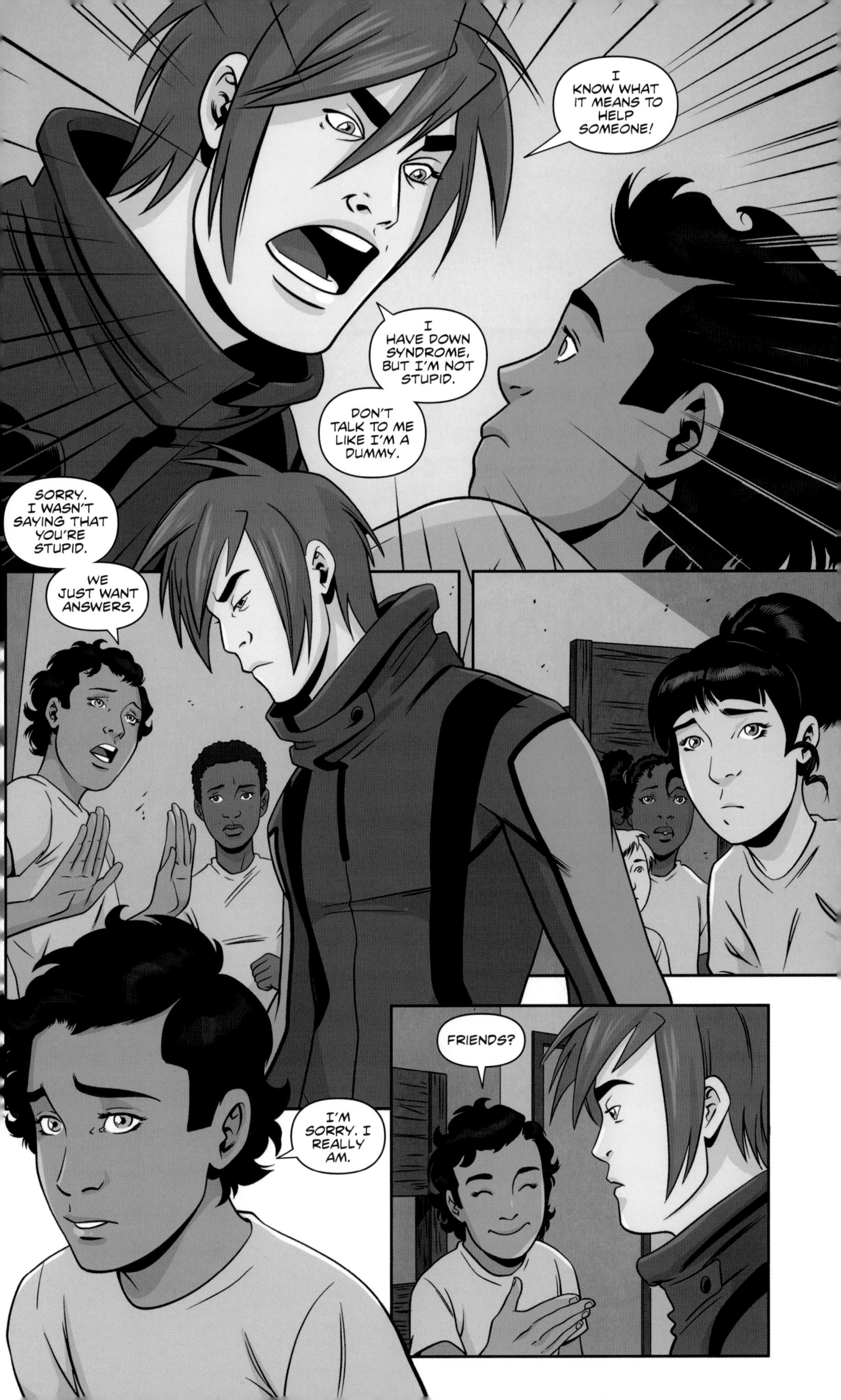
I KNOW WHAT IT MEANS TO HELP SOMEONE!
I HAVE DOWN SYNDROME, BUT I'M NOT STUPID.
DON'T TALK TO ME LIKE I'M A DUMMY.
SORRY. I WASN'T SAYING THAT YOU'RE STUPID.
WE JUST WANT ANSWERS.
I'M SORRY. I REALLY AM.
FRIENDS?

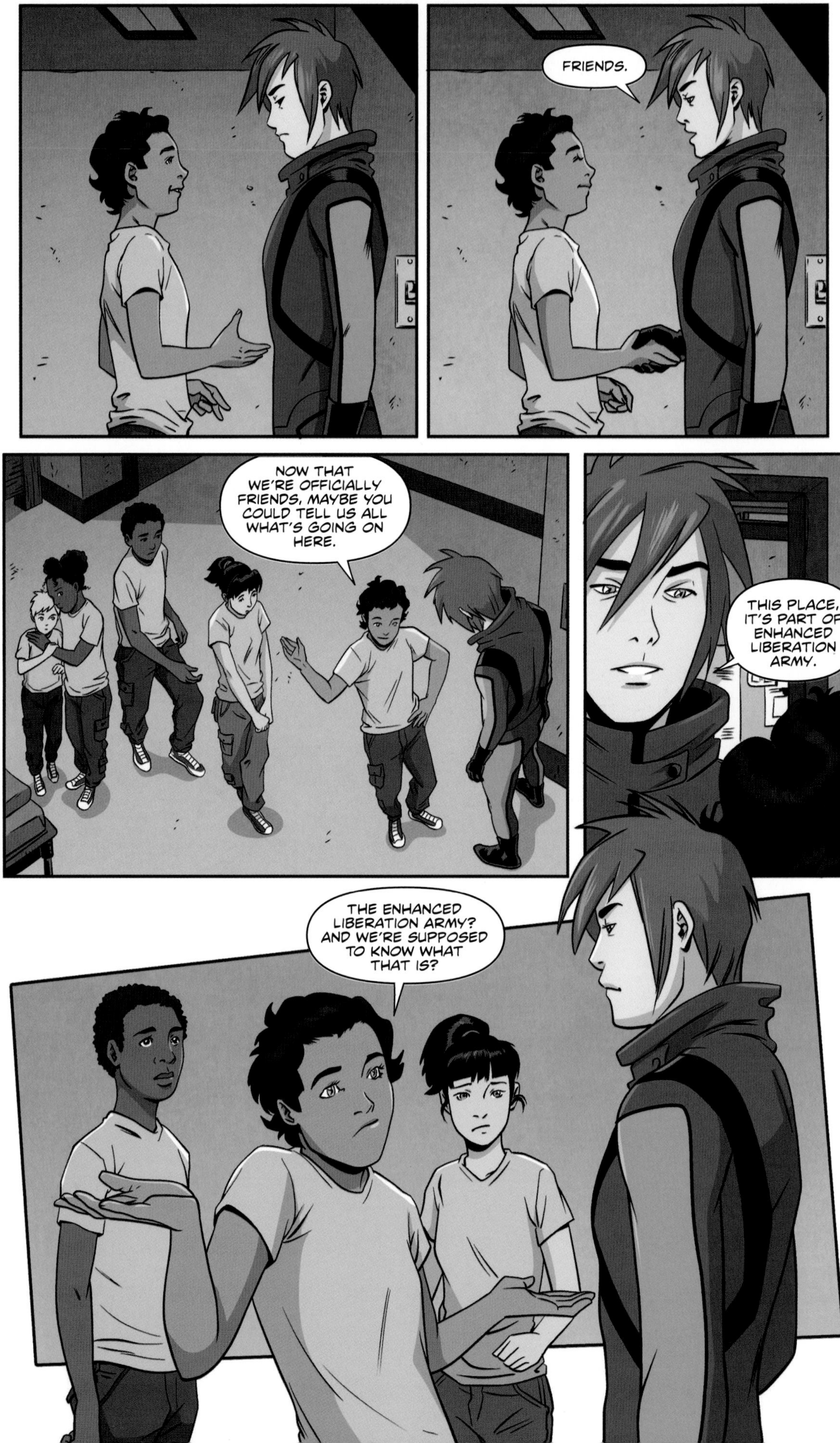
FRIENDS.
NOW THAT WE'RE OFFICIALLY FRIENDS, MAYBE YOU COULD TELL US ALL WHAT'S GOING ON HERE.
THIS PLACE, IT'S PART OF ENHANCED LIBERATION ARMY.
THE ENHANCED LIBERATION ARMY? AND WE'RE SUPPOSED TO KNOW WHAT THAT IS?

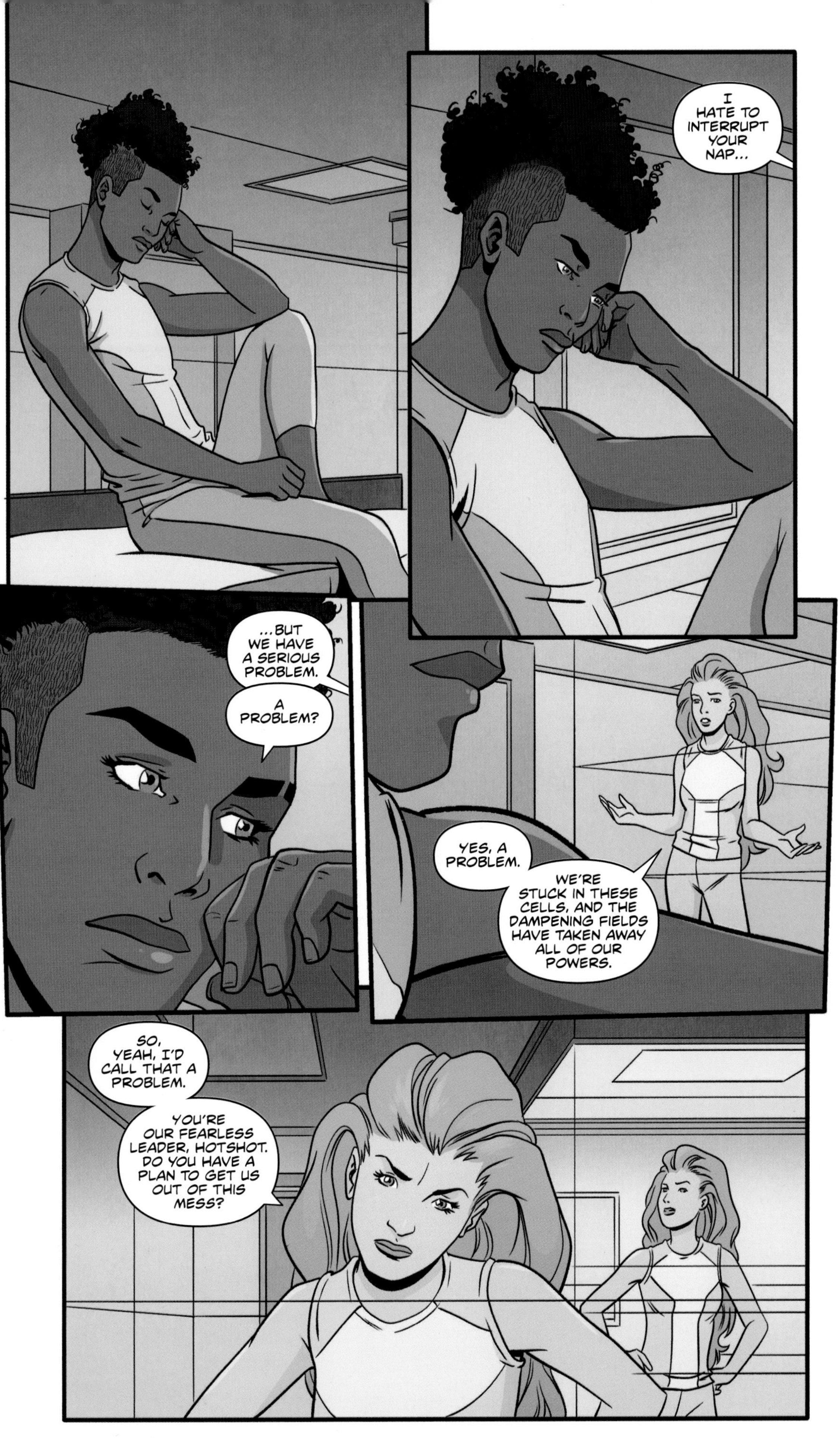
I HATE TO INTERRUPT YOUR NAP...
...BUT WE HAVE A SERIOUS PROBLEM.
A PROBLEM?
YES, A PROBLEM.
WE'RE STUCK IN THESE CELLS, AND THE DAMPENING FIELDS HAVE TAKEN AWAY ALL OF OUR POWERS.
SO, YEAH, I'D CALL THAT A PROBLEM.
YOU'RE OUR FEARLESS LEADER, HOTSHOT. DO YOU HAVE A PLAN TO GET US OUT OF THIS MESS?

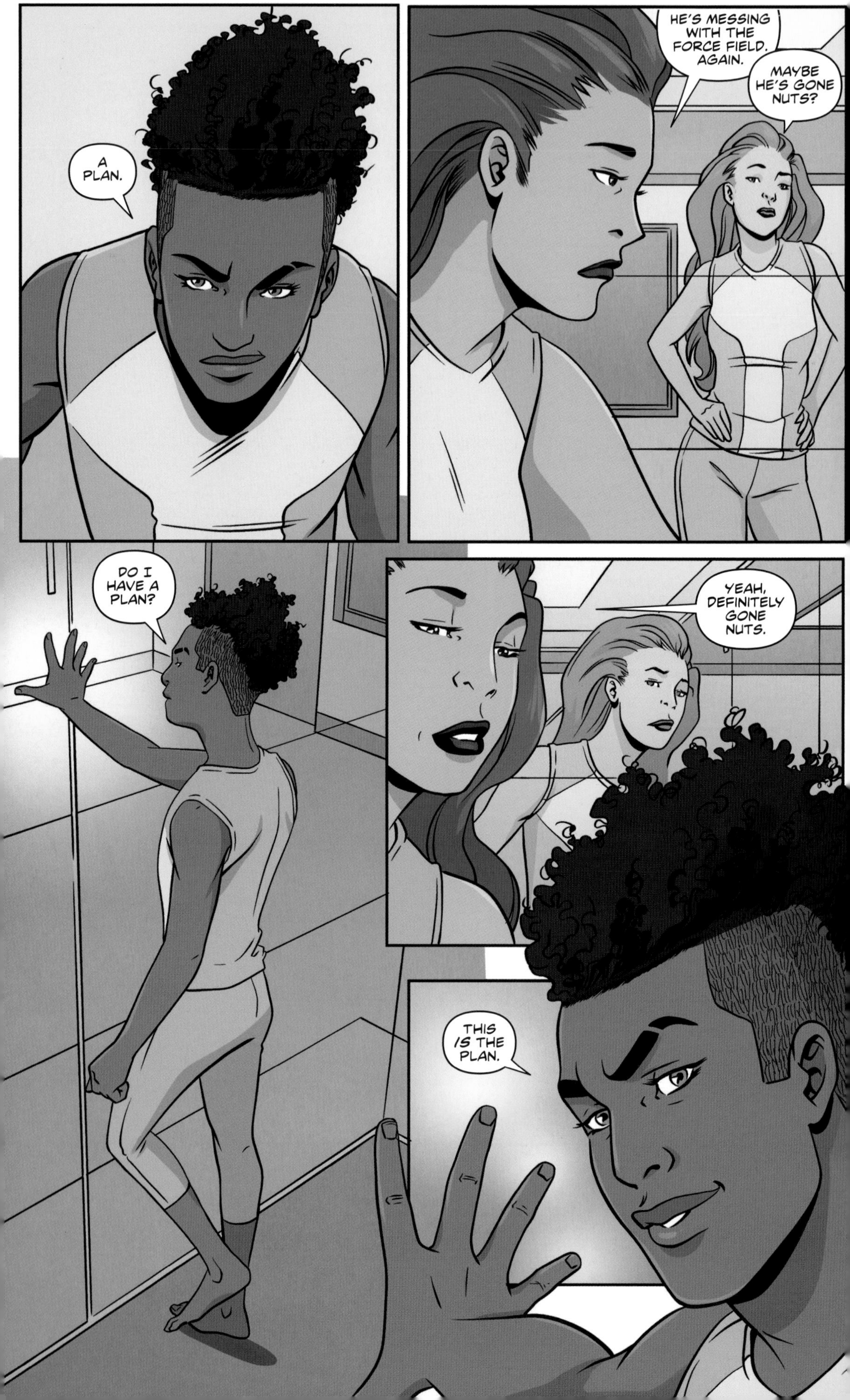
A PLAN.
HE'S MESSING WITH THE FORCE FIELD. AGAIN.
MAYBE HE'S GONE NUTS?
DO I HAVE A PLAN?
YEAH, DEFINITELY GONE NUTS.
THIS *IS* THE PLAN.

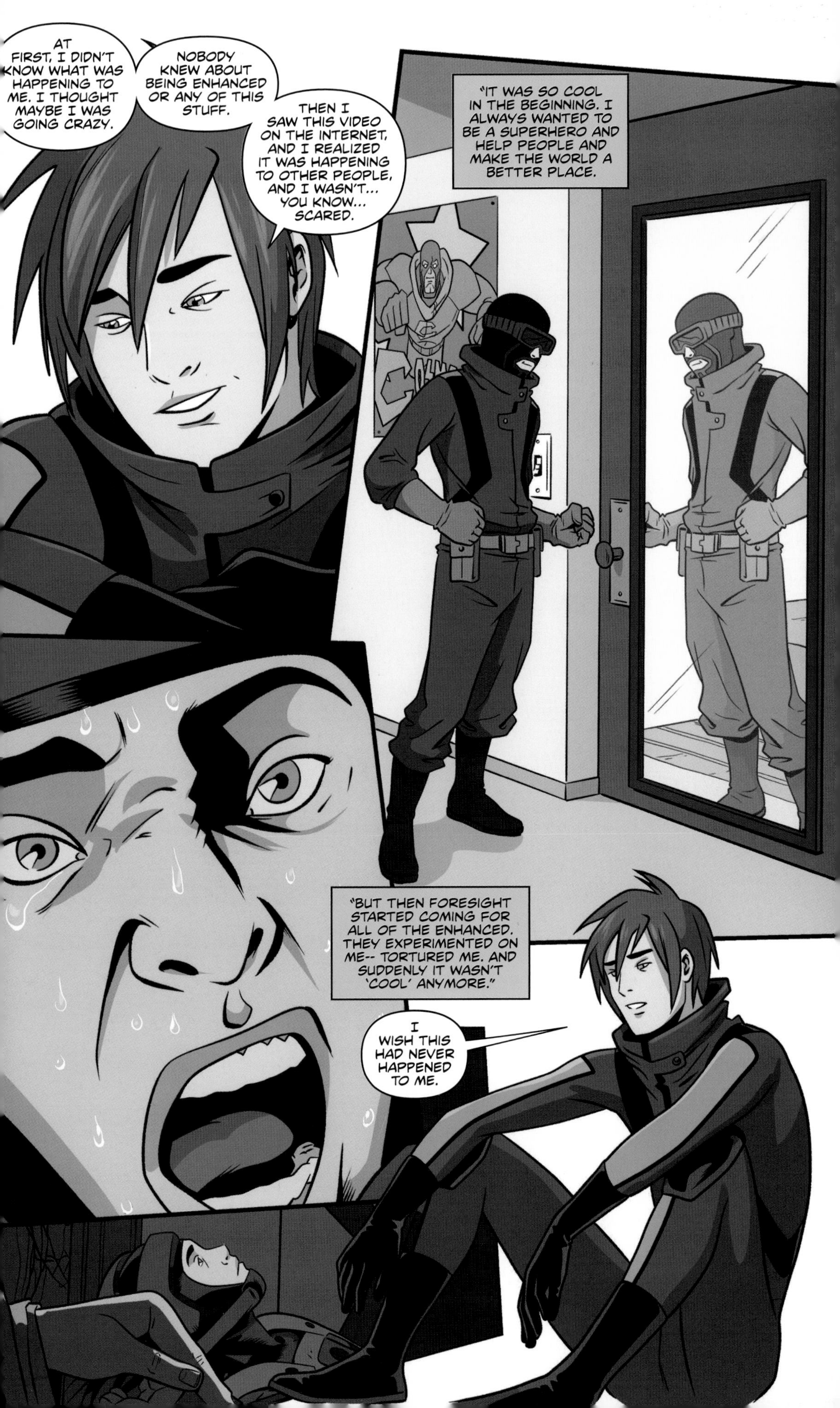
AT FIRST, I DIDN'T KNOW WHAT WAS HAPPENING TO ME. I THOUGHT MAYBE I WAS GOING CRAZY.
NOBODY KNEW ABOUT BEING ENHANCED OR ANY OF THIS STUFF.
THEN I SAW THIS VIDEO ON THE INTERNET, AND I REALIZED IT WAS HAPPENING TO OTHER PEOPLE, AND I WASN'T... YOU KNOW... SCARED.
"IT WAS SO COOL IN THE BEGINNING. I ALWAYS WANTED TO BE A SUPERHERO AND HELP PEOPLE AND MAKE THE WORLD A BETTER PLACE.
"BUT THEN FORESIGHT STARTED COMING FOR ALL OF THE ENHANCED. THEY EXPERIMENTED ON ME-- TORTURED ME. AND SUDDENLY IT WASN'T 'COOL' ANYMORE."
I WISH THIS HAD NEVER HAPPENED TO ME.

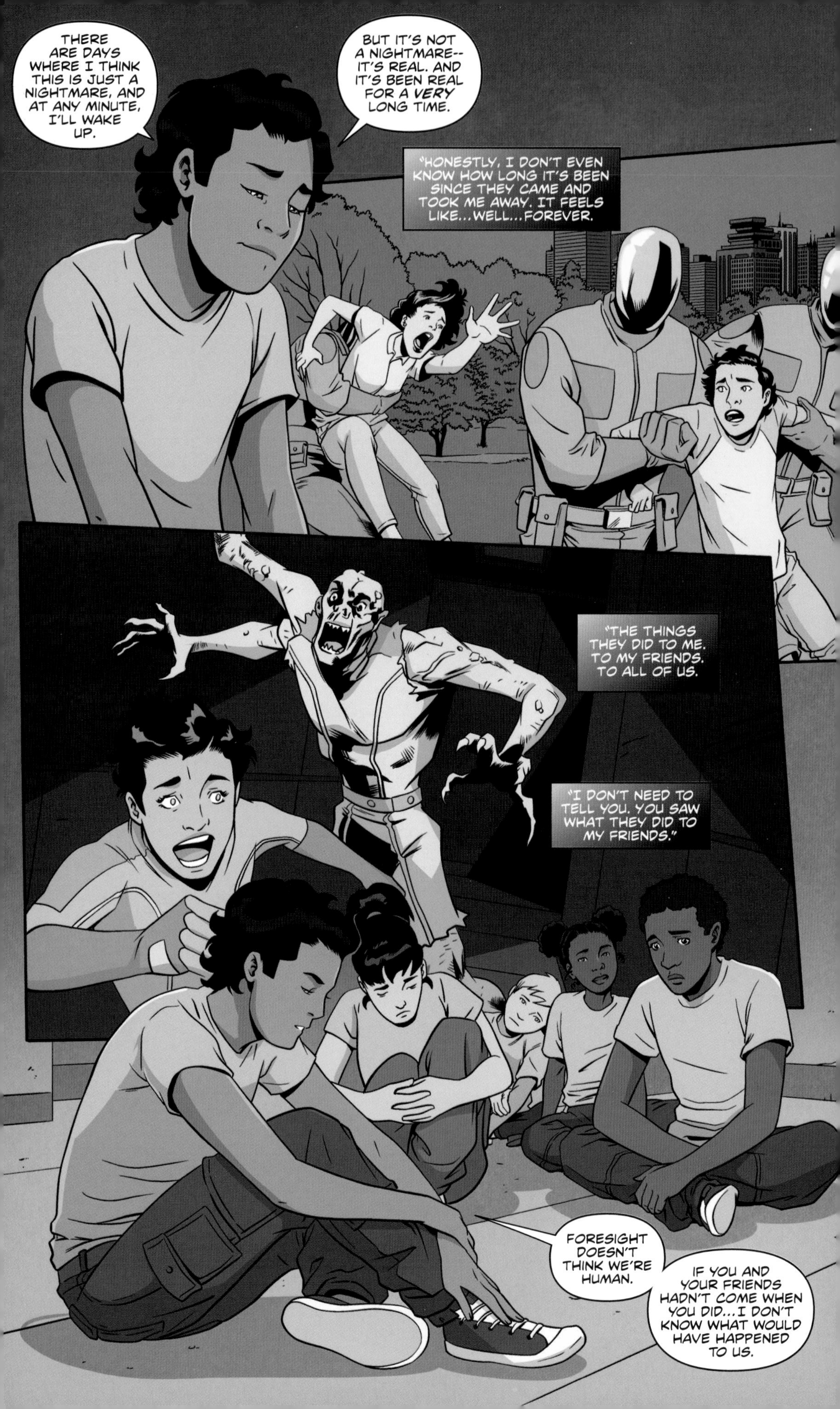
THERE ARE DAYS WHERE I THINK THIS IS JUST A NIGHTMARE, AND AT ANY MINUTE, I'LL WAKE UP.
BUT IT'S NOT A NIGHTMARE-- IT'S REAL. AND IT'S BEEN REAL FOR A *VERY* LONG TIME.
"HONESTLY, I DON'T EVEN KNOW HOW LONG IT'S BEEN SINCE THEY CAME AND TOOK ME AWAY. IT FEELS LIKE...WELL...FOREVER.
"THE THINGS THEY DID TO ME. TO MY FRIENDS. TO ALL OF US.
"I DON'T NEED TO TELL YOU. YOU SAW WHAT THEY DID TO MY FRIENDS."
FORESIGHT DOESN'T THINK WE'RE HUMAN.
IF YOU AND YOUR FRIENDS HADN'T COME WHEN YOU DID...I DON'T KNOW WHAT WOULD HAVE HAPPENED TO US.

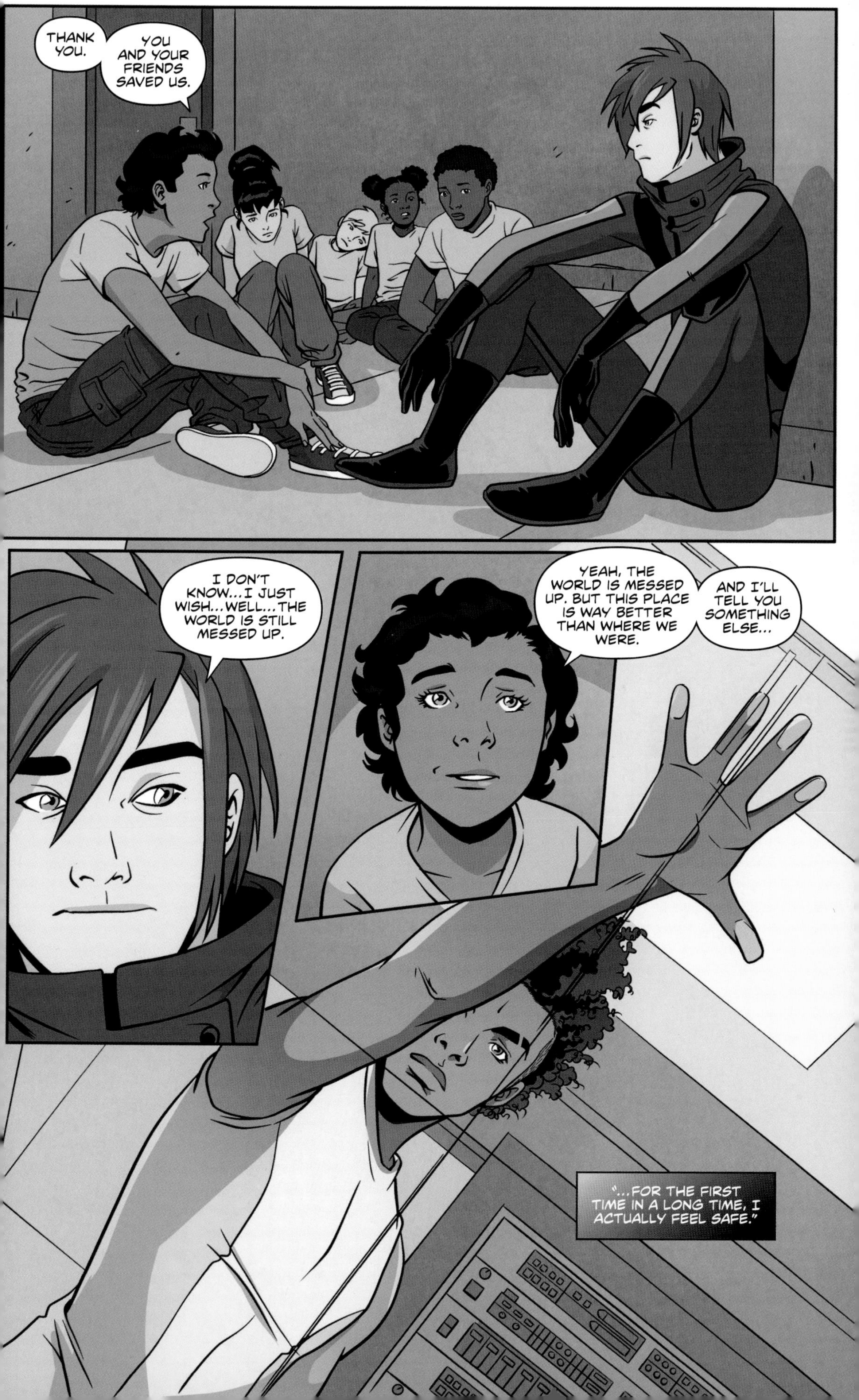
THANK YOU.
YOU AND YOUR FRIENDS SAVED US.
I DON'T KNOW...I JUST WISH...WELL...THE WORLD IS STILL MESSED UP.
YEAH, THE WORLD IS MESSED UP. BUT THIS PLACE IS WAY BETTER THAN WHERE WE WERE.
AND I'LL TELL YOU SOMETHING ELSE...
"...FOR THE FIRST TIME IN A LONG TIME, I ACTUALLY FEEL SAFE."

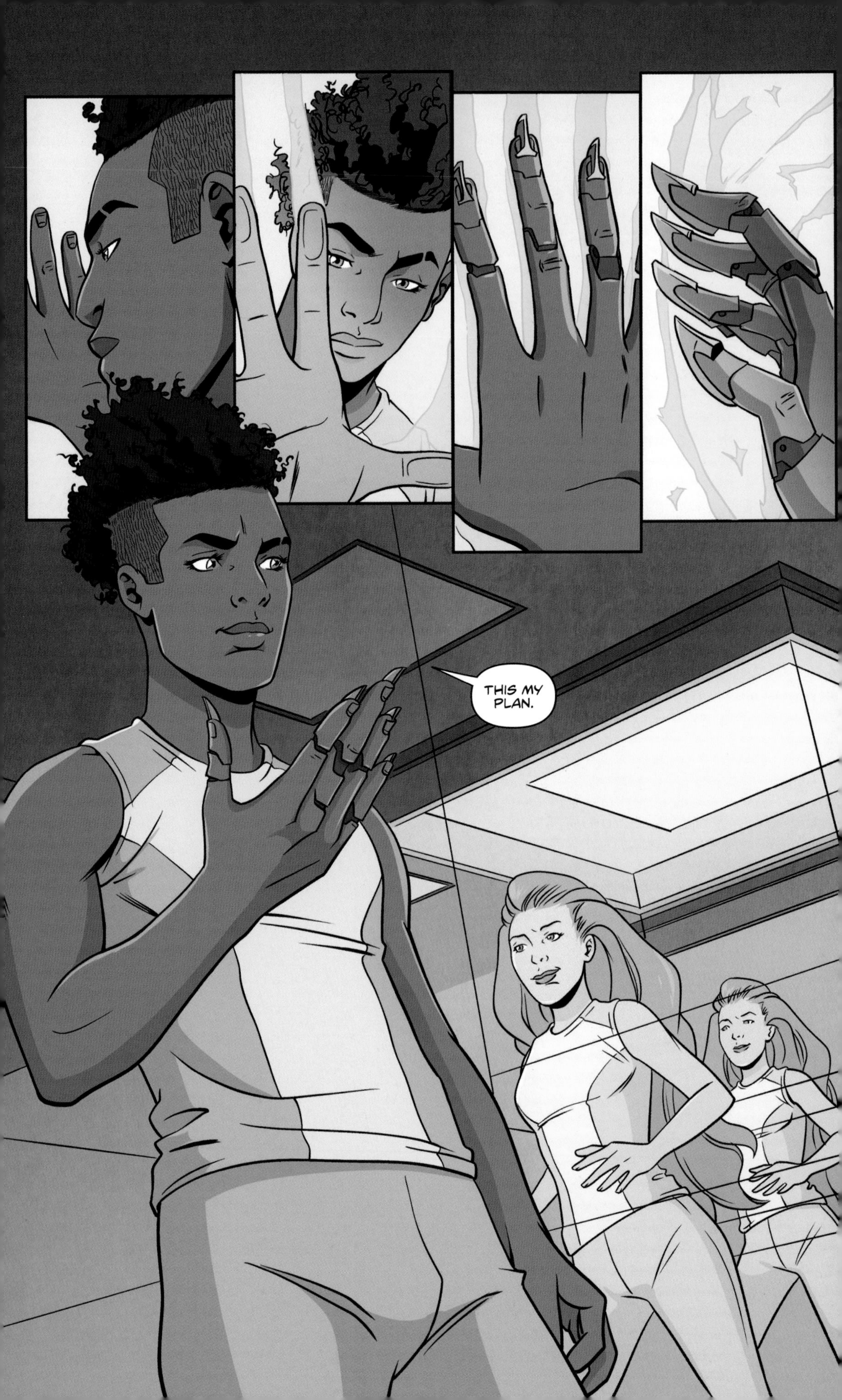
THIS MY PLAN.

CHAPTER FIVE

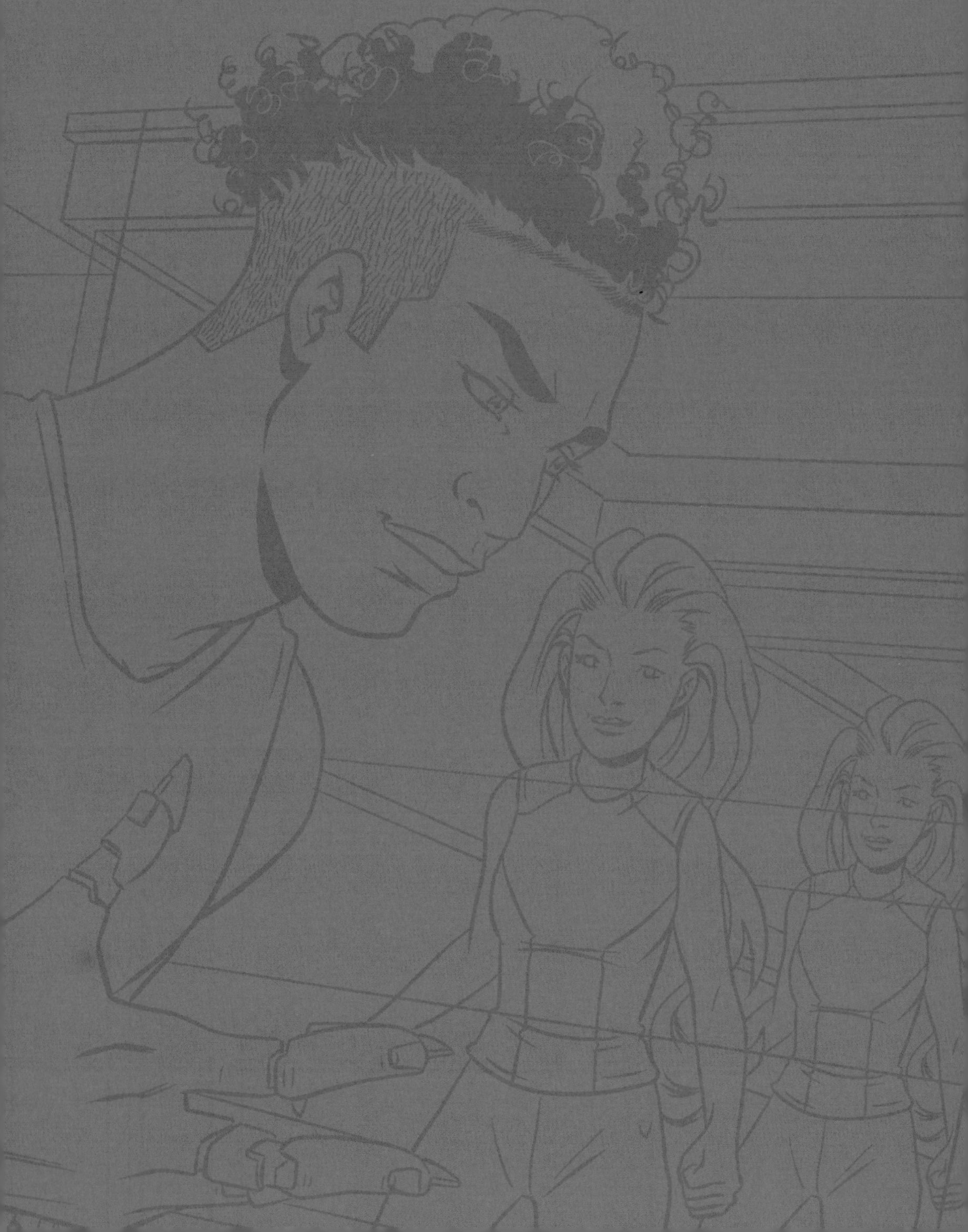

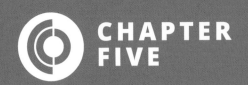

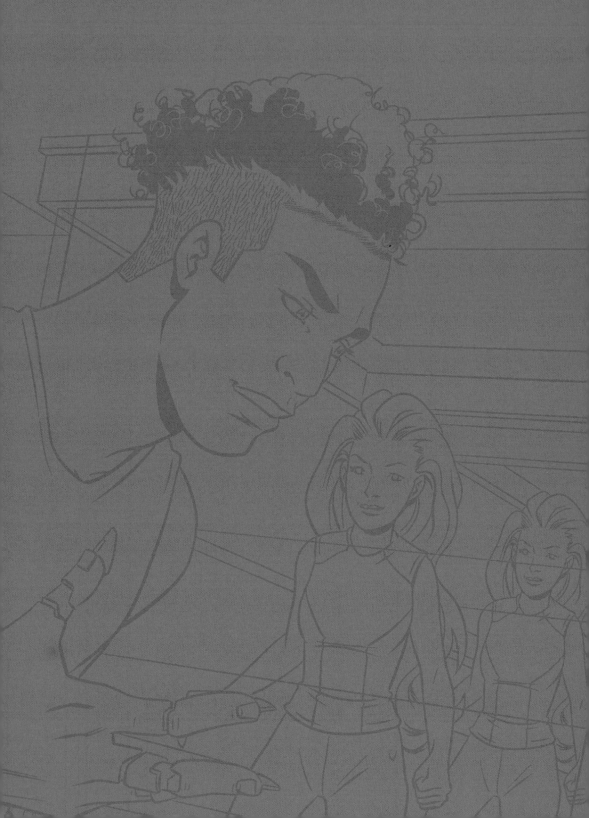

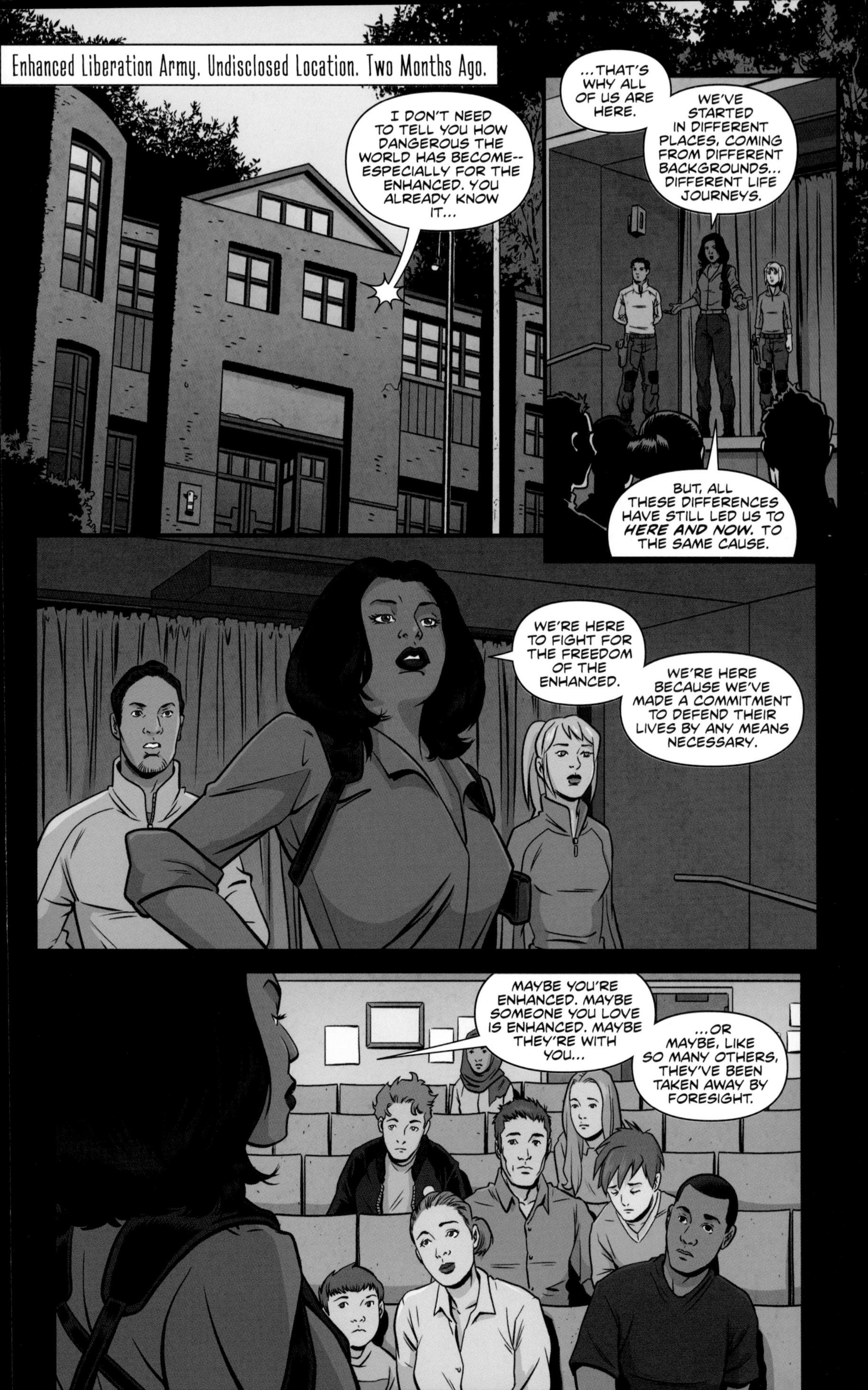
Enhanced Liberation Army. Undisclosed Location. Two Months Ago.
I DON'T NEED TO TELL YOU HOW DANGEROUS THE WORLD HAS BECOME-- ESPECIALLY FOR THE ENHANCED. YOU ALREADY KNOW IT...
...THAT'S WHY ALL OF US ARE HERE.
WE'VE STARTED IN DIFFERENT PLACES, COMING FROM DIFFERENT BACKGROUNDS... DIFFERENT LIFE JOURNEYS.
BUT, ALL THESE DIFFERENCES HAVE STILL LED US TO HERE AND NOW. TO THE SAME CAUSE.
WE'RE HERE TO FIGHT FOR THE FREEDOM OF THE ENHANCED.
WE'RE HERE BECAUSE WE'VE MADE A COMMITMENT TO DEFEND THEIR LIVES BY ANY MEANS NECESSARY.
MAYBE YOU'RE ENHANCED. MAYBE SOMEONE YOU LOVE IS ENHANCED. MAYBE THEY'RE WITH YOU...
...OR MAYBE, LIKE SO MANY OTHERS, THEY'VE BEEN TAKEN AWAY BY FORESIGHT.

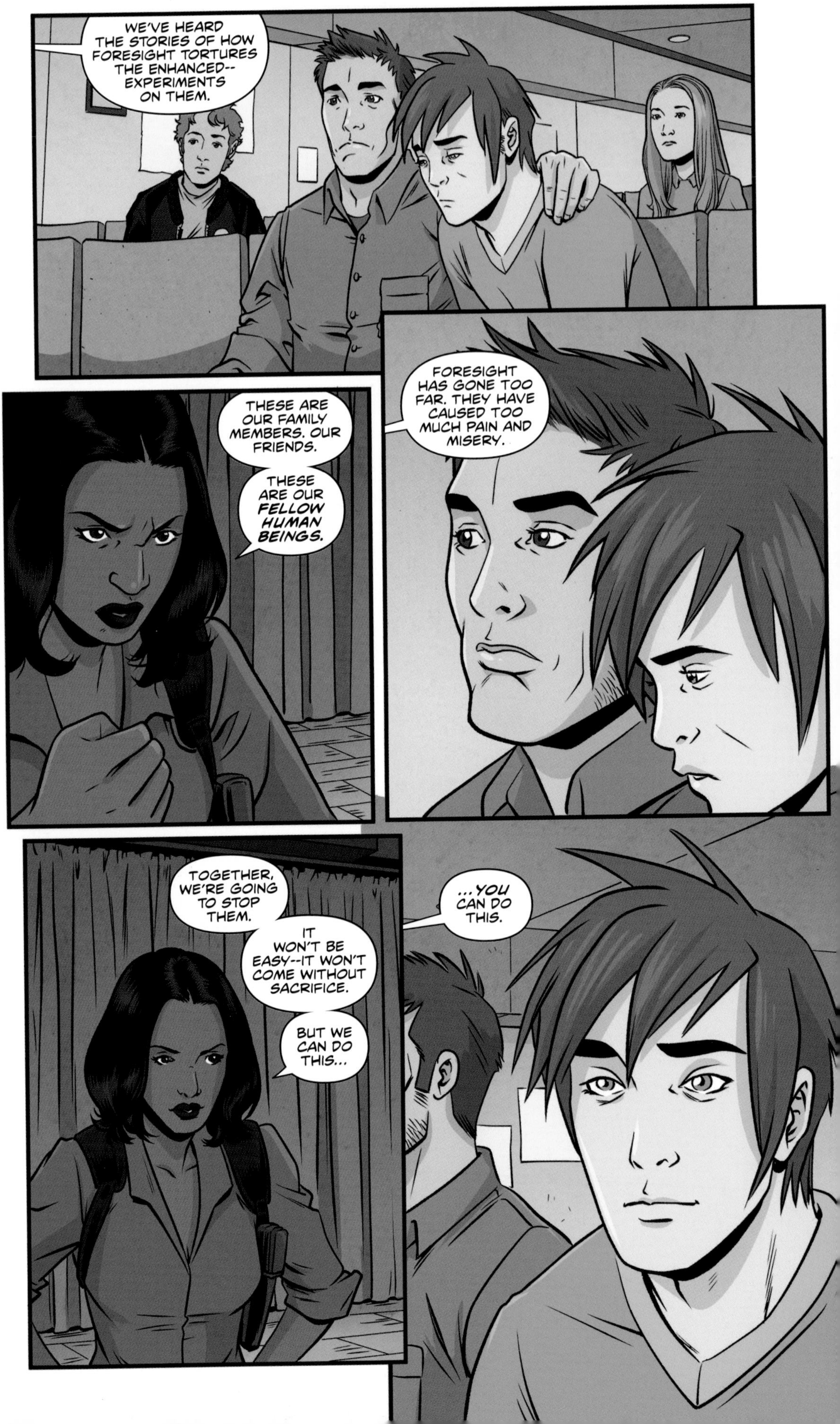
WE'VE HEARD THE STORIES OF HOW FORESIGHT TORTURES THE ENHANCED--EXPERIMENTS ON THEM.
THESE ARE OUR FAMILY MEMBERS. OUR FRIENDS.
THESE ARE OUR *FELLOW HUMAN BEINGS.*
FORESIGHT HAS GONE TOO FAR. THEY HAVE CAUSED TOO MUCH PAIN AND MISERY.
TOGETHER, WE'RE GOING TO STOP THEM.
IT WON'T BE EASY--IT WON'T COME WITHOUT SACRIFICE.
BUT WE CAN DO THIS...
...*YOU* CAN DO THIS.

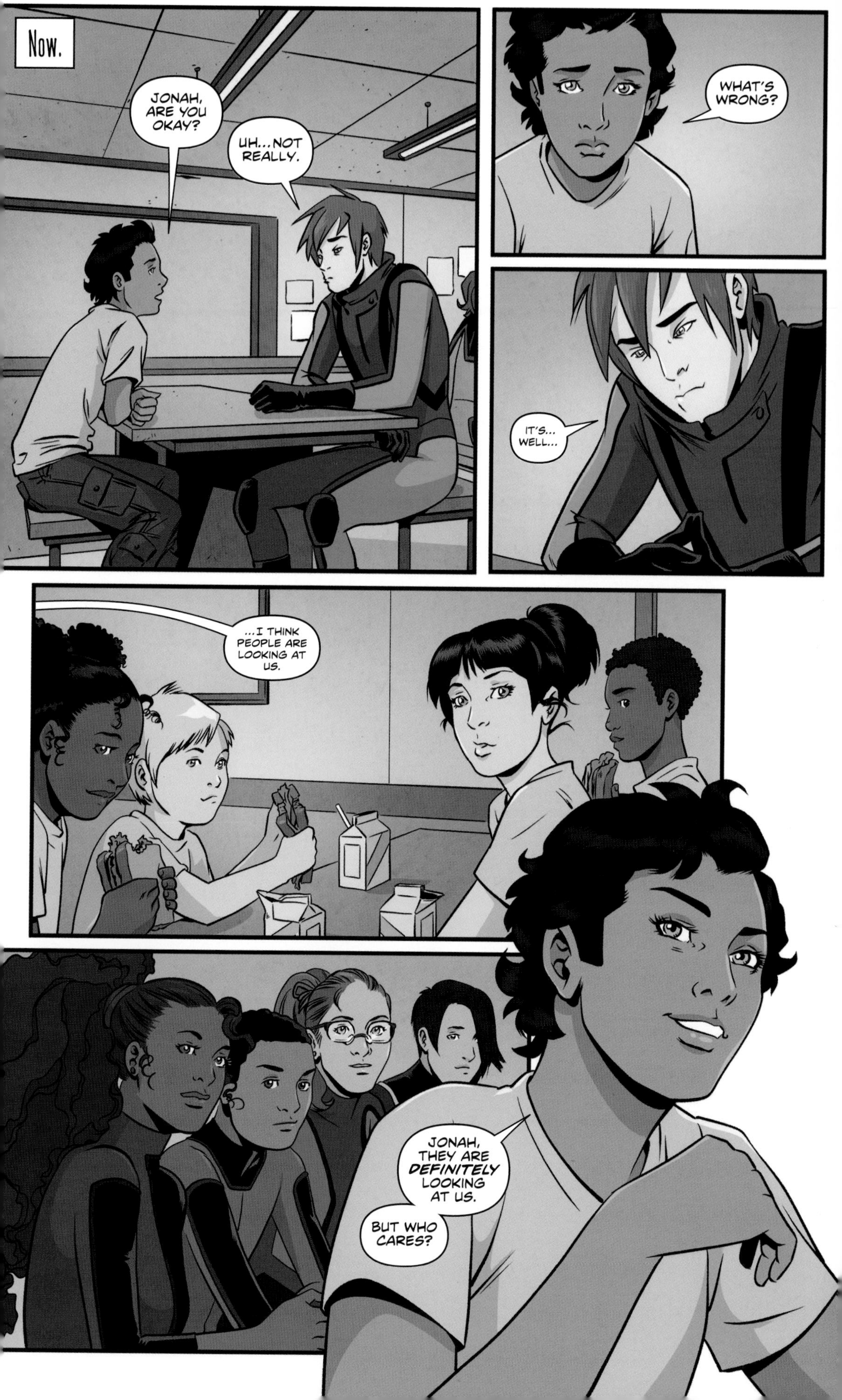
Now.
JONAH, ARE YOU OKAY?
UH...NOT REALLY.
WHAT'S WRONG?
IT'S... WELL...
...I THINK PEOPLE ARE LOOKING AT US.
JONAH, THEY ARE *DEFINITELY* LOOKING AT US.
BUT WHO CARES?

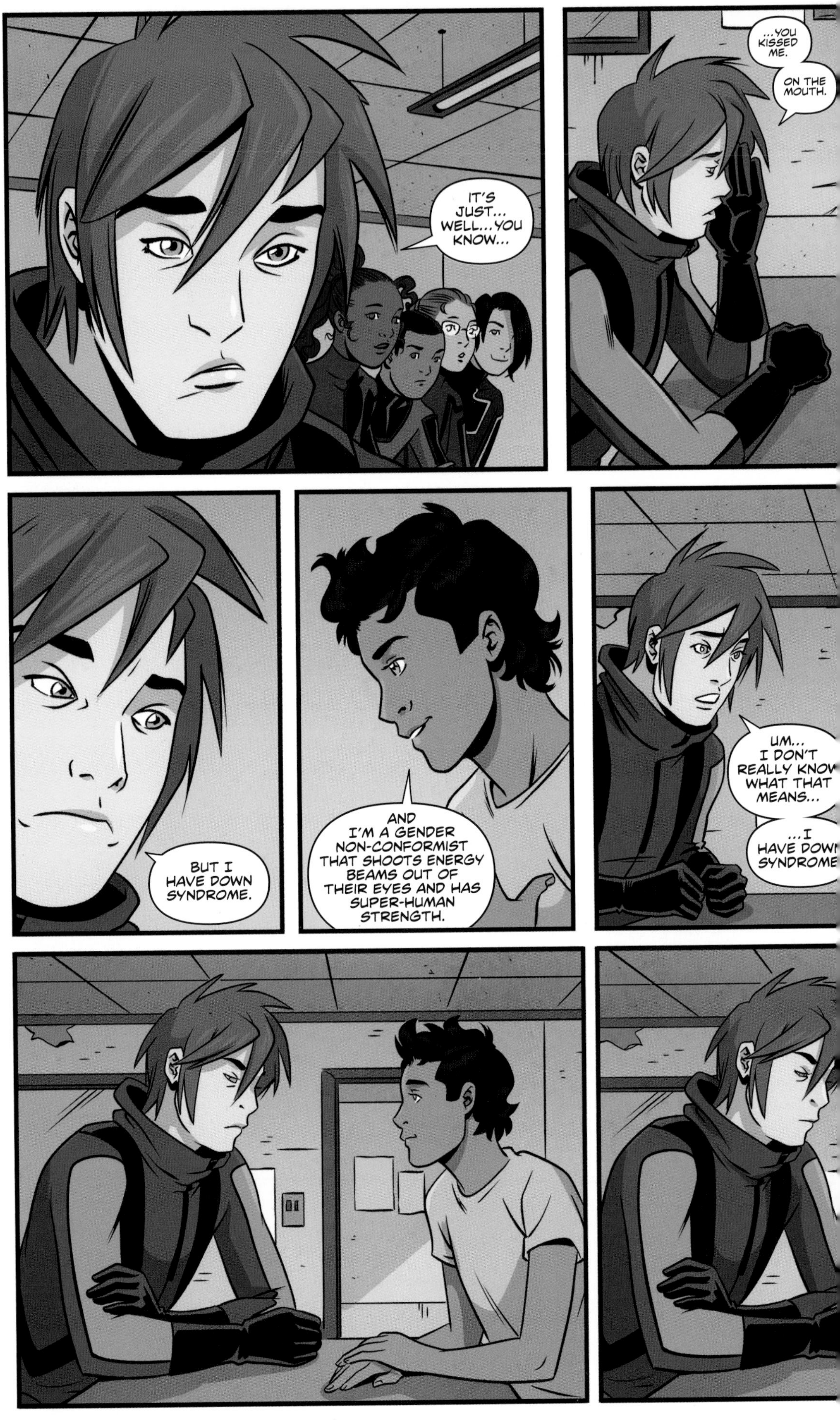
IT'S JUST... WELL...YOU KNOW...
...YOU KISSED ME.
ON THE MOUTH.
BUT I HAVE DOWN SYNDROME.
AND I'M A GENDER NON-CONFORMIST THAT SHOOTS ENERGY BEAMS OUT OF THEIR EYES AND HAS SUPER-HUMAN STRENGTH.
UM... I DON'T REALLY KNOW WHAT THAT MEANS...
...I HAVE DOWN SYNDROME

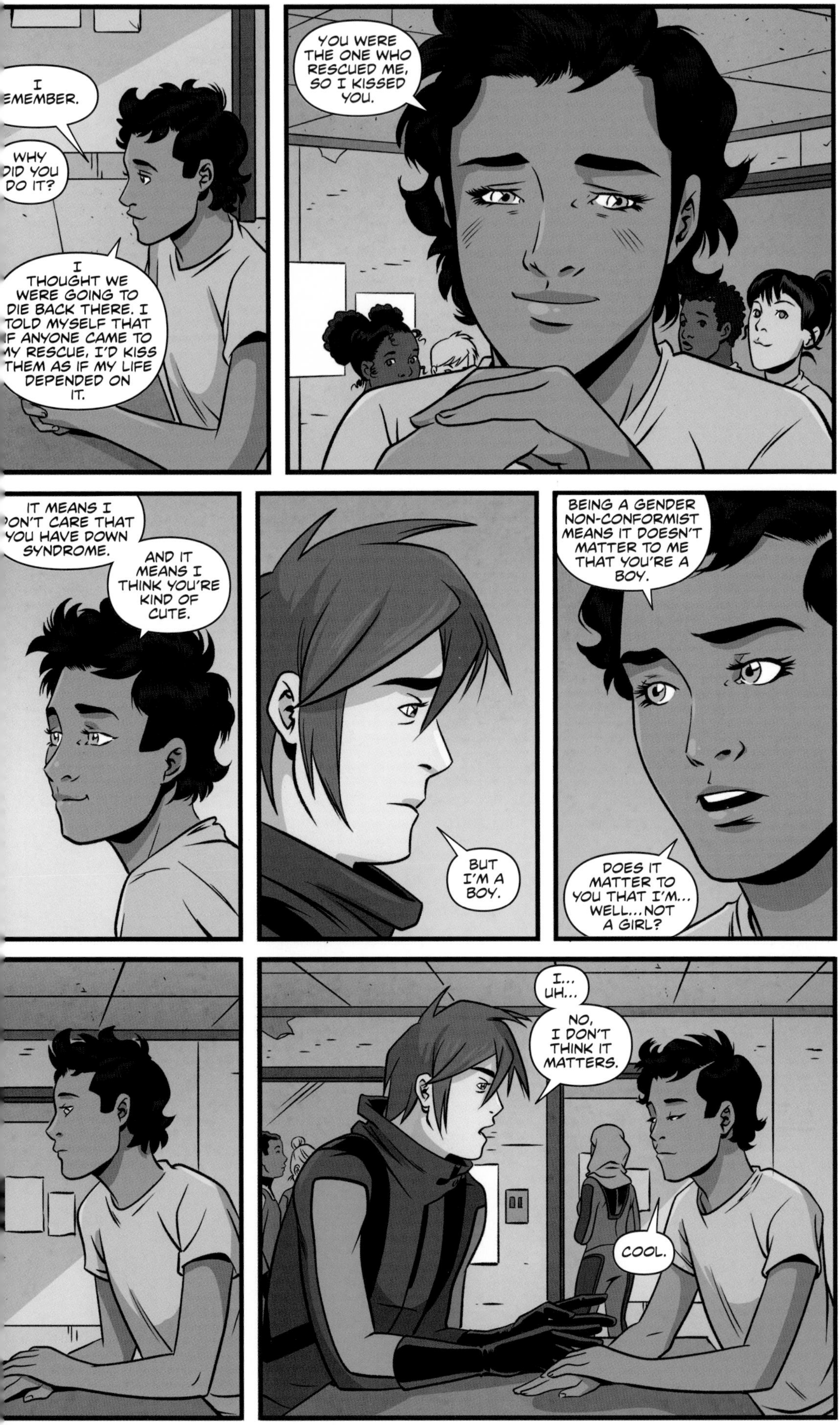

I
EMEMBER.
WHY
DID YOU
DO IT?
I THOUGHT WE WERE GOING TO DIE BACK THERE. I TOLD MYSELF THAT IF ANYONE CAME TO MY RESCUE, I'D KISS THEM AS IF MY LIFE DEPENDED ON IT.
YOU WERE THE ONE WHO RESCUED ME, SO I KISSED YOU.
IT MEANS I DON'T CARE THAT YOU HAVE DOWN SYNDROME.
AND IT MEANS I THINK YOU'RE KIND OF CUTE.
BUT I'M A BOY.
BEING A GENDER NON-CONFORMIST MEANS IT DOESN'T MATTER TO ME THAT YOU'RE A BOY.
DOES IT MATTER TO YOU THAT I'M... WELL...NOT A GIRL?
I... UH...
NO, I DON'T THINK IT MATTERS.
COOL.

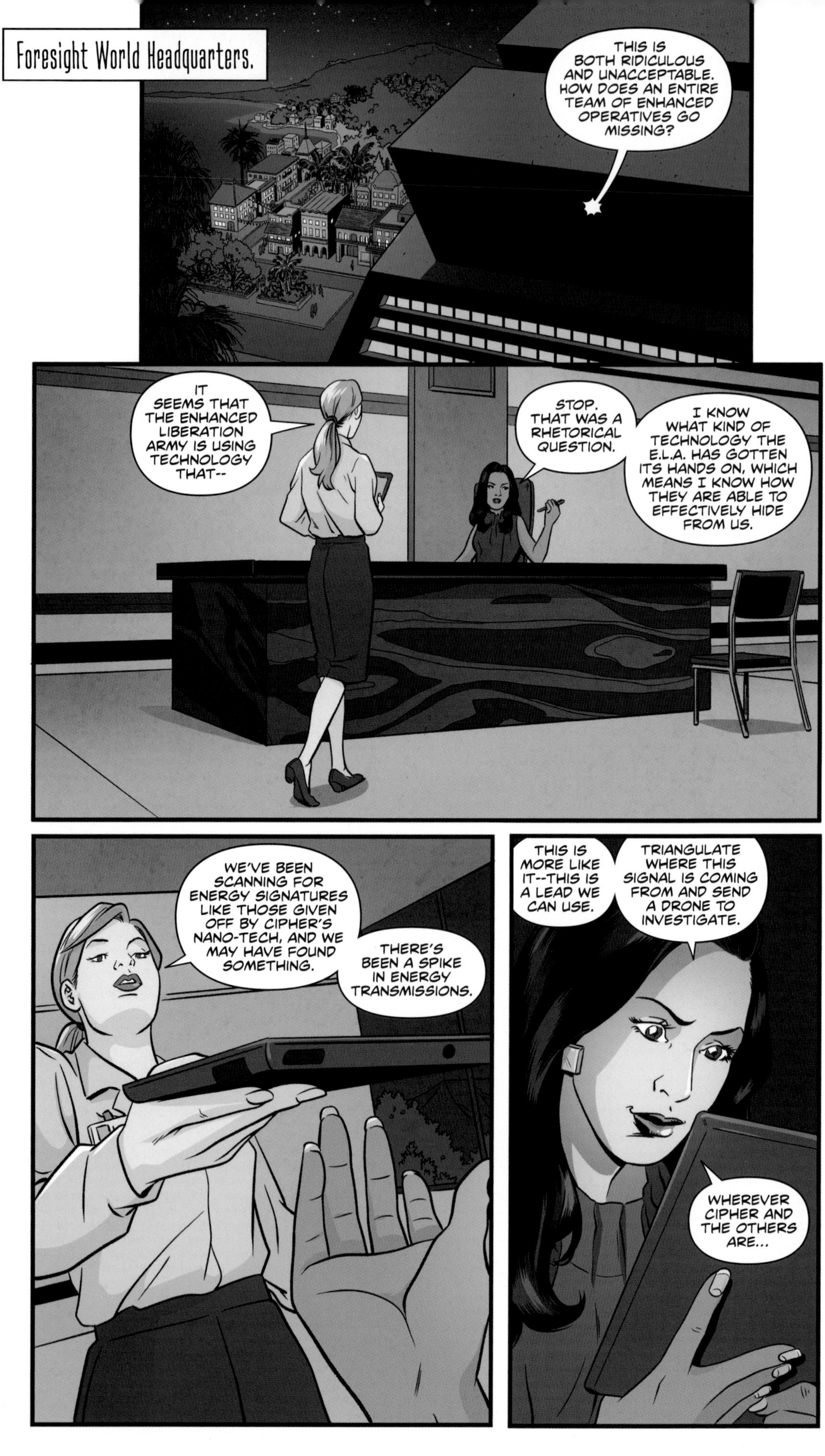
Foresight World Headquarters.
THIS IS BOTH RIDICULOUS AND UNACCEPTABLE. HOW DOES AN ENTIRE TEAM OF ENHANCED OPERATIVES GO MISSING?
IT SEEMS THAT THE ENHANCED LIBERATION ARMY IS USING TECHNOLOGY THAT--
STOP. THAT WAS A RHETORICAL QUESTION.
I KNOW WHAT KIND OF TECHNOLOGY THE E.L.A. HAS GOTTEN ITS HANDS ON, WHICH MEANS I KNOW HOW THEY ARE ABLE TO EFFECTIVELY HIDE FROM US.
WE'VE BEEN SCANNING FOR ENERGY SIGNATURES LIKE THOSE GIVEN OFF BY CIPHER'S NANO-TECH, AND WE MAY HAVE FOUND SOMETHING.
THERE'S BEEN A SPIKE IN ENERGY TRANSMISSIONS.
THIS IS MORE LIKE IT--THIS IS A LEAD WE CAN USE.
TRIANGULATE WHERE THIS SIGNAL IS COMING FROM AND SEND A DRONE TO INVESTIGATE.
WHEREVER CIPHER AND THE OTHERS ARE...

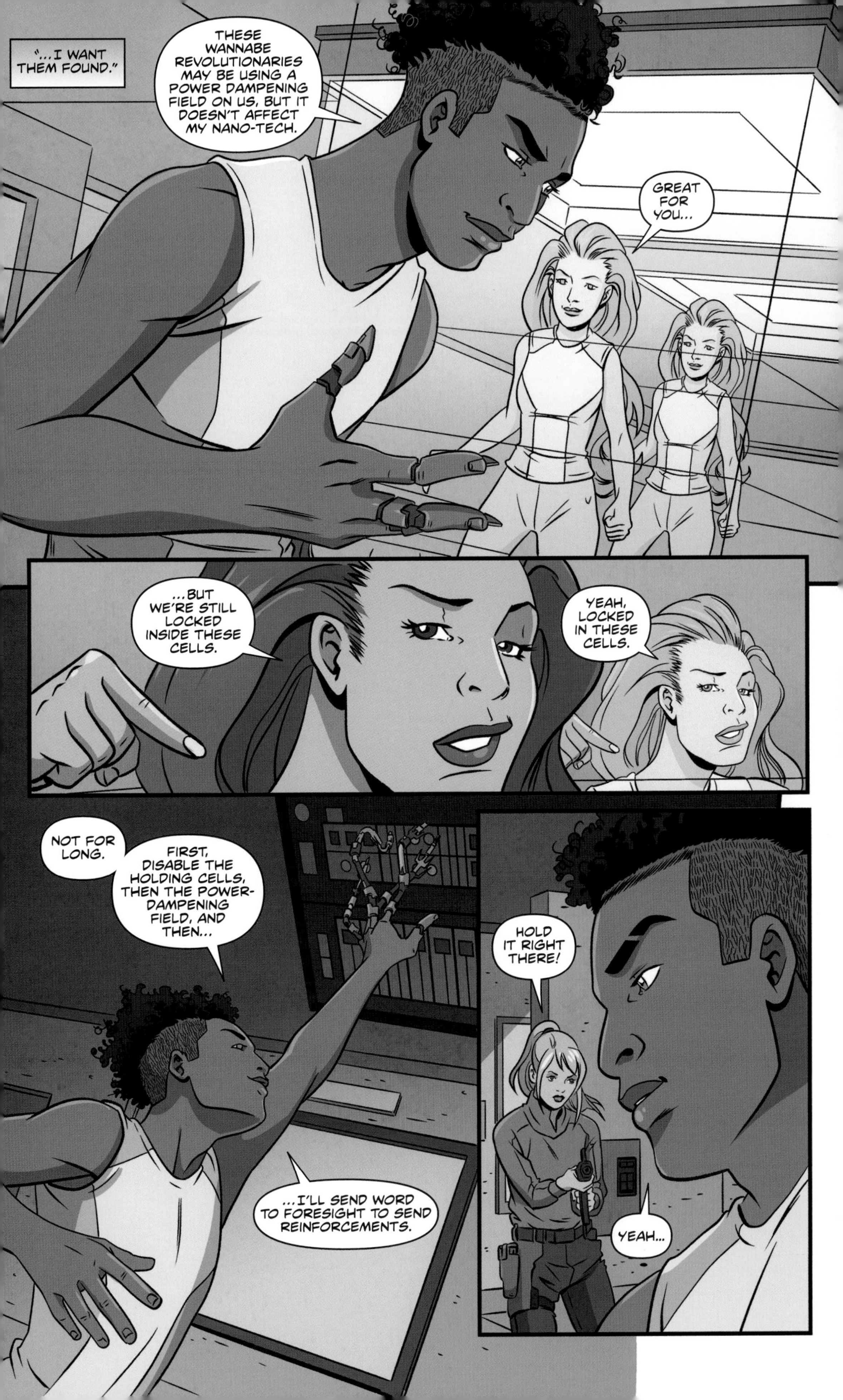
"...I WANT THEM FOUND."
THESE WANNABE REVOLUTIONARIES MAY BE USING A POWER DAMPENING FIELD ON US, BUT IT DOESN'T AFFECT MY NANO-TECH.
GREAT FOR YOU...
...BUT WE'RE STILL LOCKED INSIDE THESE CELLS.
YEAH, LOCKED IN THESE CELLS.
NOT FOR LONG.
FIRST, DISABLE THE HOLDING CELLS, THEN THE POWER-DAMPENING FIELD, AND THEN...
...I'LL SEND WORD TO FORESIGHT TO SEND REINFORCEMENTS.
HOLD IT RIGHT THERE!
YEAH...

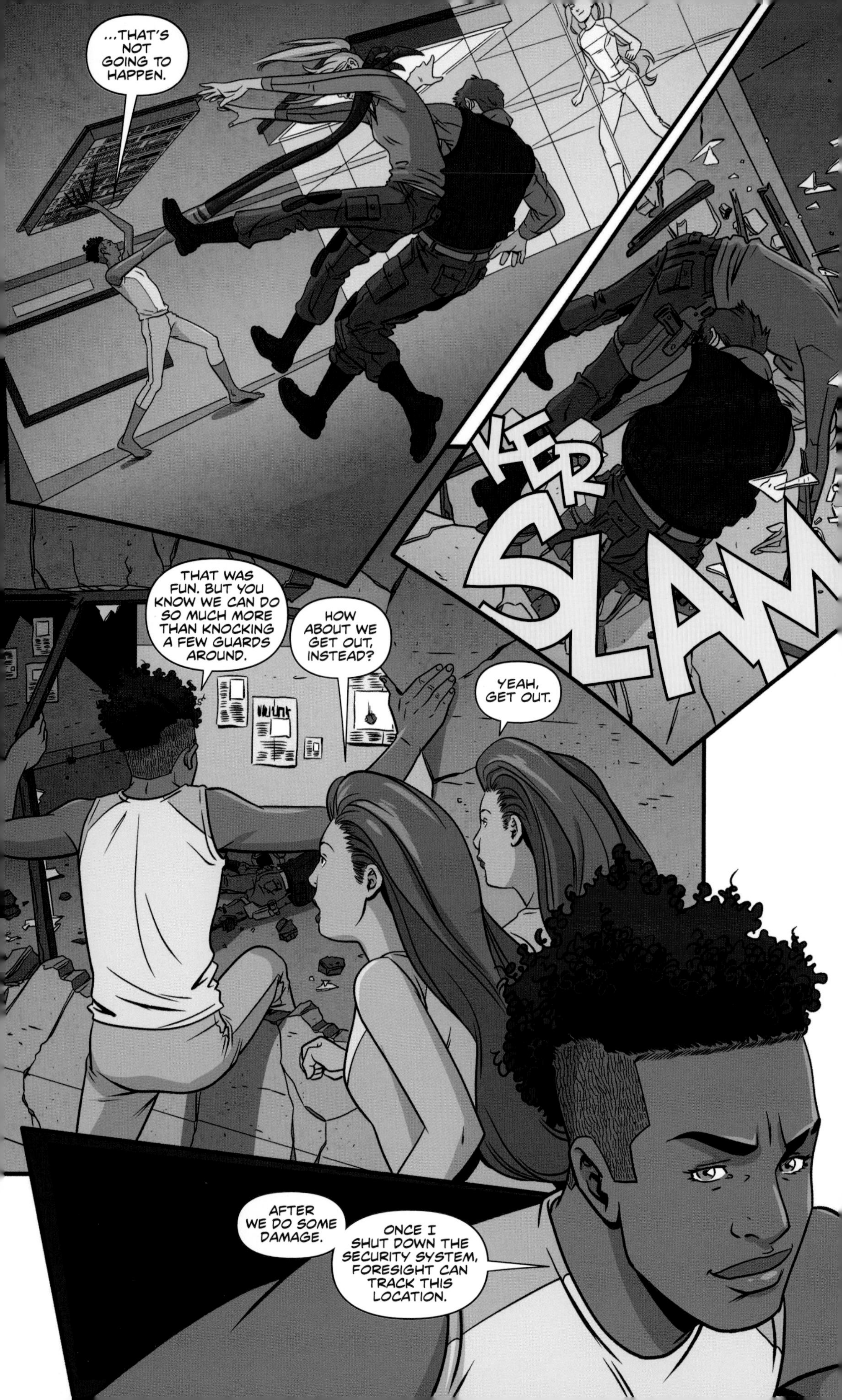

...THAT'S NOT GOING TO HAPPEN.
KER
SLAM
THAT WAS FUN. BUT YOU KNOW WE CAN DO SO MUCH MORE THAN KNOCKING A FEW GUARDS AROUND.
HOW ABOUT WE GET OUT, INSTEAD?
YEAH, GET OUT.
AFTER WE DO SOME DAMAGE.
ONCE I SHUT DOWN THE SECURITY SYSTEM, FORESIGHT CAN TRACK THIS LOCATION.

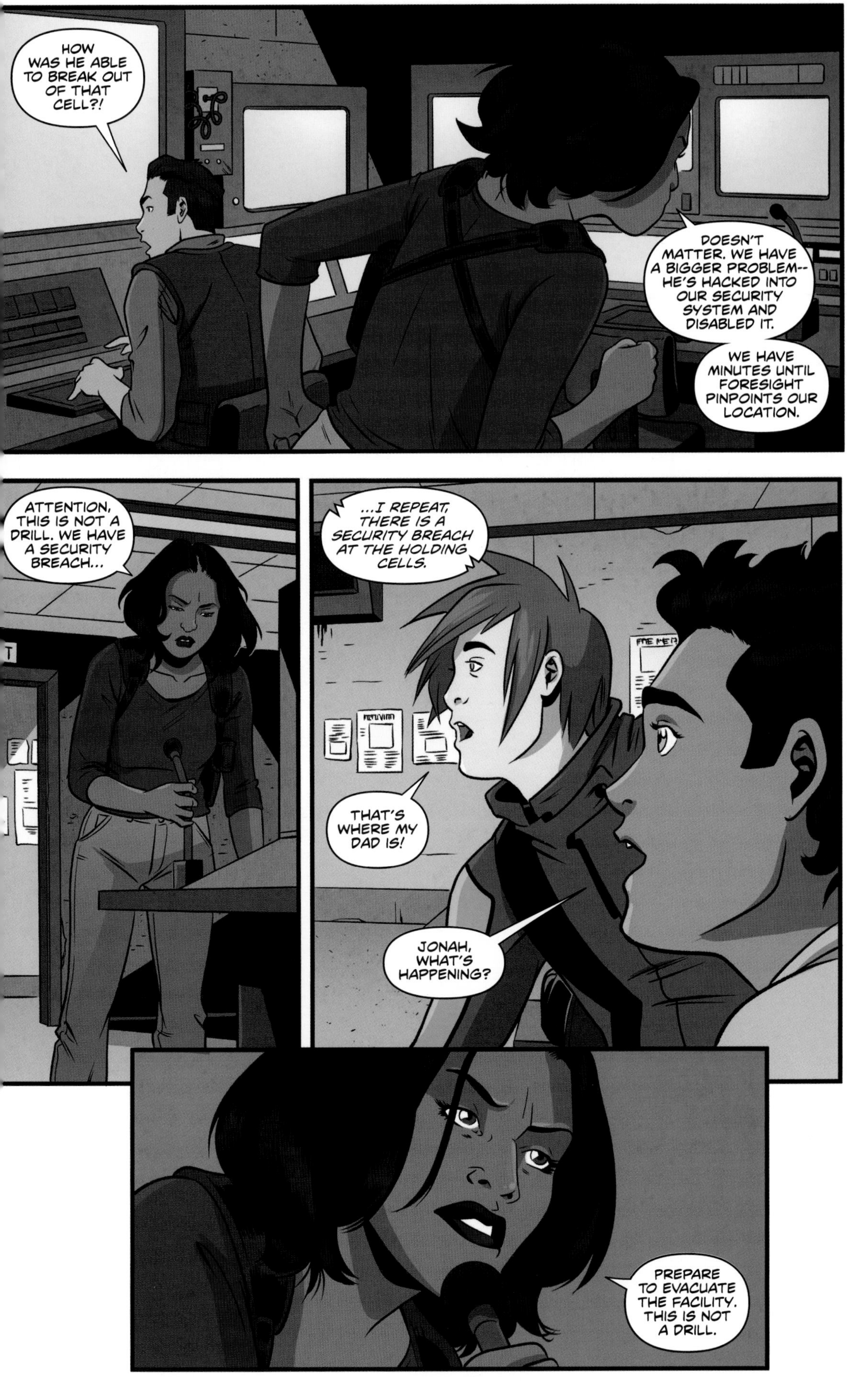
HOW WAS HE ABLE TO BREAK OUT OF THAT CELL?!
DOESN'T MATTER. WE HAVE A BIGGER PROBLEM-- HE'S HACKED INTO OUR SECURITY SYSTEM AND DISABLED IT.
WE HAVE MINUTES UNTIL FORESIGHT PINPOINTS OUR LOCATION.
ATTENTION, THIS IS NOT A DRILL. WE HAVE A SECURITY BREACH...
...I REPEAT, THERE IS A SECURITY BREACH AT THE HOLDING CELLS.
THAT'S WHERE MY DAD IS!
JONAH, WHAT'S HAPPENING?
PREPARE TO EVACUATE THE FACILITY. THIS IS NOT A DRILL.

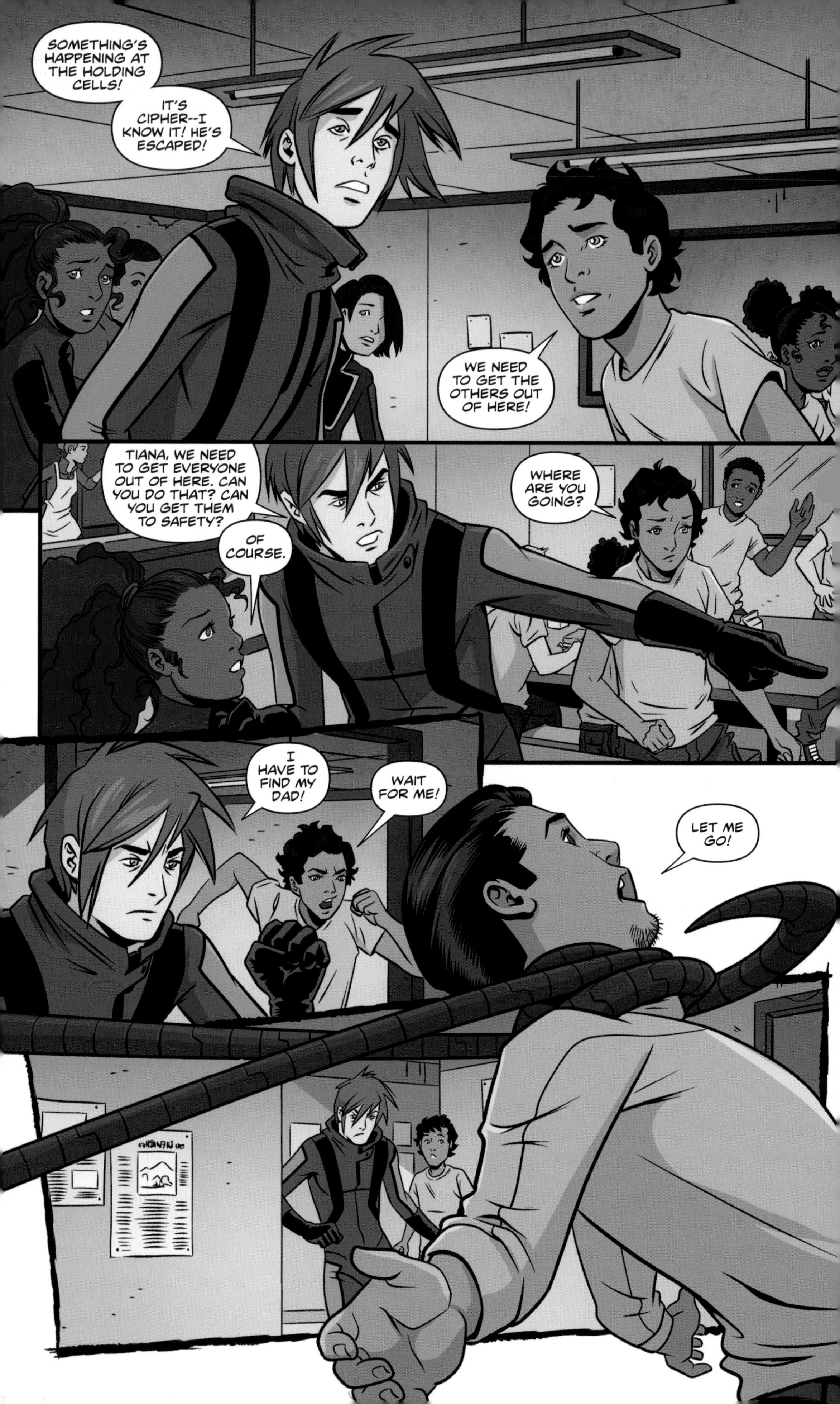
SOMETHING'S HAPPENING AT THE HOLDING CELLS!
IT'S CIPHER--I KNOW IT! HE'S ESCAPED!
WE NEED TO GET THE OTHERS OUT OF HERE!
TIANA, WE NEED TO GET EVERYONE OUT OF HERE. CAN YOU DO THAT? CAN YOU GET THEM TO SAFETY?
OF COURSE.
WHERE ARE YOU GOING?
I HAVE TO FIND MY DAD!
WAIT FOR ME!
LET ME GO!

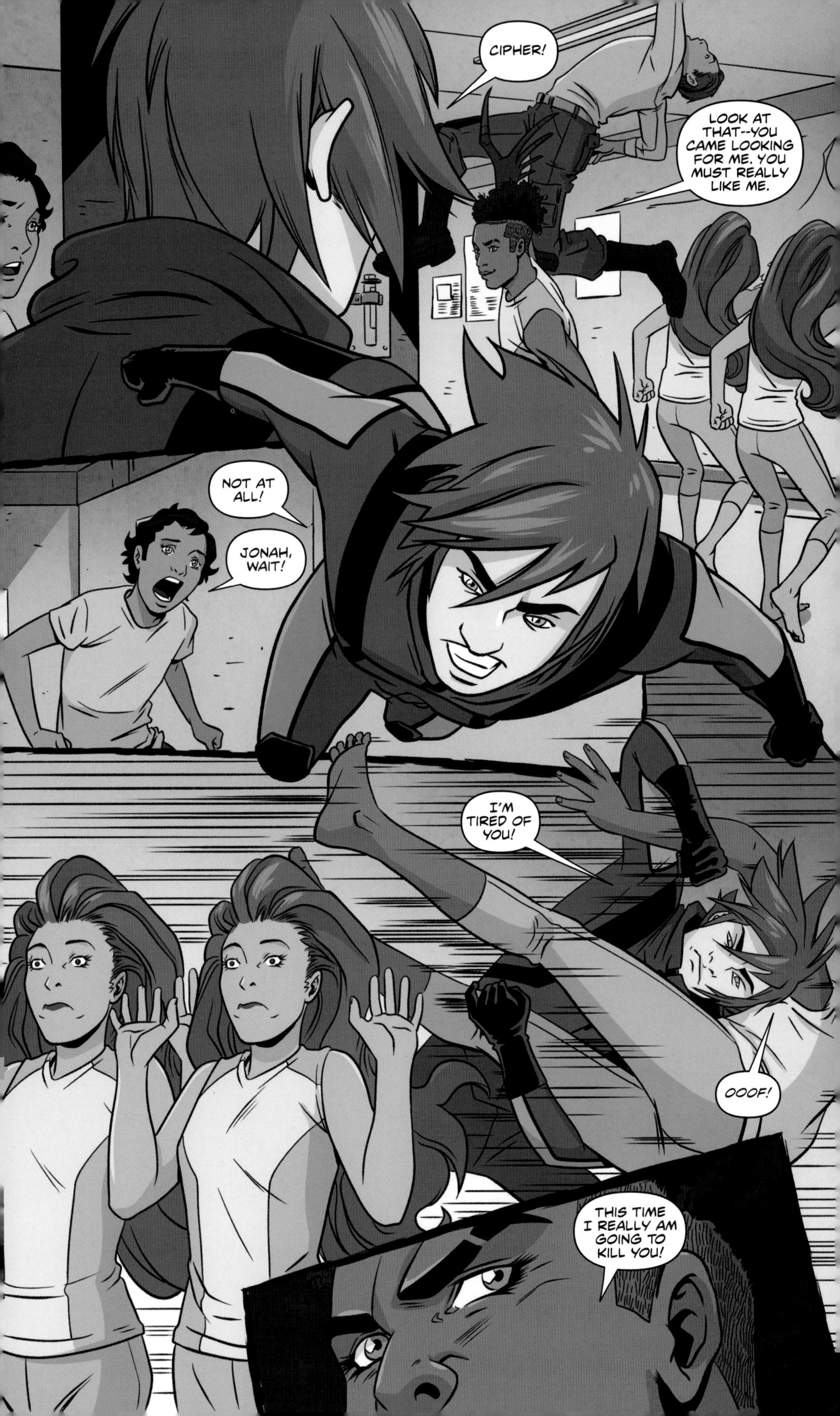
CIPHER!
LOOK AT THAT--YOU CAME LOOKING FOR ME. YOU MUST REALLY LIKE ME.
NOT AT ALL!
JONAH, WAIT!
I'M TIRED OF YOU!
OOOF!
THIS TIME I REALLY AM GOING TO KILL YOU!

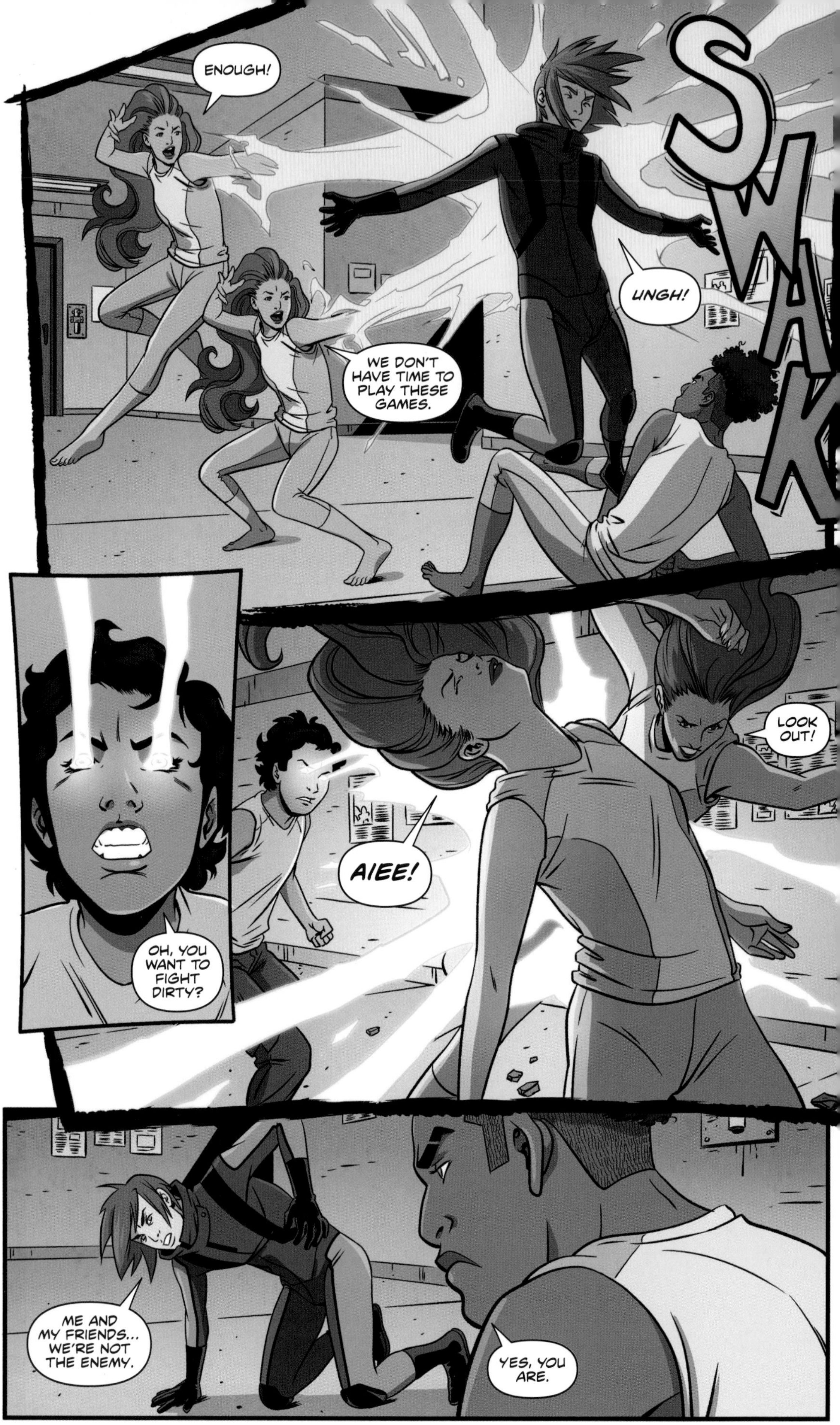
ENOUGH!
SWAK
UNGH!
WE DON'T HAVE TIME TO PLAY THESE GAMES.
OH, YOU WANT TO FIGHT DIRTY?
AIEE!
LOOK OUT!
ME AND MY FRIENDS... WE'RE NOT THE ENEMY.
YES, YOU ARE.

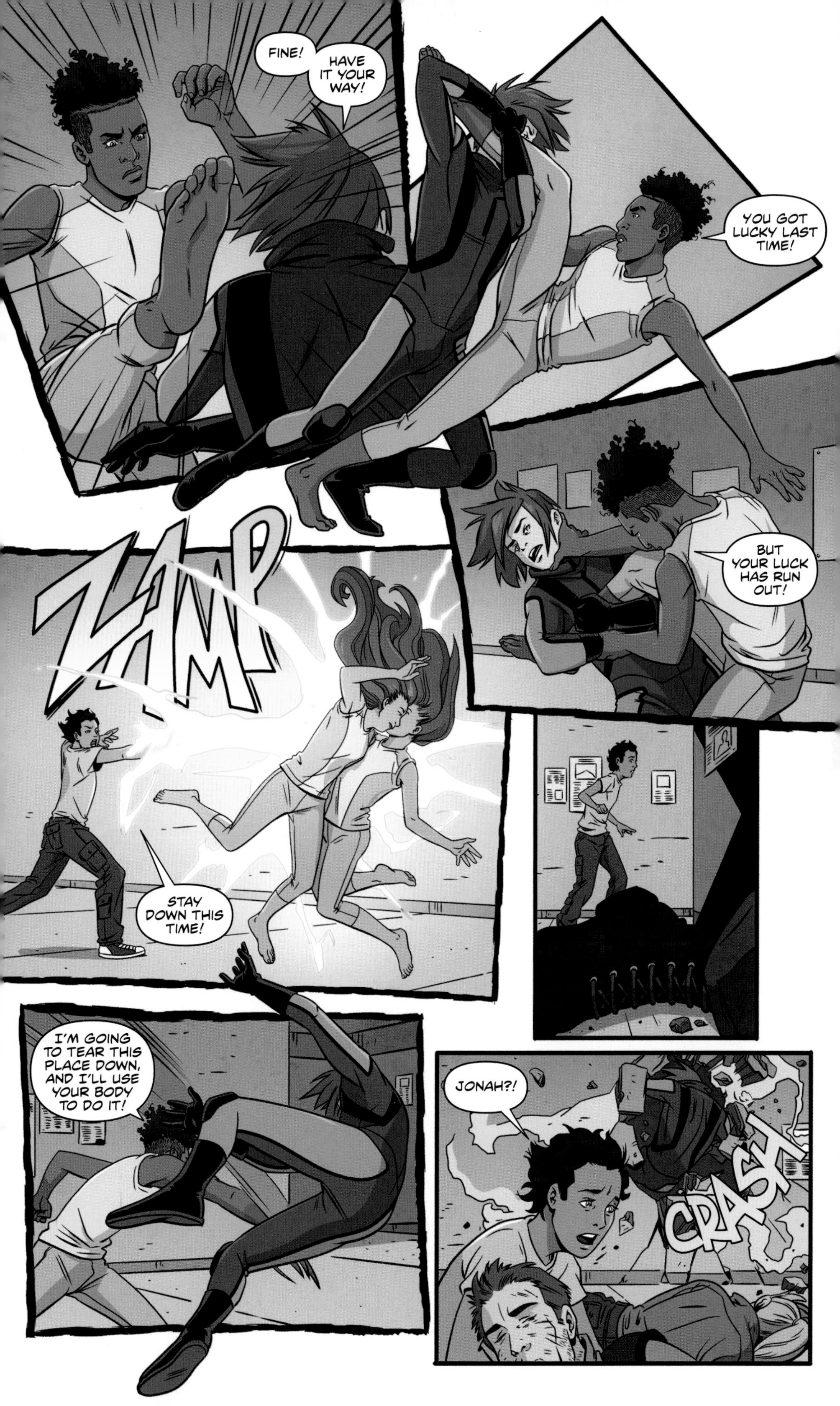

FINE!
HAVE IT YOUR WAY!
YOU GOT LUCKY LAST TIME!
BUT YOUR LUCK HAS RUN OUT!
ZAMP
STAY DOWN THIS TIME!
I'M GOING TO TEAR THIS PLACE DOWN, AND I'LL USE YOUR BODY TO DO IT!
JONAH?!
CRASH

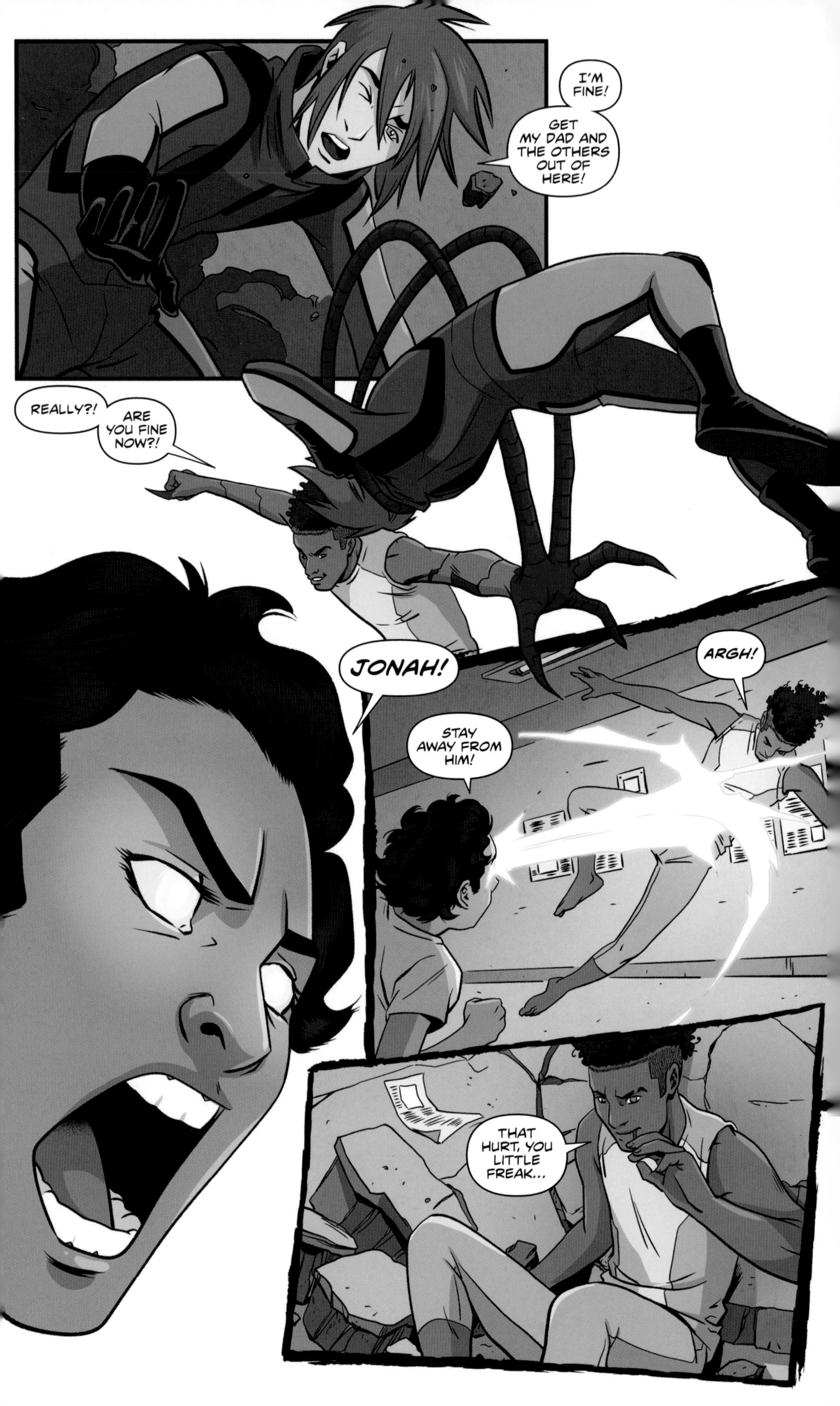

I'M FINE!
GET MY DAD AND THE OTHERS OUT OF HERE!
REALLY?!
ARE YOU FINE NOW?!
JONAH!
ARGH!
STAY AWAY FROM HIM!
THAT HURT, YOU LITTLE FREAK...

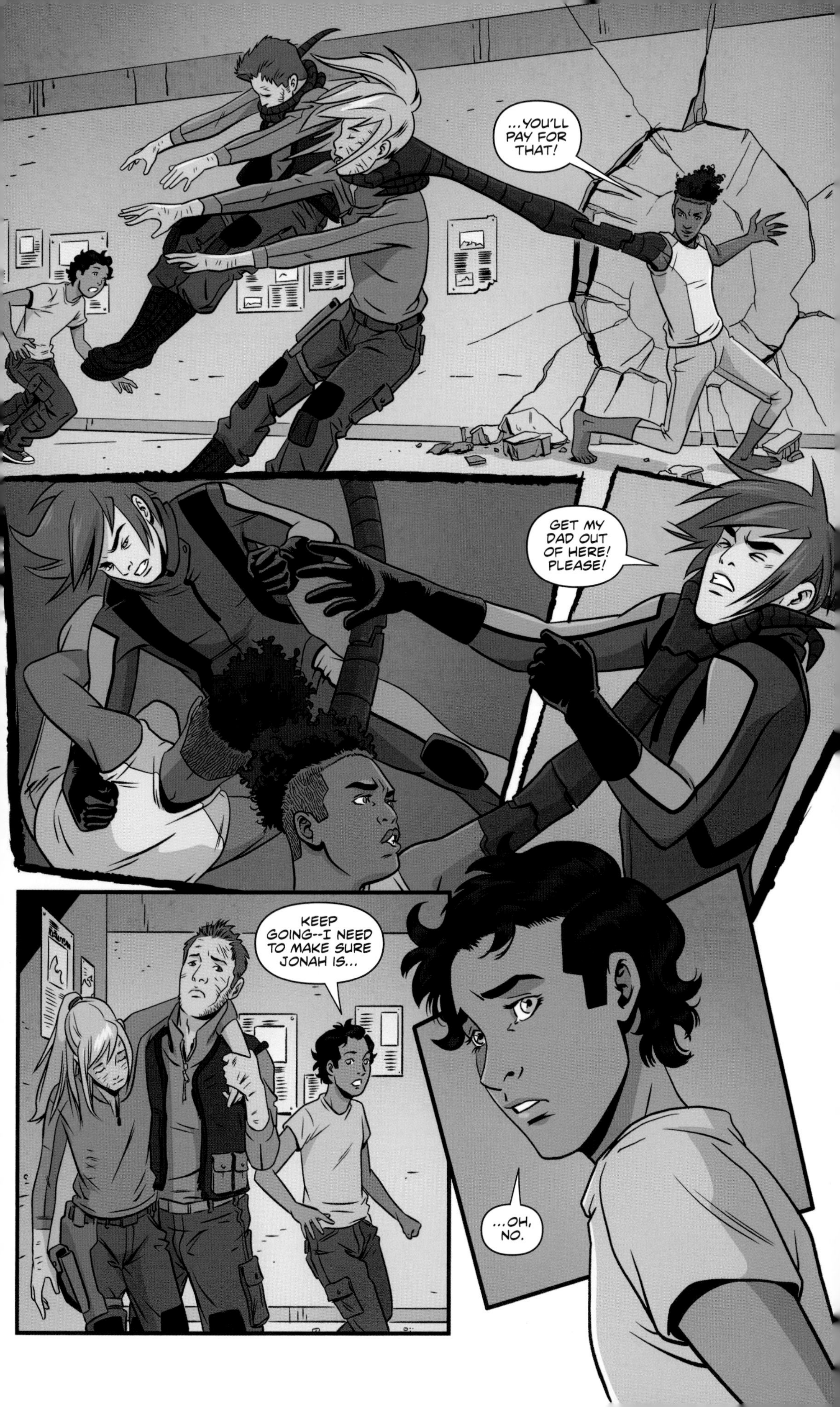
...YOU'LL PAY FOR THAT!
GET MY DAD OUT OF HERE! PLEASE!
KEEP GOING--I NEED TO MAKE SURE JONAH IS...
...OH, NO.

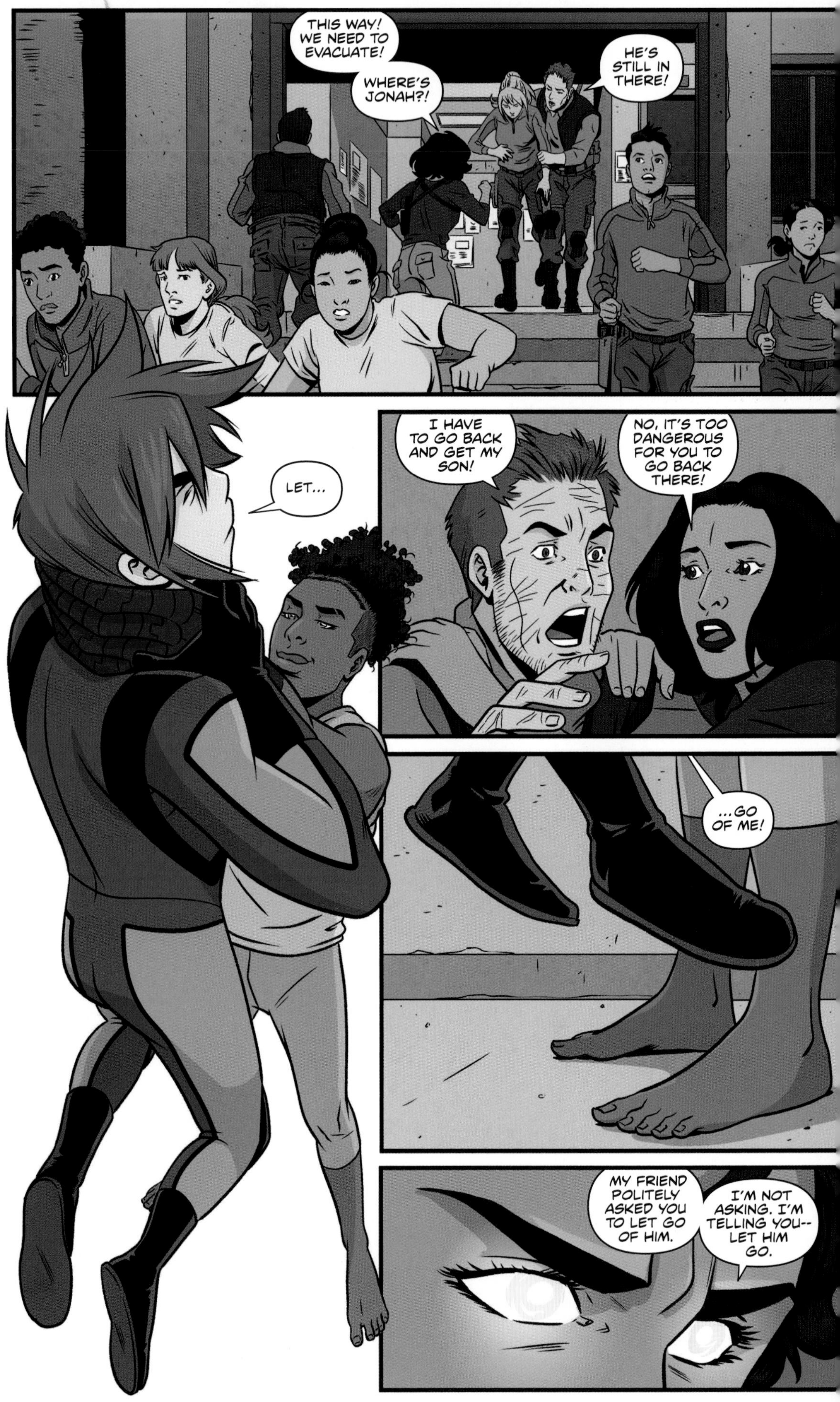
THIS WAY! WE NEED TO EVACUATE!
WHERE'S JONAH?!
HE'S STILL IN THERE!
LET...
I HAVE TO GO BACK AND GET MY SON!
NO, IT'S TOO DANGEROUS FOR YOU TO GO BACK THERE!
...GO OF ME!
MY FRIEND POLITELY ASKED YOU TO LET GO OF HIM.
I'M NOT ASKING. I'M TELLING YOU-- LET HIM GO.

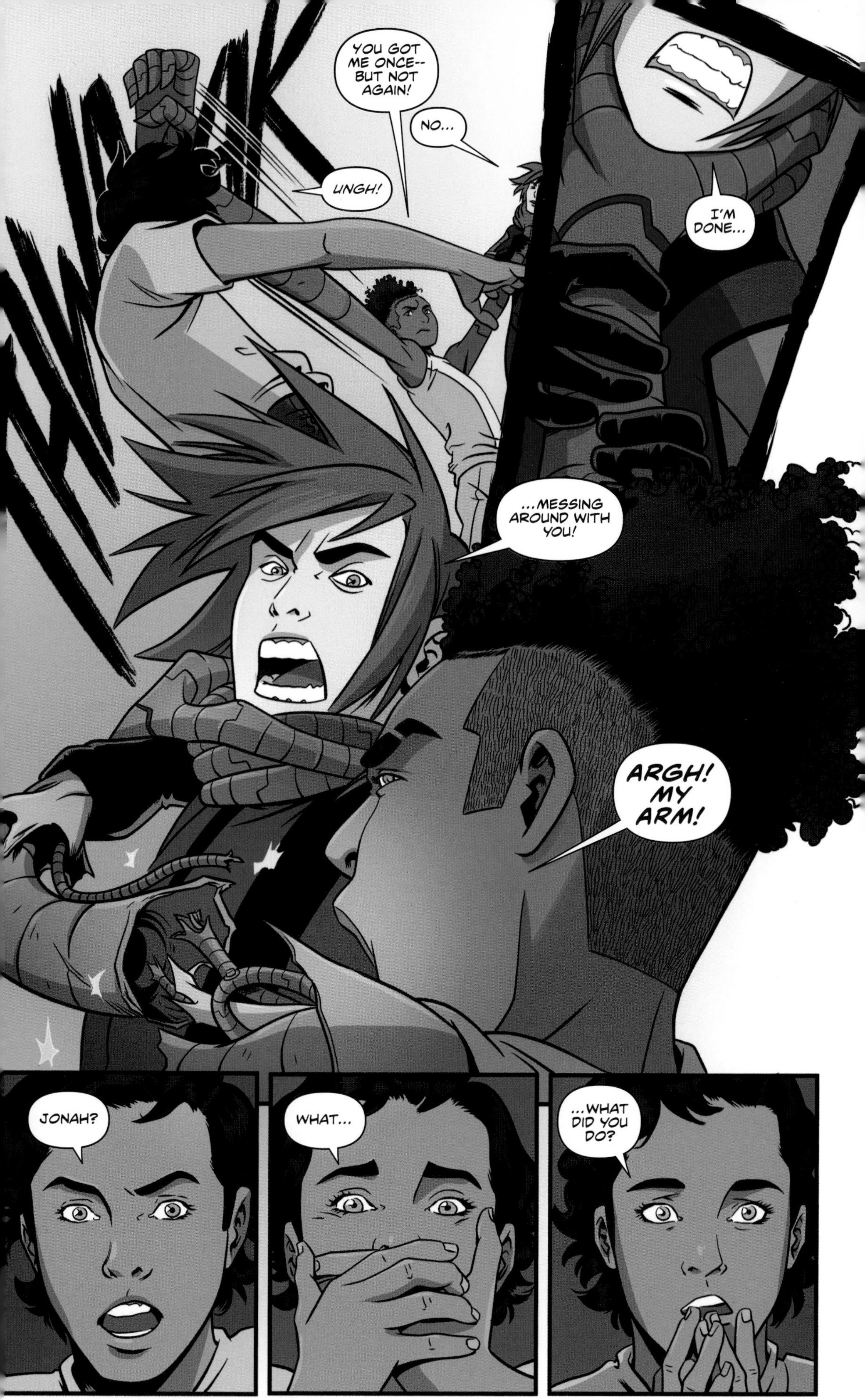

THWAK!
YOU GOT ME ONCE-- BUT NOT AGAIN!
NO...
UNGH!
I'M DONE...
...MESSING AROUND WITH YOU!
ARGH! MY ARM!
JONAH?
WHAT...
...WHAT DID YOU DO?

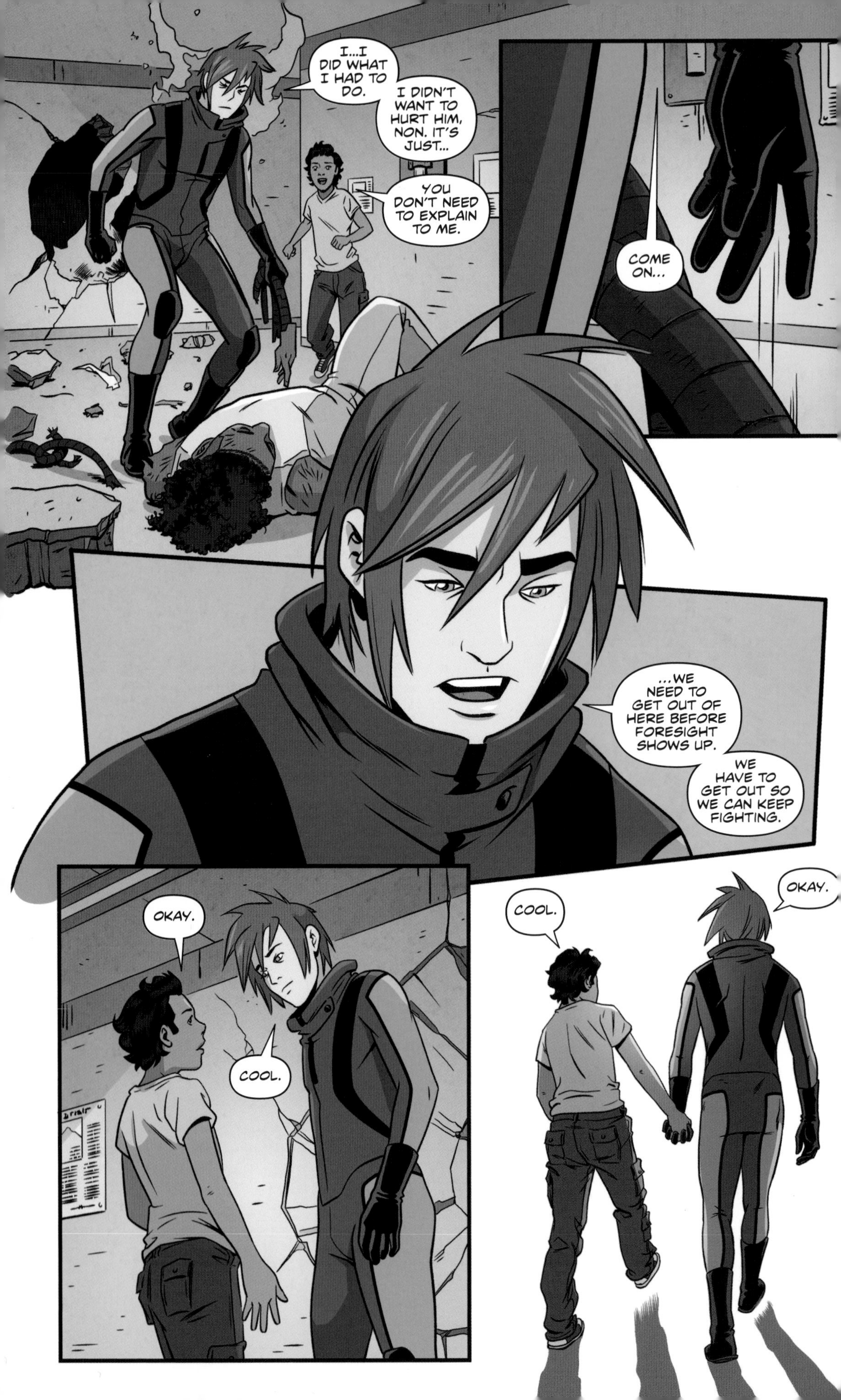
I...I DID WHAT I HAD TO DO.
I DIDN'T WANT TO HURT HIM, NON. IT'S JUST...
YOU DON'T NEED TO EXPLAIN TO ME.
COME ON...
...WE NEED TO GET OUT OF HERE BEFORE FORESIGHT SHOWS UP.
WE HAVE TO GET OUT SO WE CAN KEEP FIGHTING.
OKAY.
COOL.
COOL.
OKAY.

COSMOSIS

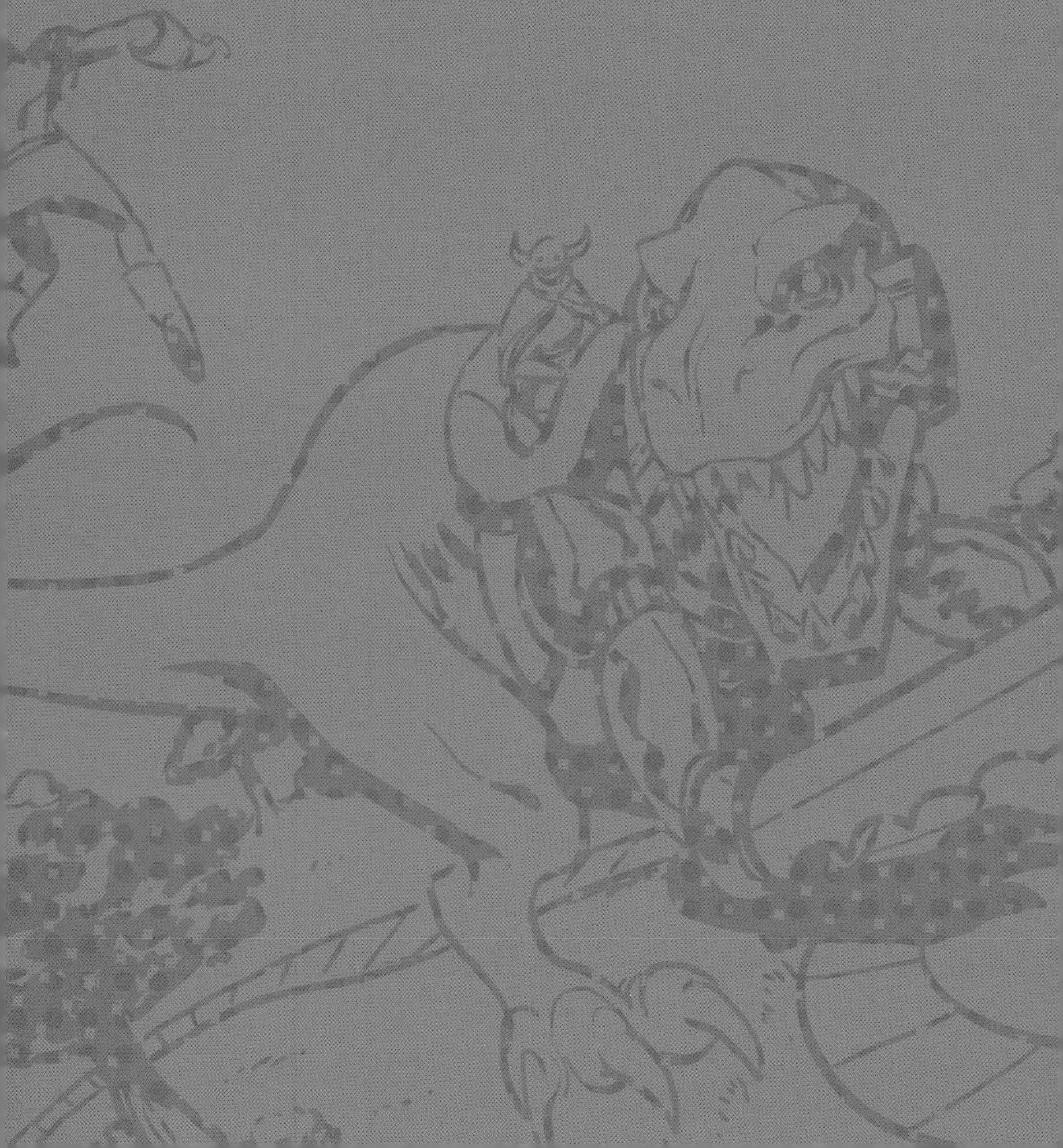

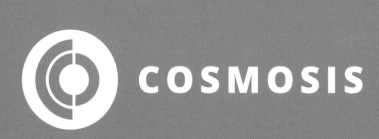

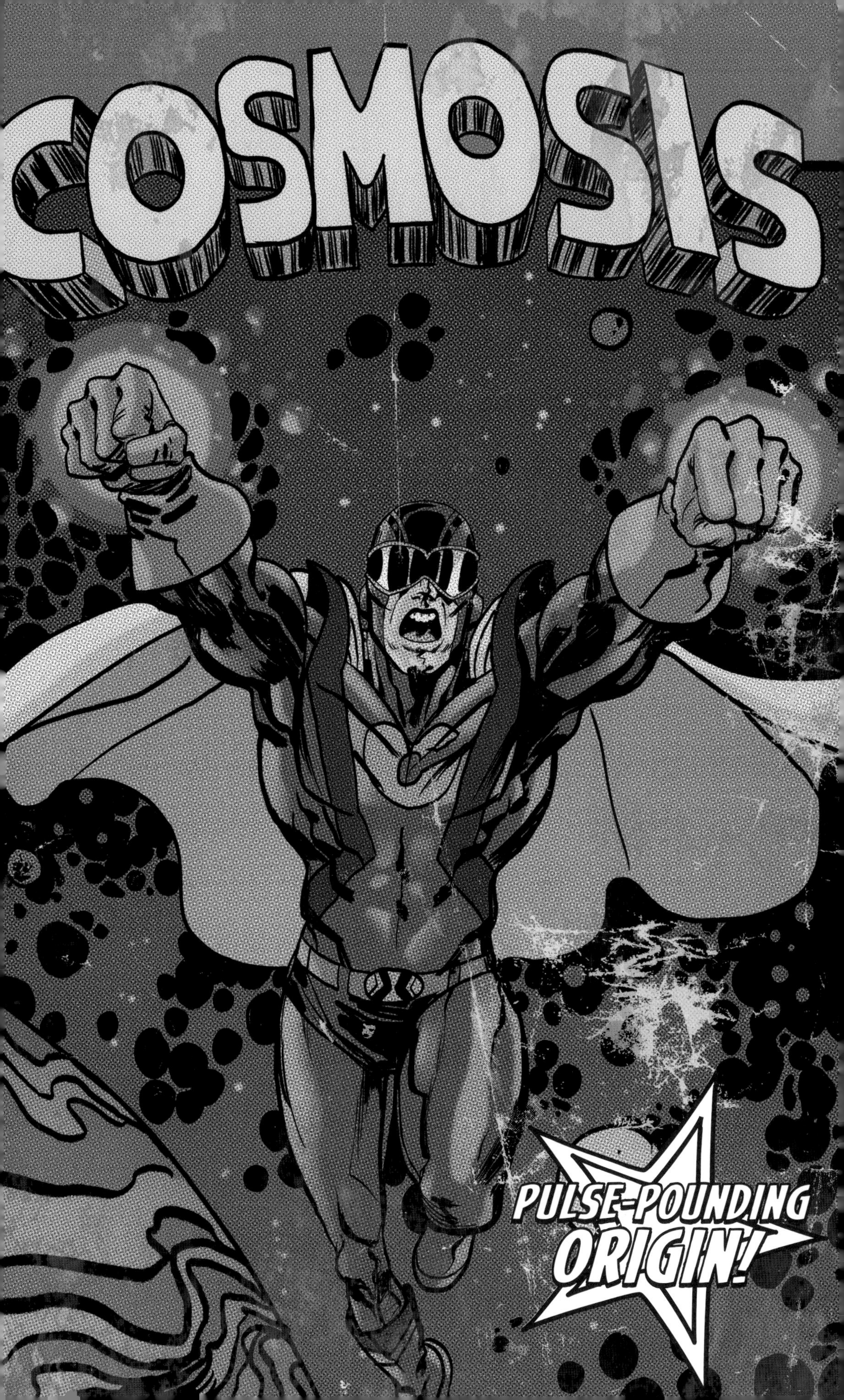
COSMOSIS
PULSE-POUNDING ORIGIN!

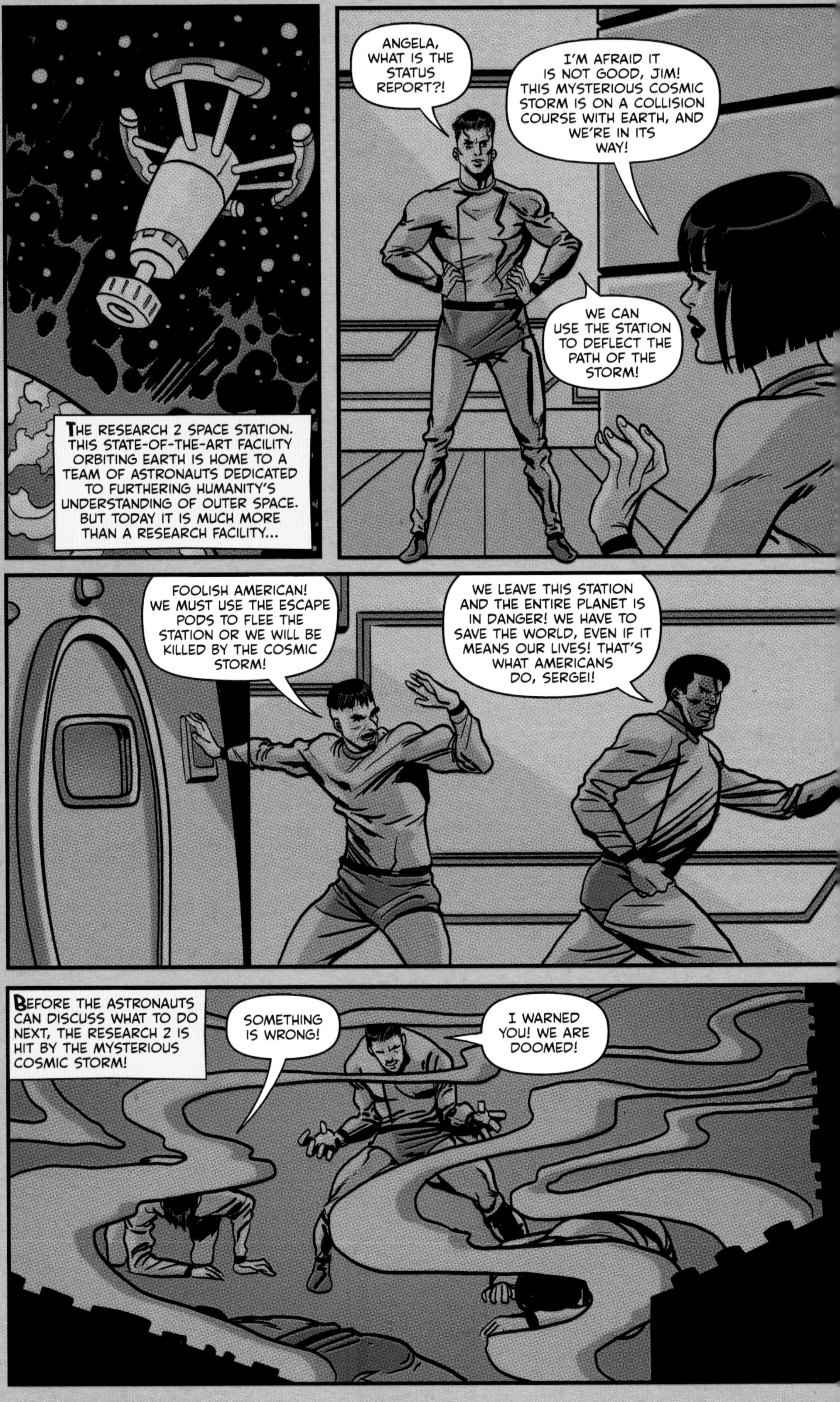
THE RESEARCH 2 SPACE STATION. THIS STATE-OF-THE-ART FACILITY ORBITING EARTH IS HOME TO A TEAM OF ASTRONAUTS DEDICATED TO FURTHERING HUMANITY'S UNDERSTANDING OF OUTER SPACE. BUT TODAY IT IS MUCH MORE THAN A RESEARCH FACILITY...
ANGELA, WHAT IS THE STATUS REPORT?!
I'M AFRAID IT IS NOT GOOD, JIM! THIS MYSTERIOUS COSMIC STORM IS ON A COLLISION COURSE WITH EARTH, AND WE'RE IN ITS WAY!
WE CAN USE THE STATION TO DEFLECT THE PATH OF THE STORM!
FOOLISH AMERICAN! WE MUST USE THE ESCAPE PODS TO FLEE THE STATION OR WE WILL BE KILLED BY THE COSMIC STORM!
WE LEAVE THIS STATION AND THE ENTIRE PLANET IS IN DANGER! WE HAVE TO SAVE THE WORLD, EVEN IF IT MEANS OUR LIVES! THAT'S WHAT AMERICANS DO, SERGEI!
BEFORE THE ASTRONAUTS CAN DISCUSS WHAT TO DO NEXT, THE RESEARCH 2 IS HIT BY THE MYSTERIOUS COSMIC STORM!
SOMETHING IS WRONG!
I WARNED YOU! WE ARE DOOMED!

ONE WEEK LATER. THE WORLD HEADQUARTERS OF THE INTERNATIONAL ASSOCIATION OF SPACE EXPLORATION (I.A.S.E.).

IT WAS TOUCH AND GO THERE FOR A FEW DAYS...

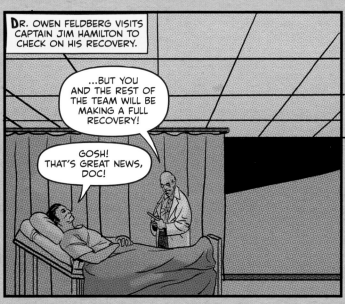

DR. OWEN FELDBERG VISITS CAPTAIN JIM HAMILTON TO CHECK ON HIS RECOVERY.

...BUT YOU AND THE REST OF THE TEAM WILL BE MAKING A FULL RECOVERY!

GOSH! THAT'S GREAT NEWS, DOC!

YOU ARE A BRAVE MAN, JIM! IF IT WEREN'T FOR YOUR ACTIONS...WHO KNOWS WHAT THAT MYSTERIOUS COSMIC STORM MIGHT HAVE DONE TO EARTH!

JUST DOING MY DUTY, DOC!

WELL, I'LL LEAVE YOU TO GET SOME SLEEP, JIM!

THANKS, DOC!

HOURS LATER, CAPTAIN JIM HAMILTON IS WOKEN BY THE SOUND OF LOUD SCREAMING.

WHAT IS THAT NOISE?! IT ALMOST SOUNDS LIKE SOMEONE SCREAMING!

IT IS SOMEONE SCREAMING! THAT NURSE--SHE'S RUNNING AWAY FROM SOMETHING! BUT WHAT COULD HAVE HER SO FRIGHTENED?!

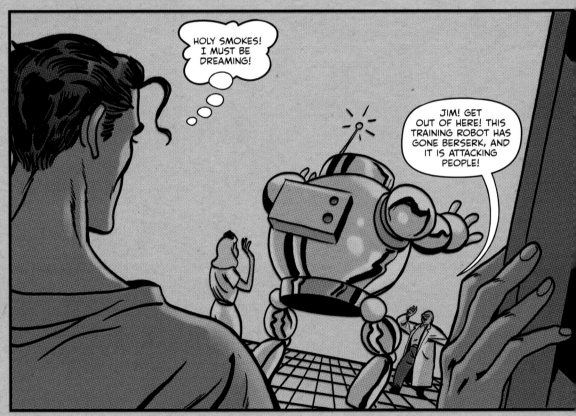

HOLY SMOKES! I MUST BE DREAMING!

JIM! GET OUT OF HERE! THIS TRAINING ROBOT HAS GONE BERSERK, AND IT IS ATTACKING PEOPLE!

I'M NOT DREAMING! THAT ROBOT IS ATTACKING THE HOSPITAL STAFF!

WITHOUT THINKING OF HIS OWN SAFETY, JIM HAMILTON MOVES INTO ACTION!

HOLD ON, DOC!

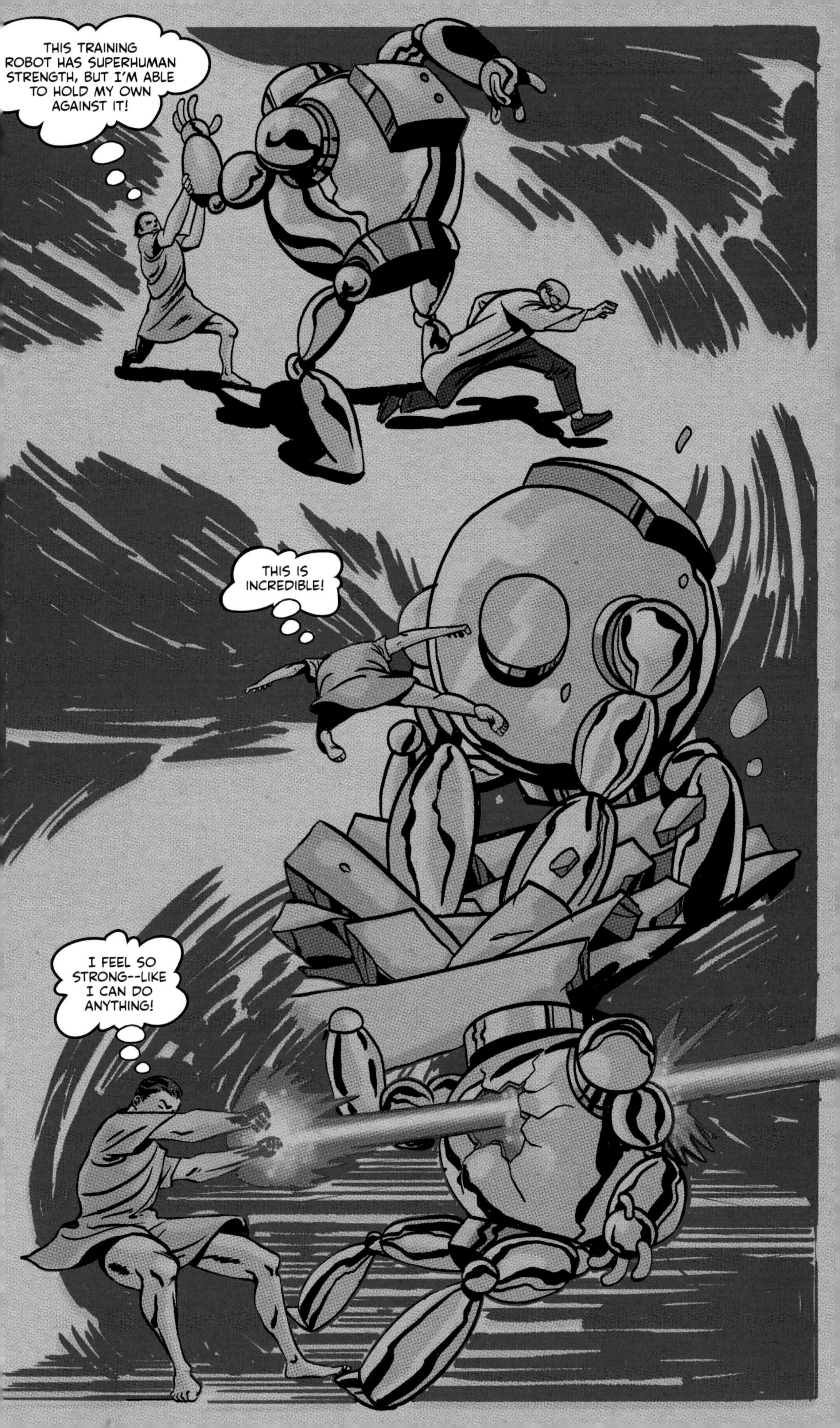
THIS TRAINING ROBOT HAS SUPERHUMAN STRENGTH, BUT I'M ABLE TO HOLD MY OWN AGAINST IT!
THIS IS INCREDIBLE!
I FEEL SO STRONG--LIKE I CAN DO ANYTHING!

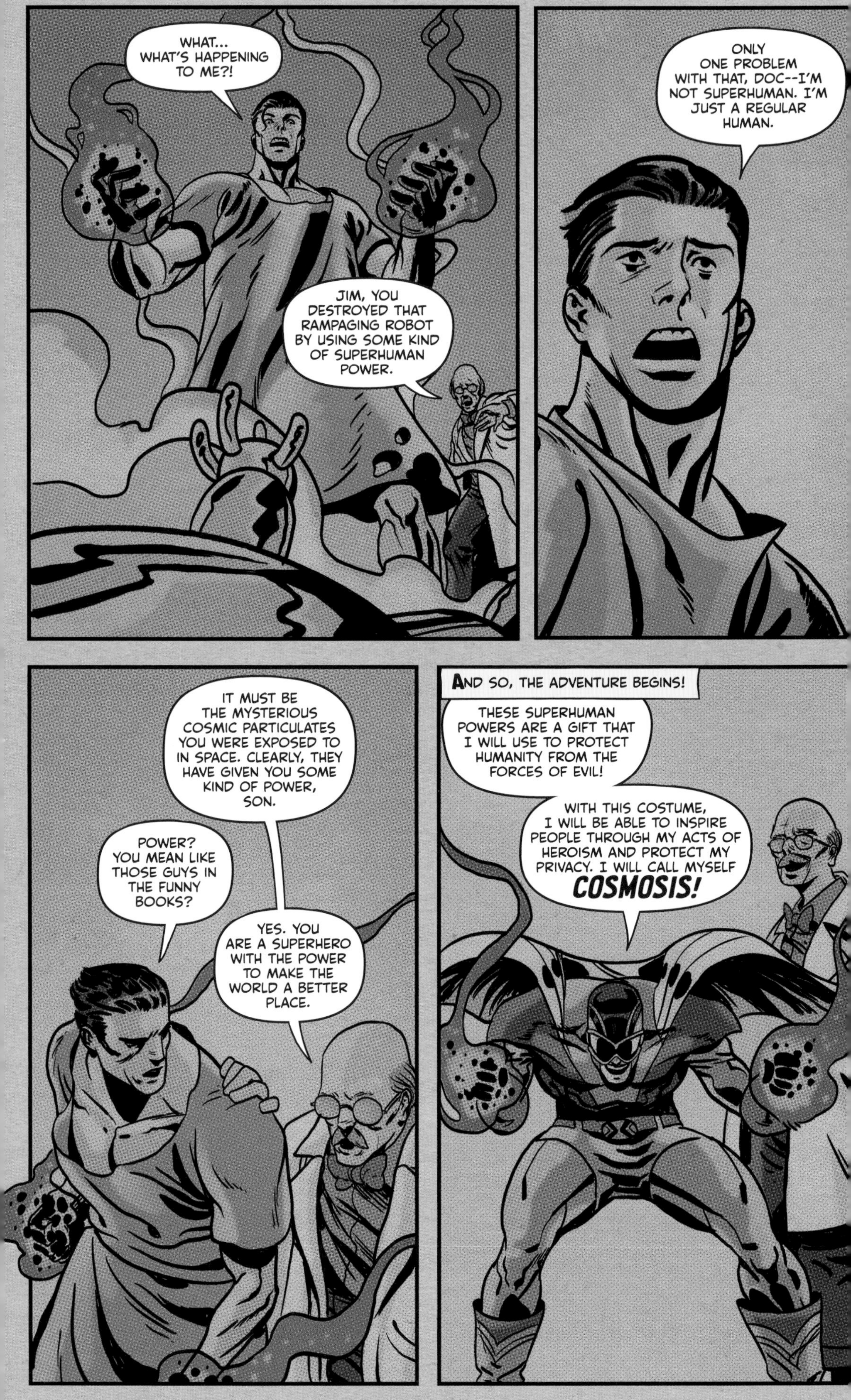
WHAT... WHAT'S HAPPENING TO ME?!
JIM, YOU DESTROYED THAT RAMPAGING ROBOT BY USING SOME KIND OF SUPERHUMAN POWER.
ONLY ONE PROBLEM WITH THAT, DOC--I'M NOT SUPERHUMAN. I'M JUST A REGULAR HUMAN.
IT MUST BE THE MYSTERIOUS COSMIC PARTICULATES YOU WERE EXPOSED TO IN SPACE. CLEARLY, THEY HAVE GIVEN YOU SOME KIND OF POWER, SON.
POWER? YOU MEAN LIKE THOSE GUYS IN THE FUNNY BOOKS?
YES. YOU ARE A SUPERHERO WITH THE POWER TO MAKE THE WORLD A BETTER PLACE.
AND SO, THE ADVENTURE BEGINS!
THESE SUPERHUMAN POWERS ARE A GIFT THAT I WILL USE TO PROTECT HUMANITY FROM THE FORCES OF EVIL!
WITH THIS COSTUME, I WILL BE ABLE TO INSPIRE PEOPLE THROUGH MY ACTS OF HEROISM AND PROTECT MY PRIVACY. I WILL CALL MYSELF COSMOSIS!

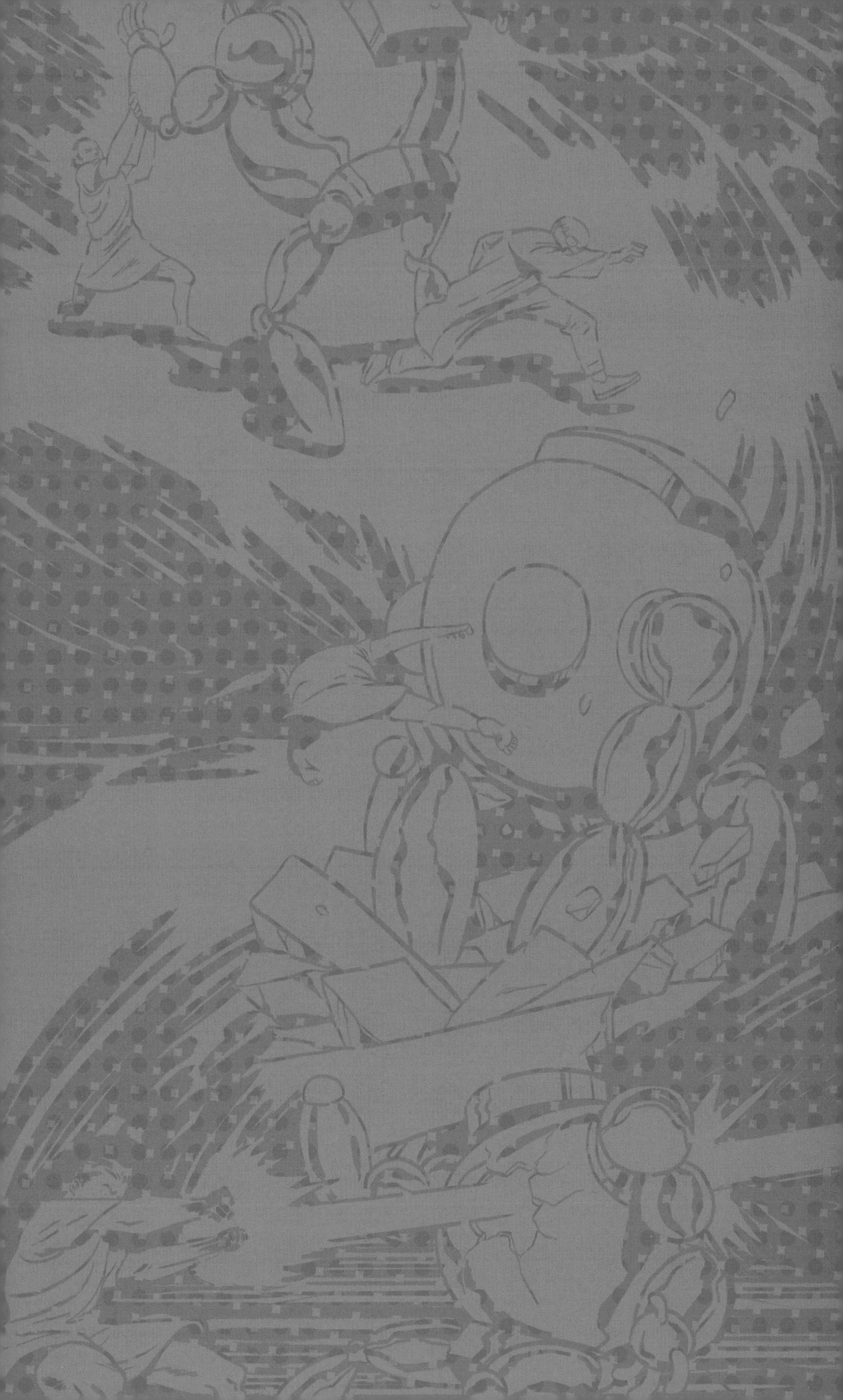

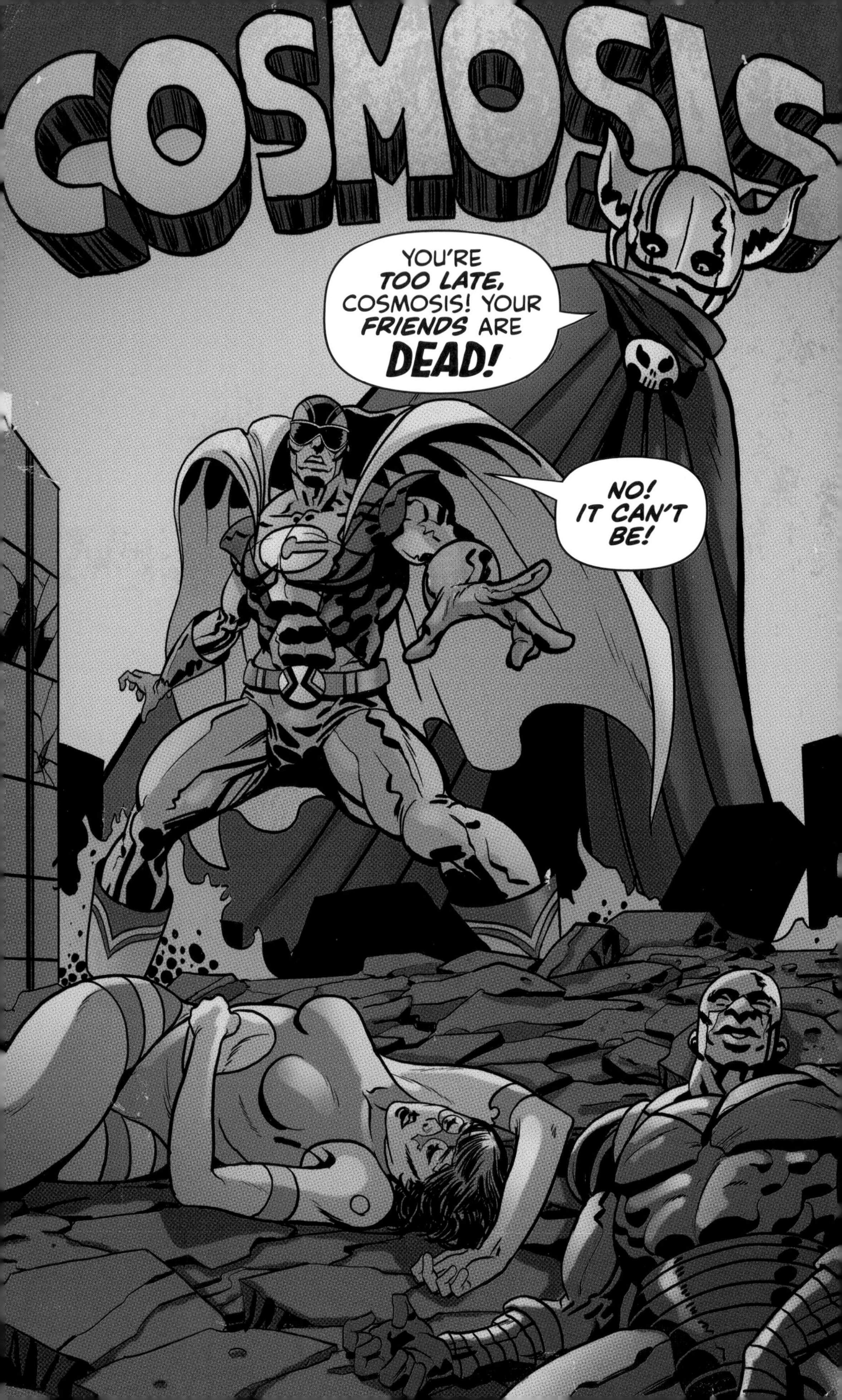
COSMOSIS
YOU'RE TOO LATE, COSMOSIS! YOUR FRIENDS ARE DEAD!
NO! IT CAN'T BE!

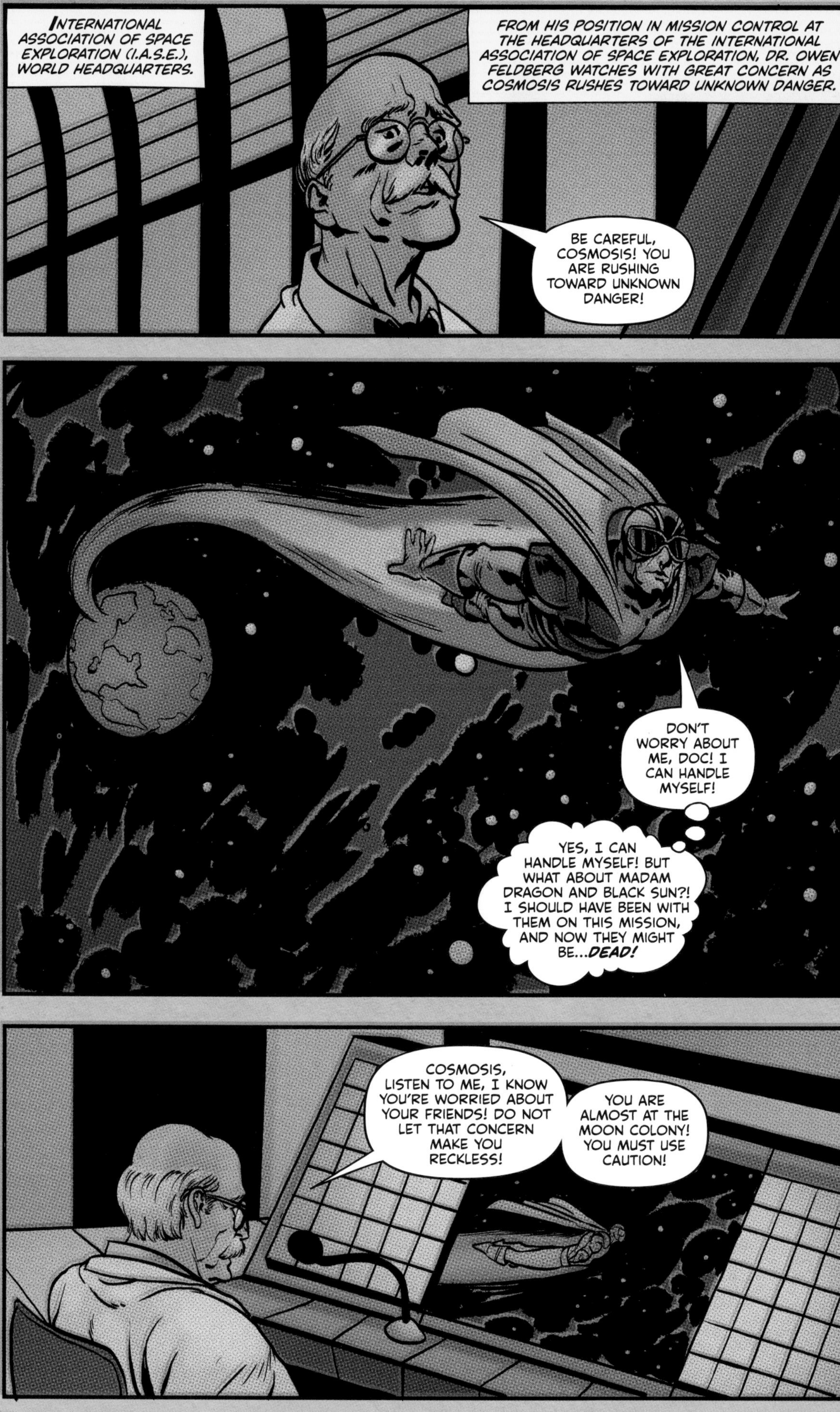
INTERNATIONAL ASSOCIATION OF SPACE EXPLORATION (I.A.S.E.), WORLD HEADQUARTERS.
FROM HIS POSITION IN MISSION CONTROL AT THE HEADQUARTERS OF THE INTERNATIONAL ASSOCIATION OF SPACE EXPLORATION, DR. OWEN FELDBERG WATCHES WITH GREAT CONCERN AS COSMOSIS RUSHES TOWARD UNKNOWN DANGER.
BE CAREFUL, COSMOSIS! YOU ARE RUSHING TOWARD UNKNOWN DANGER!
DON'T WORRY ABOUT ME, DOC! I CAN HANDLE MYSELF!
YES, I CAN HANDLE MYSELF! BUT WHAT ABOUT MADAM DRAGON AND BLACK SUN?! I SHOULD HAVE BEEN WITH THEM ON THIS MISSION, AND NOW THEY MIGHT BE...DEAD!
COSMOSIS, LISTEN TO ME, I KNOW YOU'RE WORRIED ABOUT YOUR FRIENDS! DO NOT LET THAT CONCERN MAKE YOU RECKLESS!
YOU ARE ALMOST AT THE MOON COLONY! YOU MUST USE CAUTION!

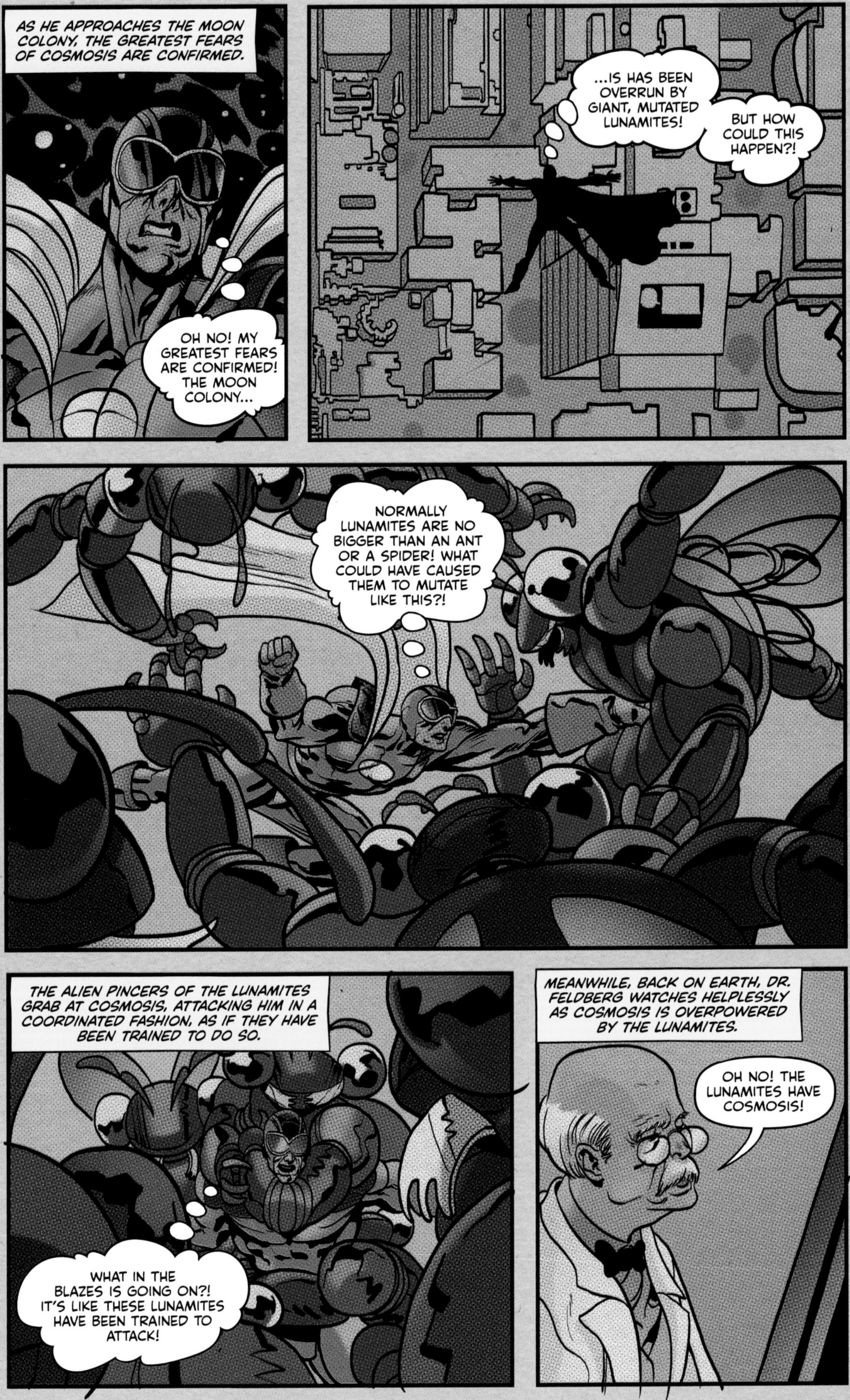
AS HE APPROACHES THE MOON COLONY, THE GREATEST FEARS OF COSMOSIS ARE CONFIRMED.
OH NO! MY GREATEST FEARS ARE CONFIRMED! THE MOON COLONY...
...IS HAS BEEN OVERRUN BY GIANT, MUTATED LUNAMITES!
BUT HOW COULD THIS HAPPEN?!
NORMALLY LUNAMITES ARE NO BIGGER THAN AN ANT OR A SPIDER! WHAT COULD HAVE CAUSED THEM TO MUTATE LIKE THIS?!
THE ALIEN PINCERS OF THE LUNAMITES GRAB AT COSMOSIS, ATTACKING HIM IN A COORDINATED FASHION, AS IF THEY HAVE BEEN TRAINED TO DO SO.
WHAT IN THE BLAZES IS GOING ON?! IT'S LIKE THESE LUNAMITES HAVE BEEN TRAINED TO ATTACK!
MEANWHILE, BACK ON EARTH, DR. FELDBERG WATCHES HELPLESSLY AS COSMOSIS IS OVERPOWERED BY THE LUNAMITES.
OH NO! THE LUNAMITES HAVE COSMOSIS!

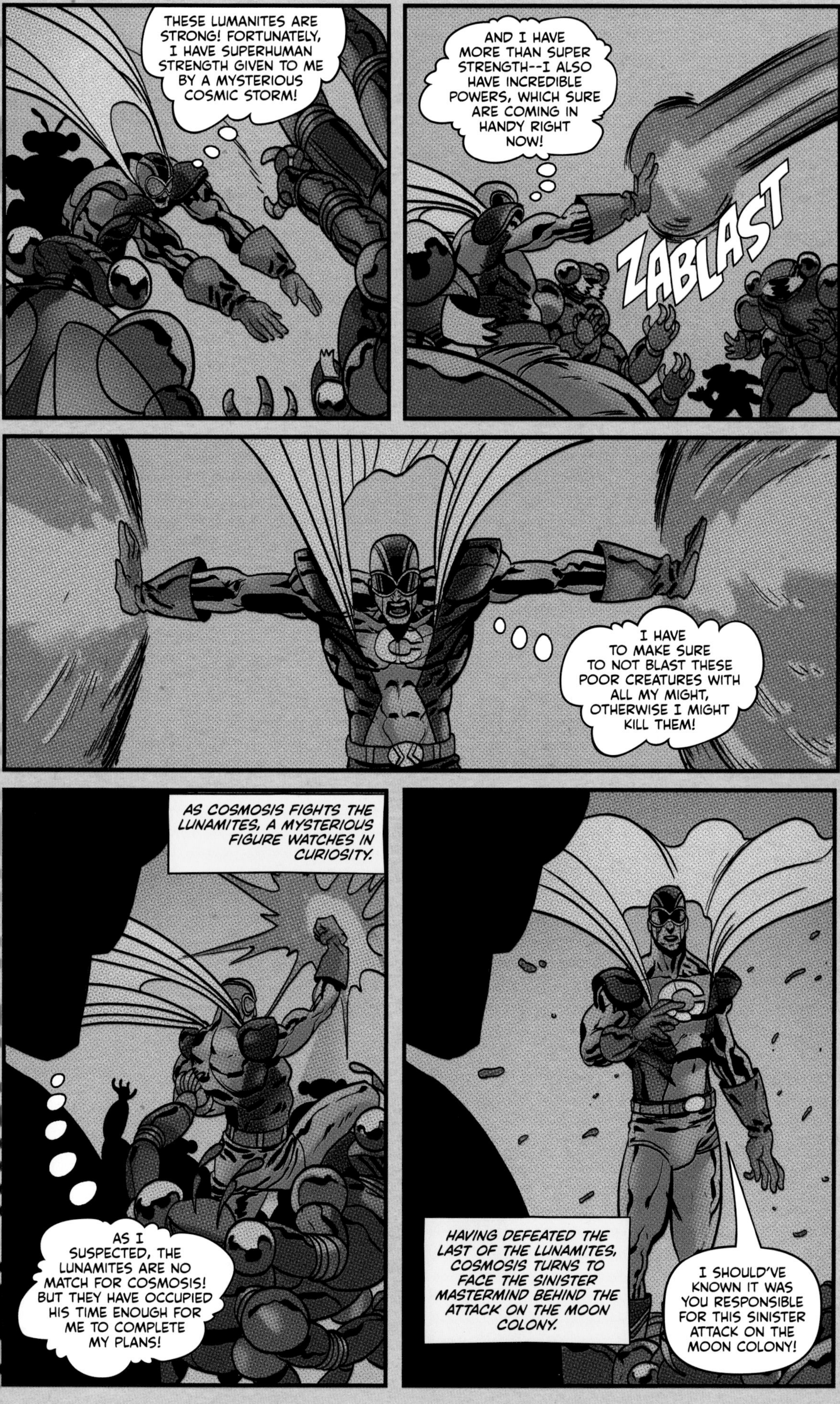
THESE LUMANITES ARE STRONG! FORTUNATELY, I HAVE SUPERHUMAN STRENGTH GIVEN TO ME BY A MYSTERIOUS COSMIC STORM!
AND I HAVE MORE THAN SUPER STRENGTH--I ALSO HAVE INCREDIBLE POWERS, WHICH SURE ARE COMING IN HANDY RIGHT NOW!
ZABLAST
I HAVE TO MAKE SURE TO NOT BLAST THESE POOR CREATURES WITH ALL MY MIGHT, OTHERWISE I MIGHT KILL THEM!
AS COSMOSIS FIGHTS THE LUNAMITES, A MYSTERIOUS FIGURE WATCHES IN CURIOSITY.
AS I SUSPECTED, THE LUNAMITES ARE NO MATCH FOR COSMOSIS! BUT THEY HAVE OCCUPIED HIS TIME ENOUGH FOR ME TO COMPLETE MY PLANS!
HAVING DEFEATED THE LAST OF THE LUNAMITES, COSMOSIS TURNS TO FACE THE SINISTER MASTERMIND BEHIND THE ATTACK ON THE MOON COLONY.
I SHOULD'VE KNOWN IT WAS YOU RESPONSIBLE FOR THIS SINISTER ATTACK ON THE MOON COLONY!

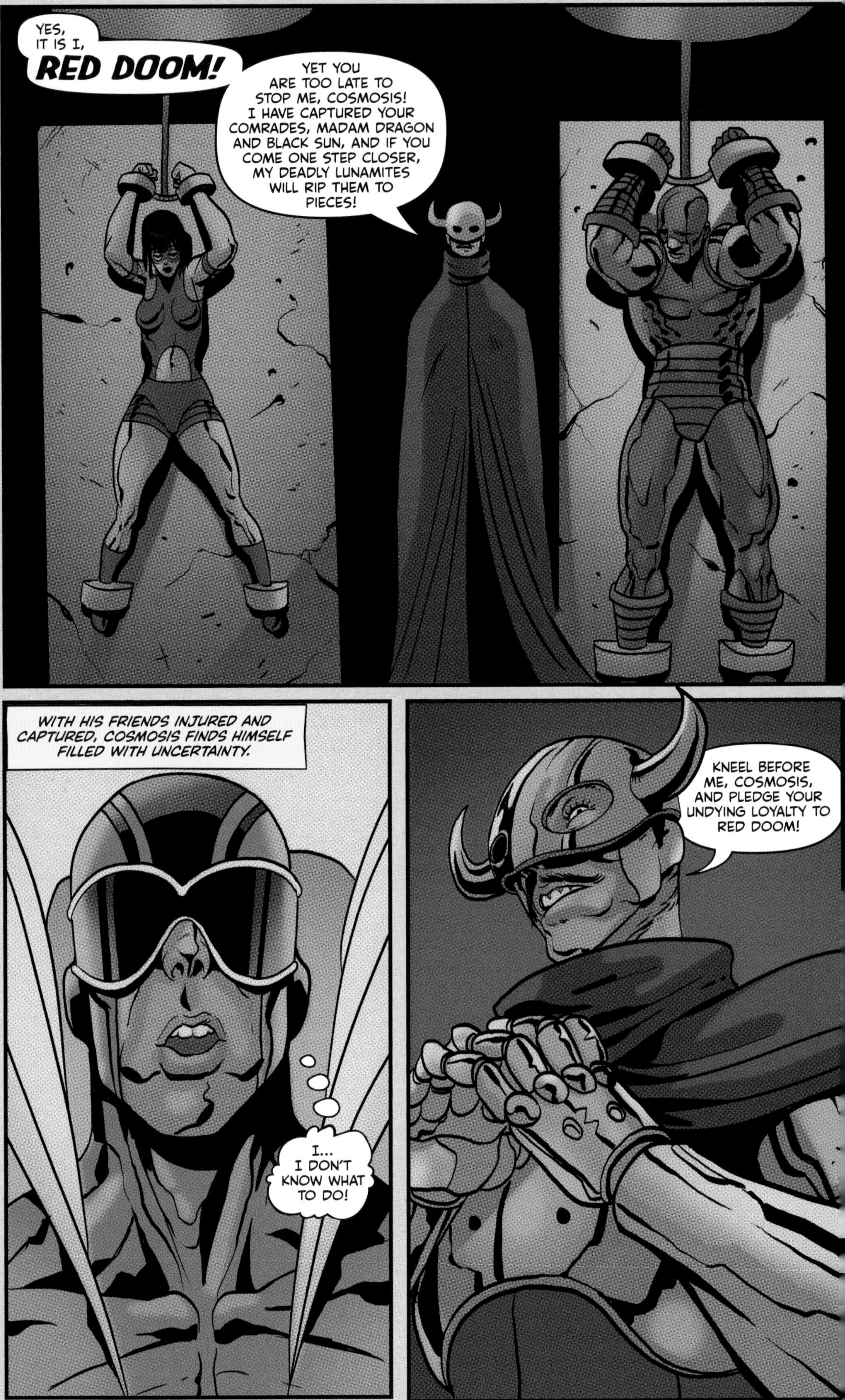
YES, IT IS I, RED DOOM!
YET YOU ARE TOO LATE TO STOP ME, COSMOSIS! I HAVE CAPTURED YOUR COMRADES, MADAM DRAGON AND BLACK SUN, AND IF YOU COME ONE STEP CLOSER, MY DEADLY LUNAMITES WILL RIP THEM TO PIECES!
WITH HIS FRIENDS INJURED AND CAPTURED, COSMOSIS FINDS HIMSELF FILLED WITH UNCERTAINTY.
I... I DON'T KNOW WHAT TO DO!
KNEEL BEFORE ME, COSMOSIS, AND PLEDGE YOUR UNDYING LOYALTY TO RED DOOM!

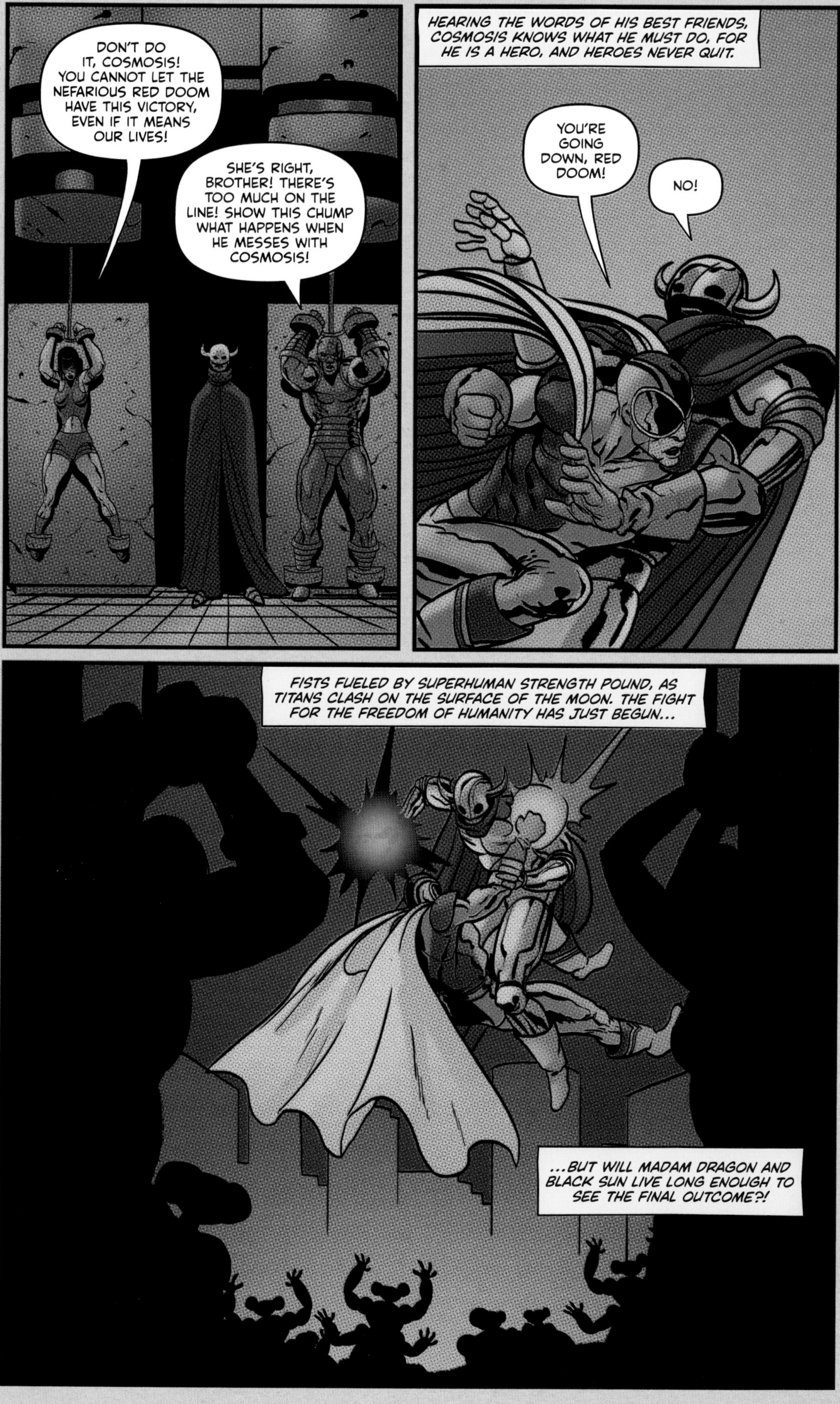

DON'T DO IT, COSMOSIS! YOU CANNOT LET THE NEFARIOUS RED DOOM HAVE THIS VICTORY, EVEN IF IT MEANS OUR LIVES!
SHE'S RIGHT, BROTHER! THERE'S TOO MUCH ON THE LINE! SHOW THIS CHUMP WHAT HAPPENS WHEN HE MESSES WITH COSMOSIS!
HEARING THE WORDS OF HIS BEST FRIENDS, COSMOSIS KNOWS WHAT HE MUST DO, FOR HE IS A HERO, AND HEROES NEVER QUIT.
YOU'RE GOING DOWN, RED DOOM!
NO!
FISTS FUELED BY SUPERHUMAN STRENGTH POUND, AS TITANS CLASH ON THE SURFACE OF THE MOON. THE FIGHT FOR THE FREEDOM OF HUMANITY HAS JUST BEGUN...
...BUT WILL MADAM DRAGON AND BLACK SUN LIVE LONG ENOUGH TO SEE THE FINAL OUTCOME?!

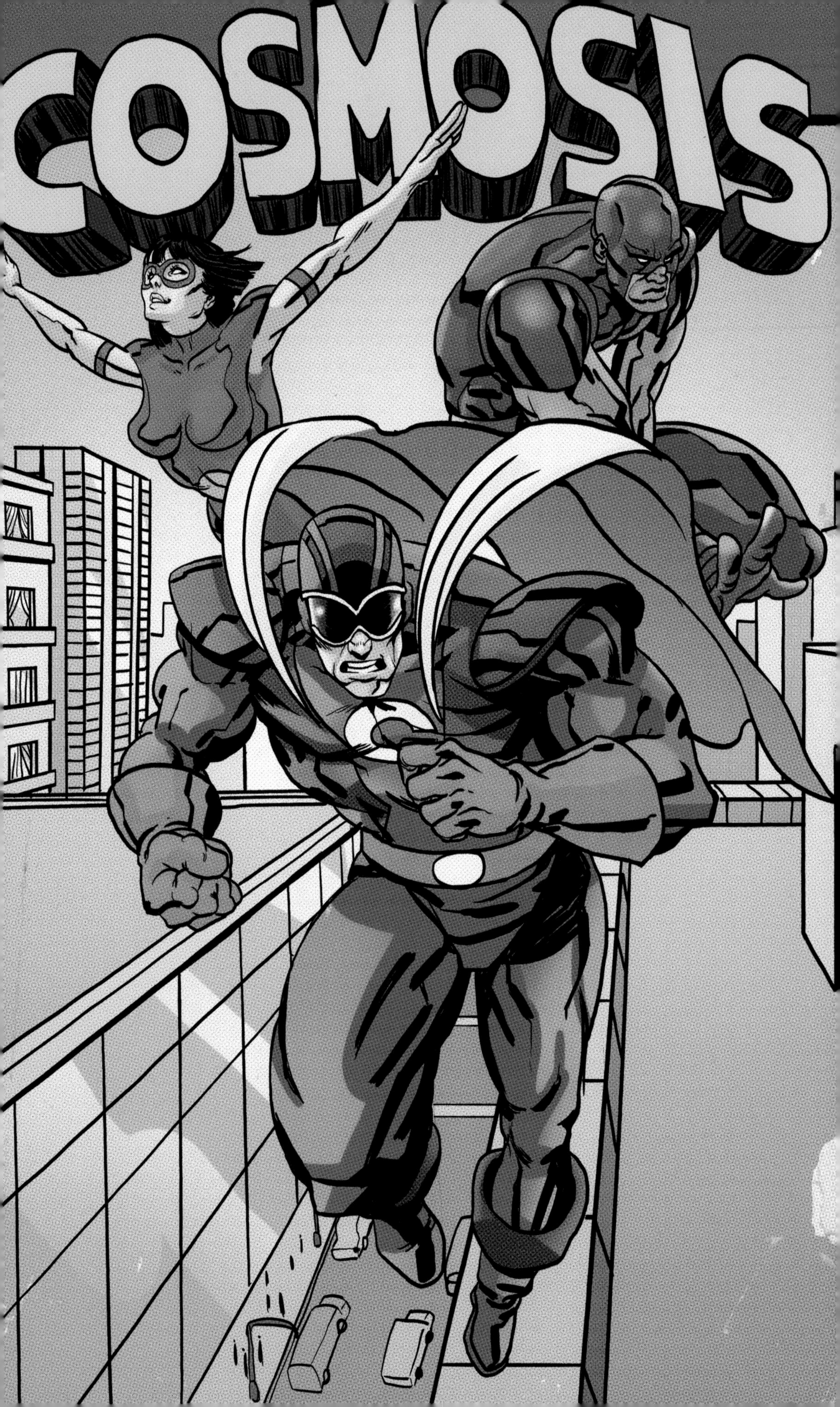
COSMOSIS

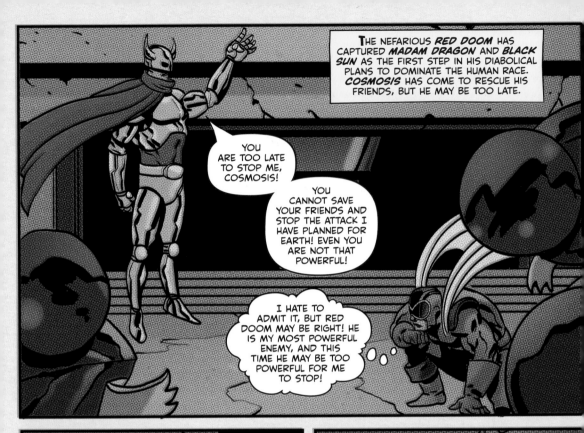

THE NEFARIOUS **RED DOOM** HAS CAPTURED **MADAM DRAGON** AND **BLACK SUN** AS THE FIRST STEP IN HIS DIABOLICAL PLANS TO DOMINATE THE HUMAN RACE. **COSMOSIS** HAS COME TO RESCUE HIS FRIENDS, BUT HE MAY BE TOO LATE.

YOU ARE TOO LATE TO STOP ME, COSMOSIS!

YOU CANNOT SAVE YOUR FRIENDS AND STOP THE ATTACK I HAVE PLANNED FOR EARTH! EVEN YOU ARE NOT THAT POWERFUL!

I HATE TO ADMIT IT, BUT RED DOOM MAY BE RIGHT! HE IS MY MOST POWERFUL ENEMY, AND THIS TIME HE MAY BE TOO POWERFUL FOR ME TO STOP!

WE HAVE TO DO SOMETHING, BLACK SUN! IF WE DON'T HELP COSMOSIS, NOT ONLY WILL HE DIE, WE'LL DIE AS WELL! AND THE HUMAN RACE WILL BE ENSLAVED!

I HEAR YA TALKIN', SISTER! AND LET ME TELL YA, I'VE GOT A PLAN!

IF I CONCENTRATE ALL MY ENERGY INTO ONE POWERFUL **SUPER SOLAR BLAST,** I CAN BREAK THESE BINDS AND GET US FREE, EVEN THOUGH IT WILL DRAIN MUCH OF MY ENERGY! IT'S WORTH THE RISK!

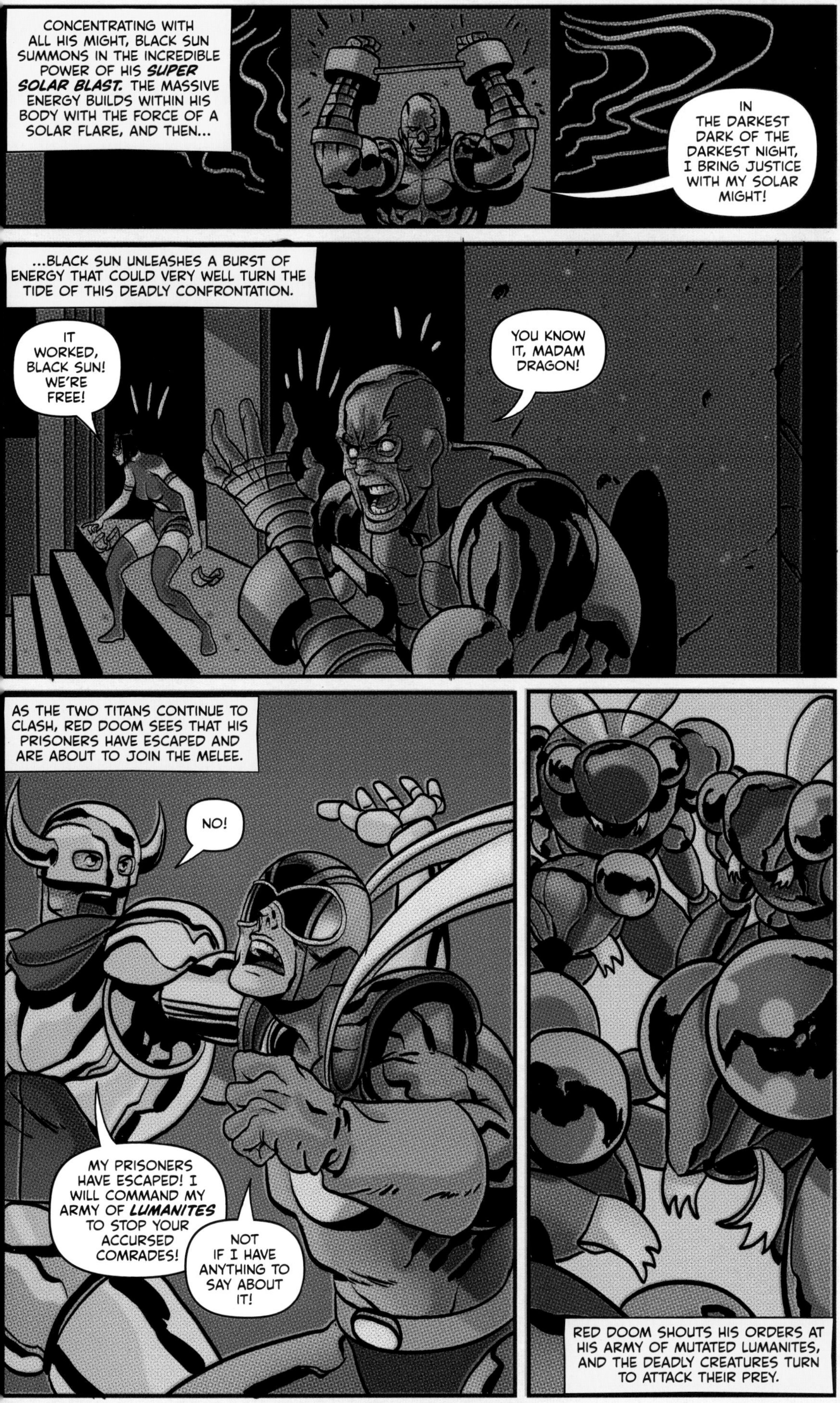

CONCENTRATING WITH ALL HIS MIGHT, BLACK SUN SUMMONS IN THE INCREDIBLE POWER OF HIS ***SUPER SOLAR BLAST.*** THE MASSIVE ENERGY BUILDS WITHIN HIS BODY WITH THE FORCE OF A SOLAR FLARE, AND THEN...
IN THE DARKEST DARK OF THE DARKEST NIGHT, I BRING JUSTICE WITH MY SOLAR MIGHT!
...BLACK SUN UNLEASHES A BURST OF ENERGY THAT COULD VERY WELL TURN THE TIDE OF THIS DEADLY CONFRONTATION.
IT WORKED, BLACK SUN! WE'RE FREE!
YOU KNOW IT, MADAM DRAGON!
AS THE TWO TITANS CONTINUE TO CLASH, RED DOOM SEES THAT HIS PRISONERS HAVE ESCAPED AND ARE ABOUT TO JOIN THE MELEE.
NO!
MY PRISONERS HAVE ESCAPED! I WILL COMMAND MY ARMY OF ***LUMANITES*** TO STOP YOUR ACCURSED COMRADES!
NOT IF I HAVE ANYTHING TO SAY ABOUT IT!
RED DOOM SHOUTS HIS ORDERS AT HIS ARMY OF MUTATED LUMANITES, AND THE DEADLY CREATURES TURN TO ATTACK THEIR PREY.

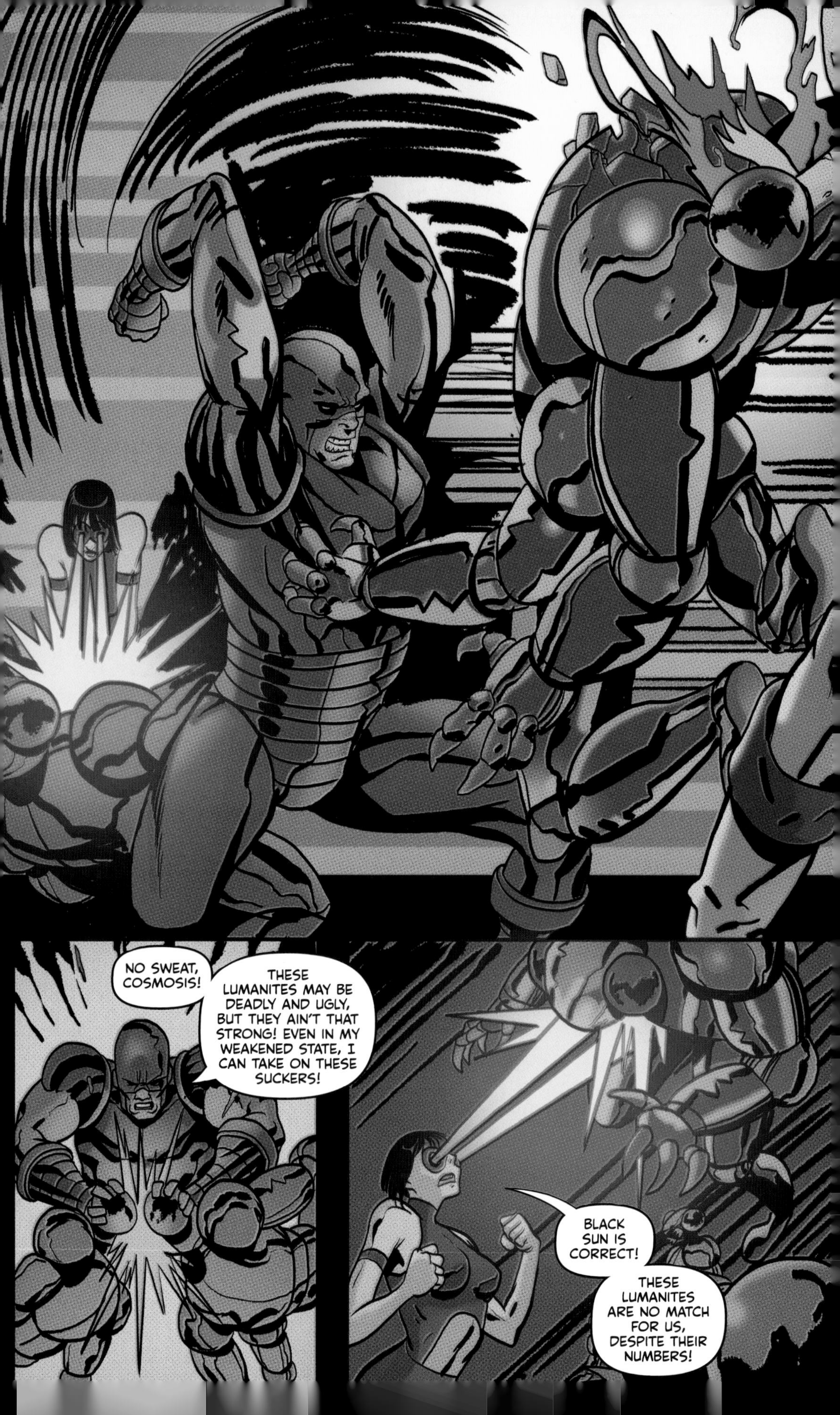

NO SWEAT, COSMOSIS!
THESE LUMANITES MAY BE DEADLY AND UGLY, BUT THEY AIN'T THAT STRONG! EVEN IN MY WEAKENED STATE, I CAN TAKE ON THESE SUCKERS!
BLACK SUN IS CORRECT!
THESE LUMANITES ARE NO MATCH FOR US, DESPITE THEIR NUMBERS!

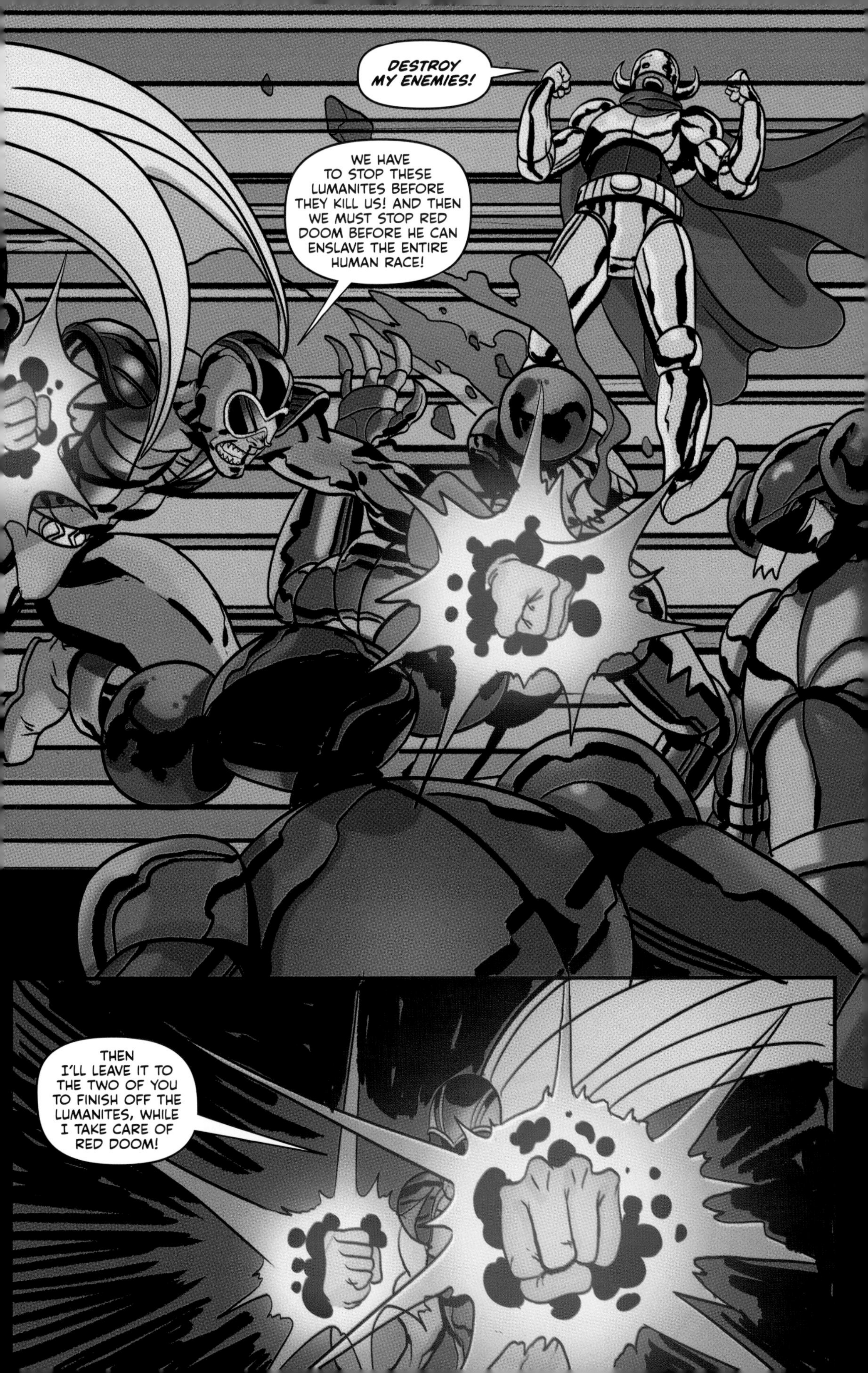
DESTROY MY ENEMIES!
WE HAVE TO STOP THESE LUMANITES BEFORE THEY KILL US! AND THEN WE MUST STOP RED DOOM BEFORE HE CAN ENSLAVE THE ENTIRE HUMAN RACE!
THEN I'LL LEAVE IT TO THE TWO OF YOU TO FINISH OFF THE LUMANITES, WHILE I TAKE CARE OF RED DOOM!

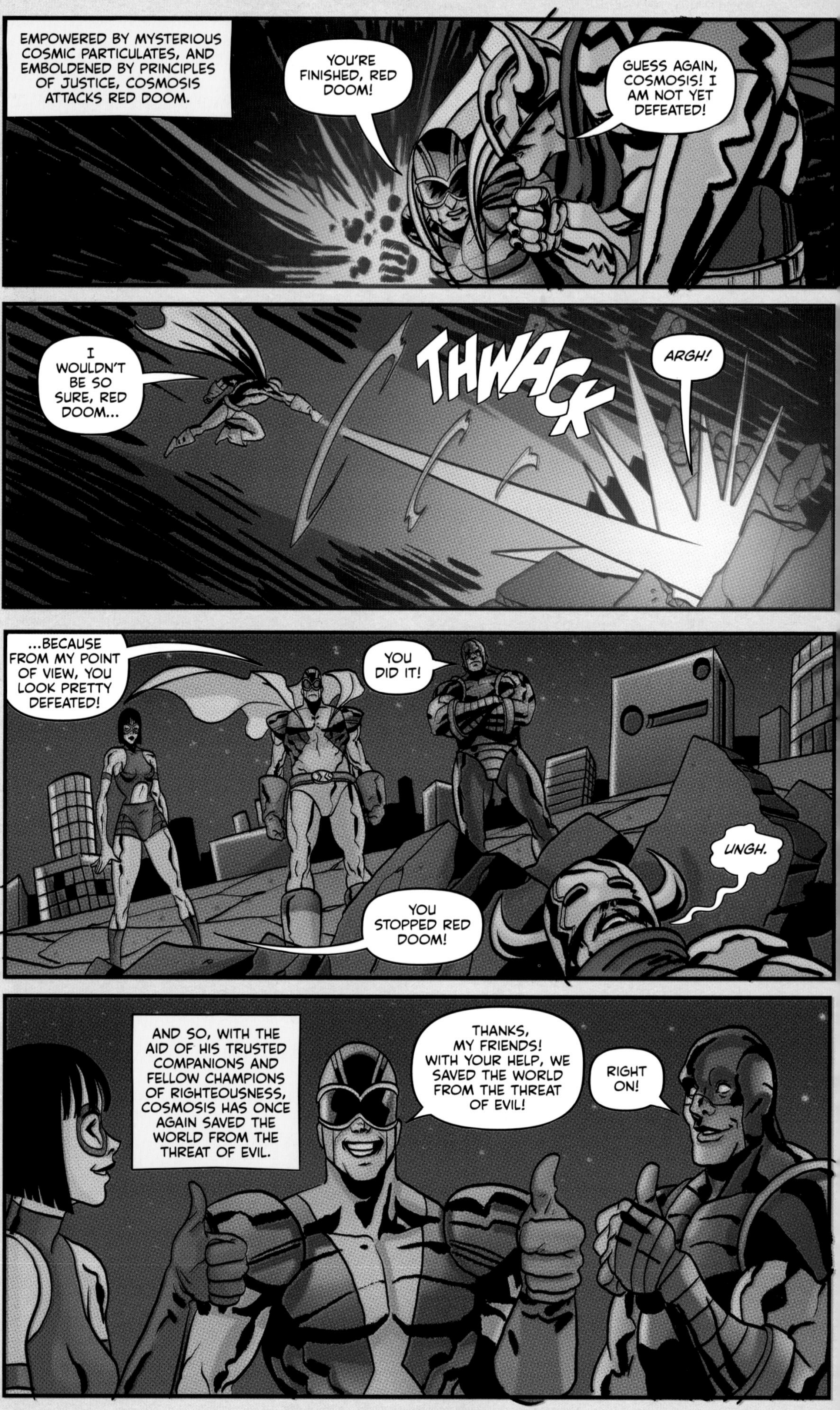
EMPOWERED BY MYSTERIOUS COSMIC PARTICULATES, AND EMBOLDENED BY PRINCIPLES OF JUSTICE, COSMOSIS ATTACKS RED DOOM.
YOU'RE FINISHED, RED DOOM!
GUESS AGAIN, COSMOSIS! I AM NOT YET DEFEATED!
I WOULDN'T BE SO SURE, RED DOOM...
THWACK
ARGH!
...BECAUSE FROM MY POINT OF VIEW, YOU LOOK PRETTY DEFEATED!
YOU DID IT!
UNGH.
YOU STOPPED RED DOOM!
AND SO, WITH THE AID OF HIS TRUSTED COMPANIONS AND FELLOW CHAMPIONS OF RIGHTEOUSNESS, COSMOSIS HAS ONCE AGAIN SAVED THE WORLD FROM THE THREAT OF EVIL.
THANKS, MY FRIENDS! WITH YOUR HELP, WE SAVED THE WORLD FROM THE THREAT OF EVIL!
RIGHT ON!

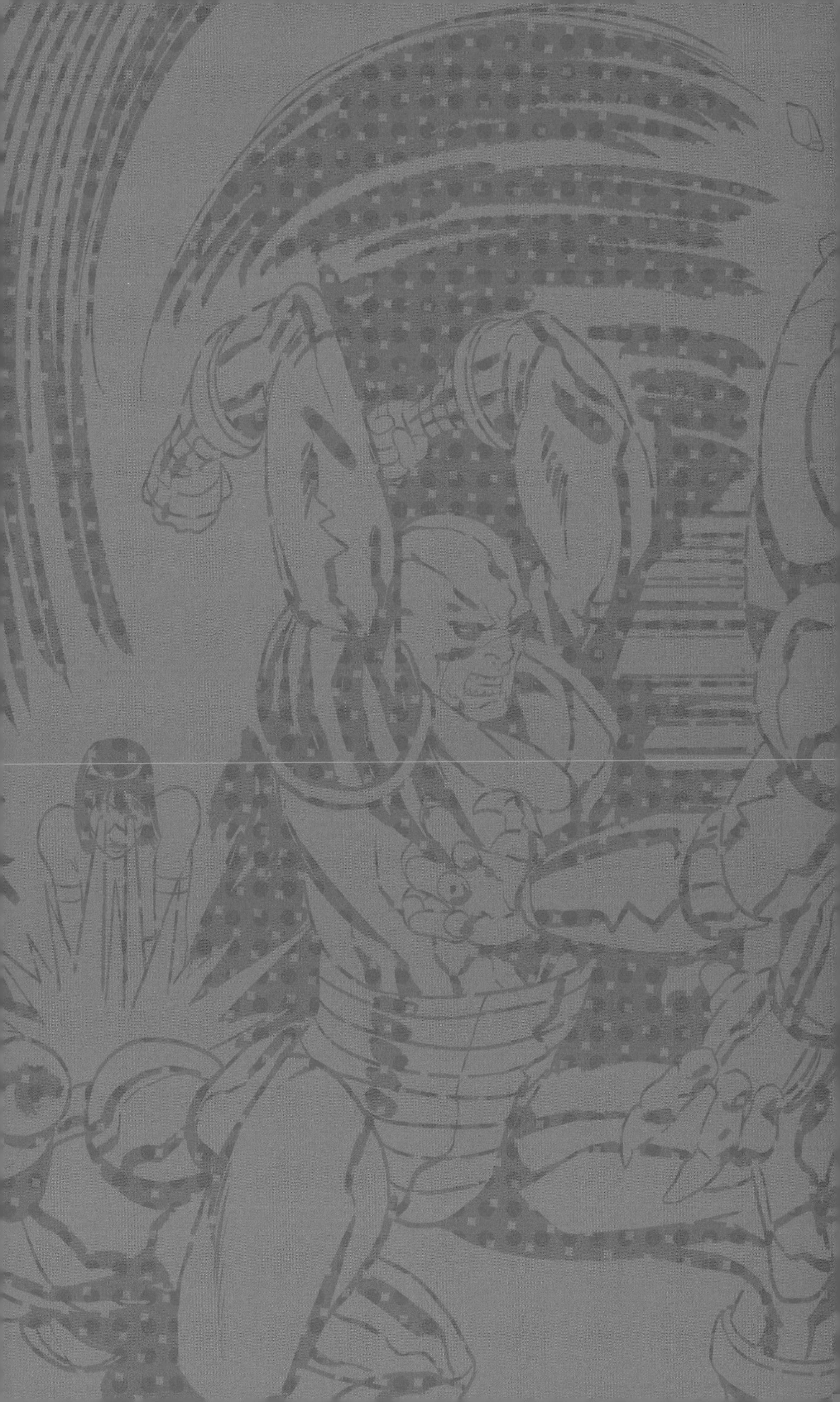

COSMOSIS
IT'S THE DRUGS!
ALL MY POWERS, AND I COULDN'T SAVE THEM!
THE RETURN OF DOCTOR DRUGS!

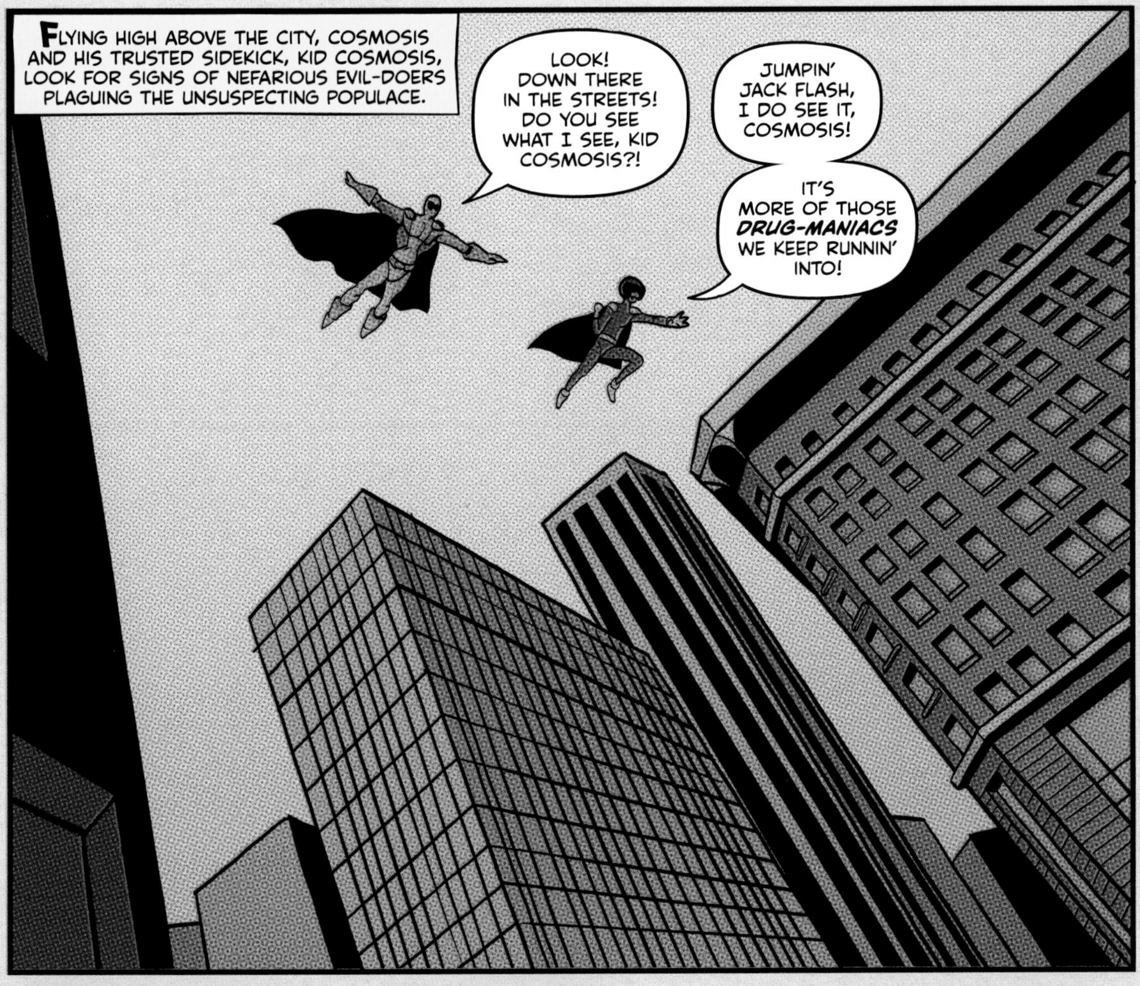
FLYING HIGH ABOVE THE CITY, COSMOSIS AND HIS TRUSTED SIDEKICK, KID COSMOSIS, LOOK FOR SIGNS OF NEFARIOUS EVIL-DOERS PLAGUING THE UNSUSPECTING POPULACE.
LOOK! DOWN THERE IN THE STREETS! DO YOU SEE WHAT I SEE, KID COSMOSIS?!
JUMPIN' JACK FLASH, I DO SEE IT, COSMOSIS!
IT'S MORE OF THOSE *DRUG-MANIACS* WE KEEP RUNNIN' INTO!

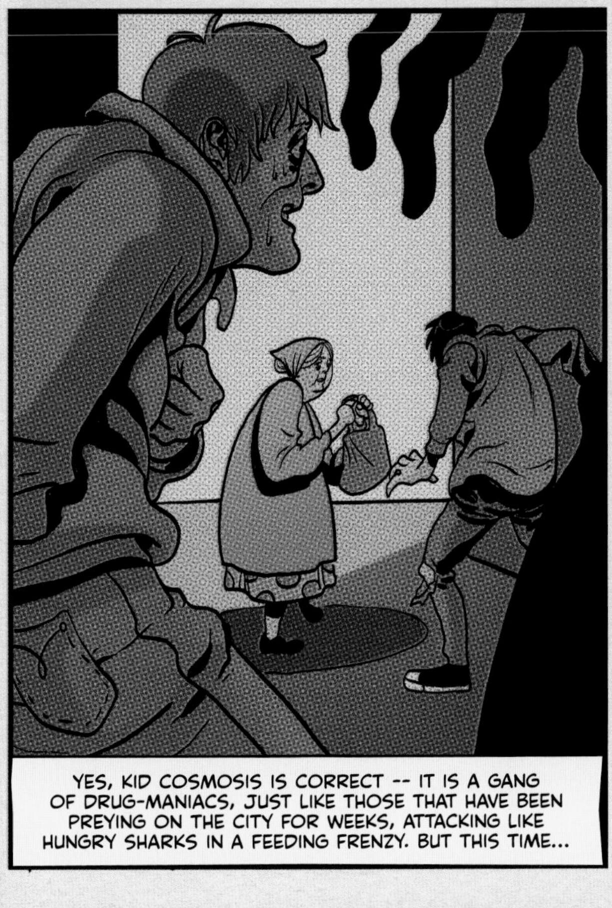
YES, KID COSMOSIS IS CORRECT -- IT IS A GANG OF DRUG-MANIACS, JUST LIKE THOSE THAT HAVE BEEN PREYING ON THE CITY FOR WEEKS, ATTACKING LIKE HUNGRY SHARKS IN A FEEDING FRENZY. BUT THIS TIME...

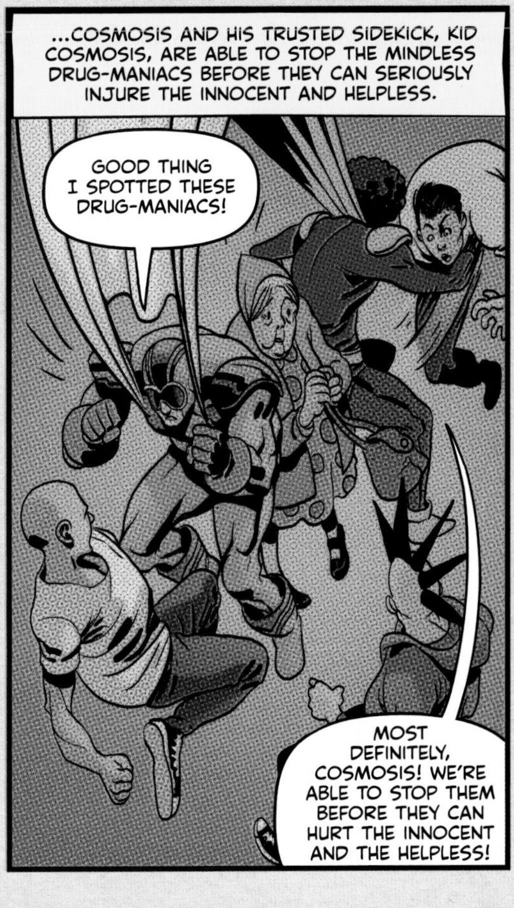
...COSMOSIS AND HIS TRUSTED SIDEKICK, KID COSMOSIS, ARE ABLE TO STOP THE MINDLESS DRUG-MANIACS BEFORE THEY CAN SERIOUSLY INJURE THE INNOCENT AND HELPLESS.
GOOD THING I SPOTTED THESE DRUG-MANIACS!
MOST DEFINITELY, COSMOSIS! WE'RE ABLE TO STOP THEM BEFORE THEY CAN HURT THE INNOCENT AND THE HELPLESS!

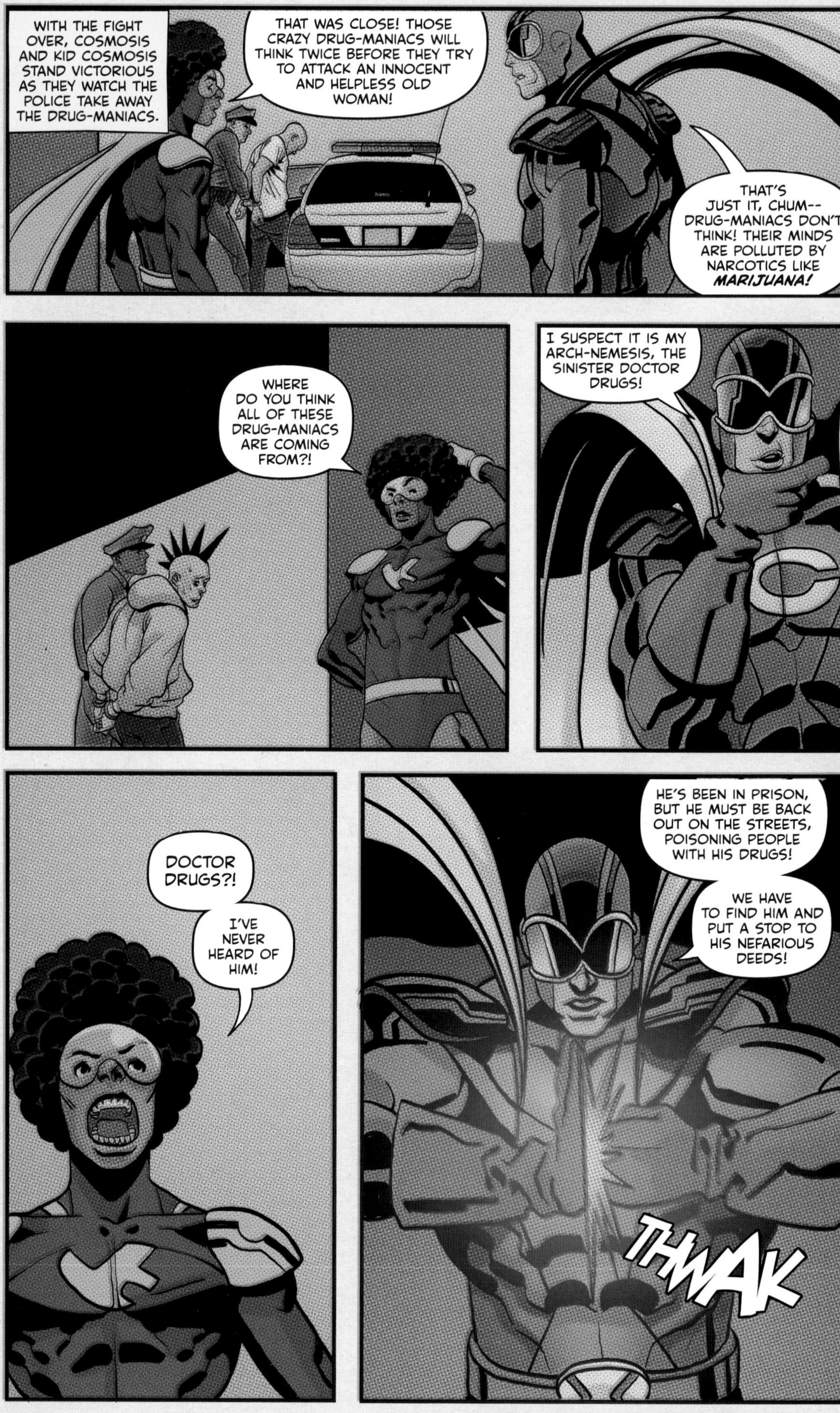
WITH THE FIGHT OVER, COSMOSIS AND KID COSMOSIS STAND VICTORIOUS AS THEY WATCH THE POLICE TAKE AWAY THE DRUG-MANIACS.
THAT WAS CLOSE! THOSE CRAZY DRUG-MANIACS WILL THINK TWICE BEFORE THEY TRY TO ATTACK AN INNOCENT AND HELPLESS OLD WOMAN!
THAT'S JUST IT, CHUM-- DRUG-MANIACS DON'T THINK! THEIR MINDS ARE POLLUTED BY NARCOTICS LIKE ***MARIJUANA!***
WHERE DO YOU THINK ALL OF THESE DRUG-MANIACS ARE COMING FROM?!
I SUSPECT IT IS MY ARCH-NEMESIS, THE SINISTER DOCTOR DRUGS!
DOCTOR DRUGS?!
I'VE NEVER HEARD OF HIM!
HE'S BEEN IN PRISON, BUT HE MUST BE BACK OUT ON THE STREETS, POISONING PEOPLE WITH HIS DRUGS!
WE HAVE TO FIND HIM AND PUT A STOP TO HIS NEFARIOUS DEEDS!
THWAK

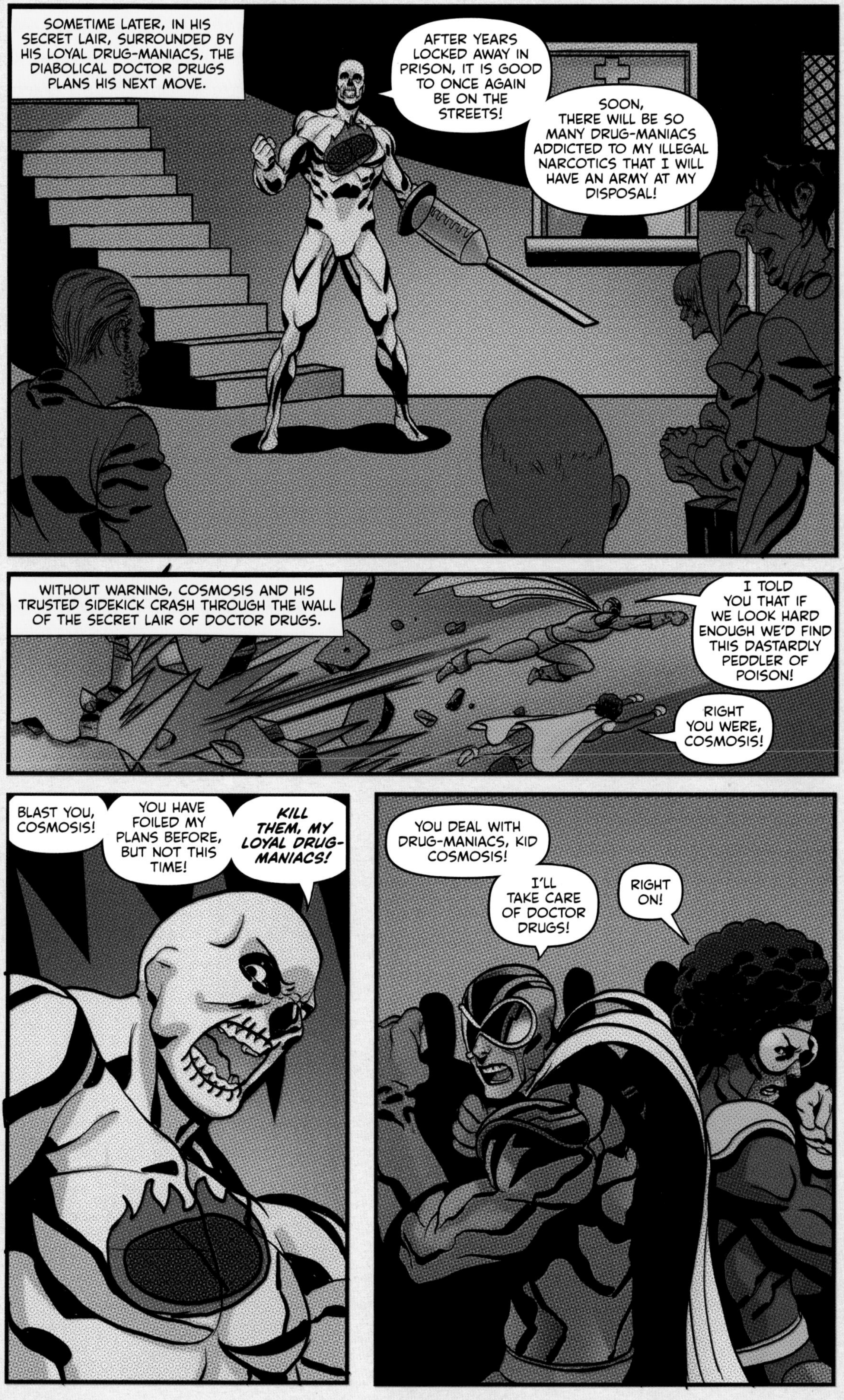
SOMETIME LATER, IN HIS SECRET LAIR, SURROUNDED BY HIS LOYAL DRUG-MANIACS, THE DIABOLICAL DOCTOR DRUGS PLANS HIS NEXT MOVE.
AFTER YEARS LOCKED AWAY IN PRISON, IT IS GOOD TO ONCE AGAIN BE ON THE STREETS!
SOON, THERE WILL BE SO MANY DRUG-MANIACS ADDICTED TO MY ILLEGAL NARCOTICS THAT I WILL HAVE AN ARMY AT MY DISPOSAL!
WITHOUT WARNING, COSMOSIS AND HIS TRUSTED SIDEKICK CRASH THROUGH THE WALL OF THE SECRET LAIR OF DOCTOR DRUGS.
I TOLD YOU THAT IF WE LOOK HARD ENOUGH WE'D FIND THIS DASTARDLY PEDDLER OF POISON!
RIGHT YOU WERE, COSMOSIS!
BLAST YOU, COSMOSIS!
YOU HAVE FOILED MY PLANS BEFORE, BUT NOT THIS TIME!
KILL THEM, MY LOYAL DRUG-MANIACS!
YOU DEAL WITH DRUG-MANIACS, KID COSMOSIS!
I'LL TAKE CARE OF DOCTOR DRUGS!
RIGHT ON!

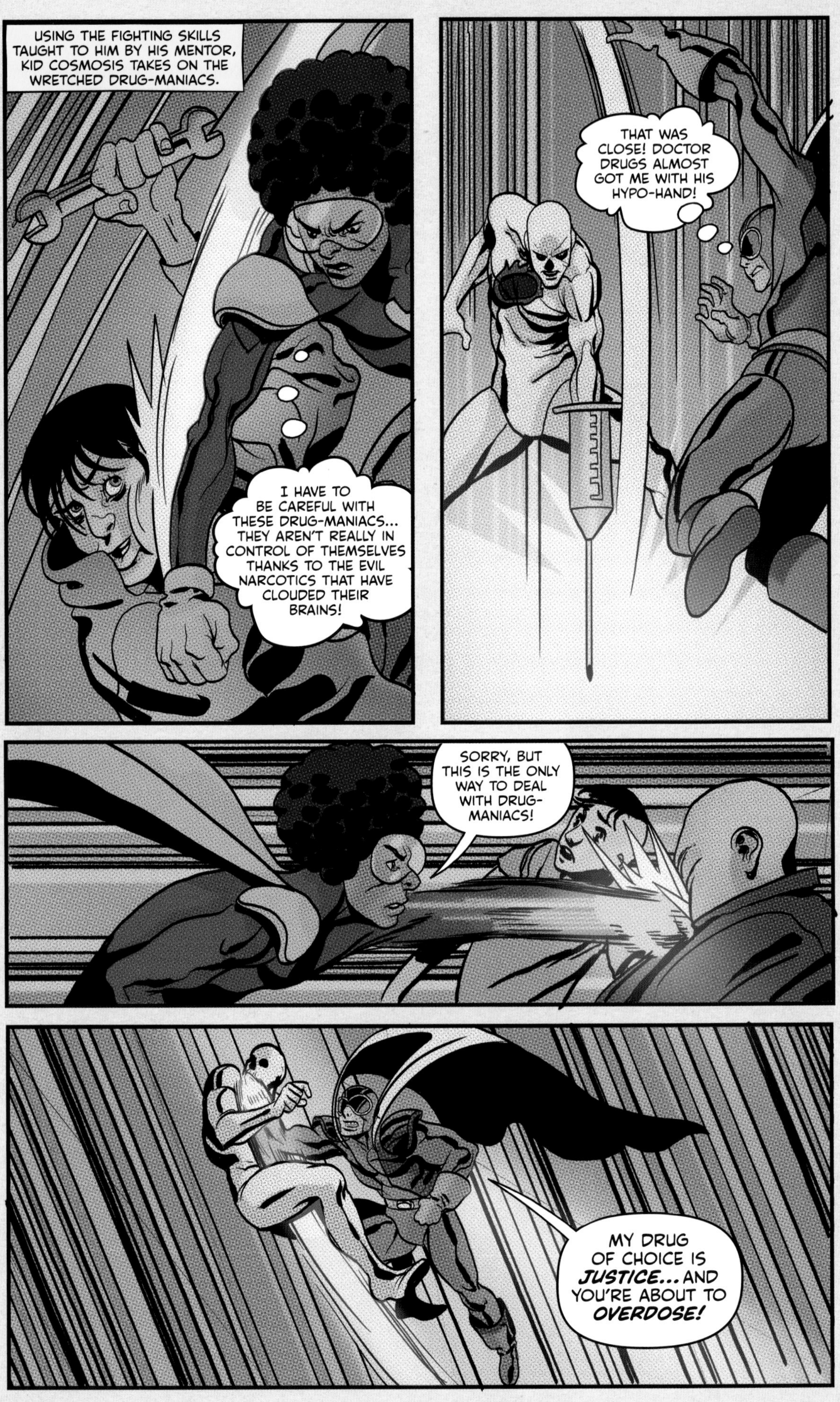
USING THE FIGHTING SKILLS TAUGHT TO HIM BY HIS MENTOR, KID COSMOSIS TAKES ON THE WRETCHED DRUG-MANIACS.
I HAVE TO BE CAREFUL WITH THESE DRUG-MANIACS... THEY AREN'T REALLY IN CONTROL OF THEMSELVES THANKS TO THE EVIL NARCOTICS THAT HAVE CLOUDED THEIR BRAINS!
THAT WAS CLOSE! DOCTOR DRUGS ALMOST GOT ME WITH HIS HYPO-HAND!
SORRY, BUT THIS IS THE ONLY WAY TO DEAL WITH DRUG-MANIACS!
MY DRUG OF CHOICE IS ***JUSTICE...*** AND YOU'RE ABOUT TO ***OVERDOSE!***

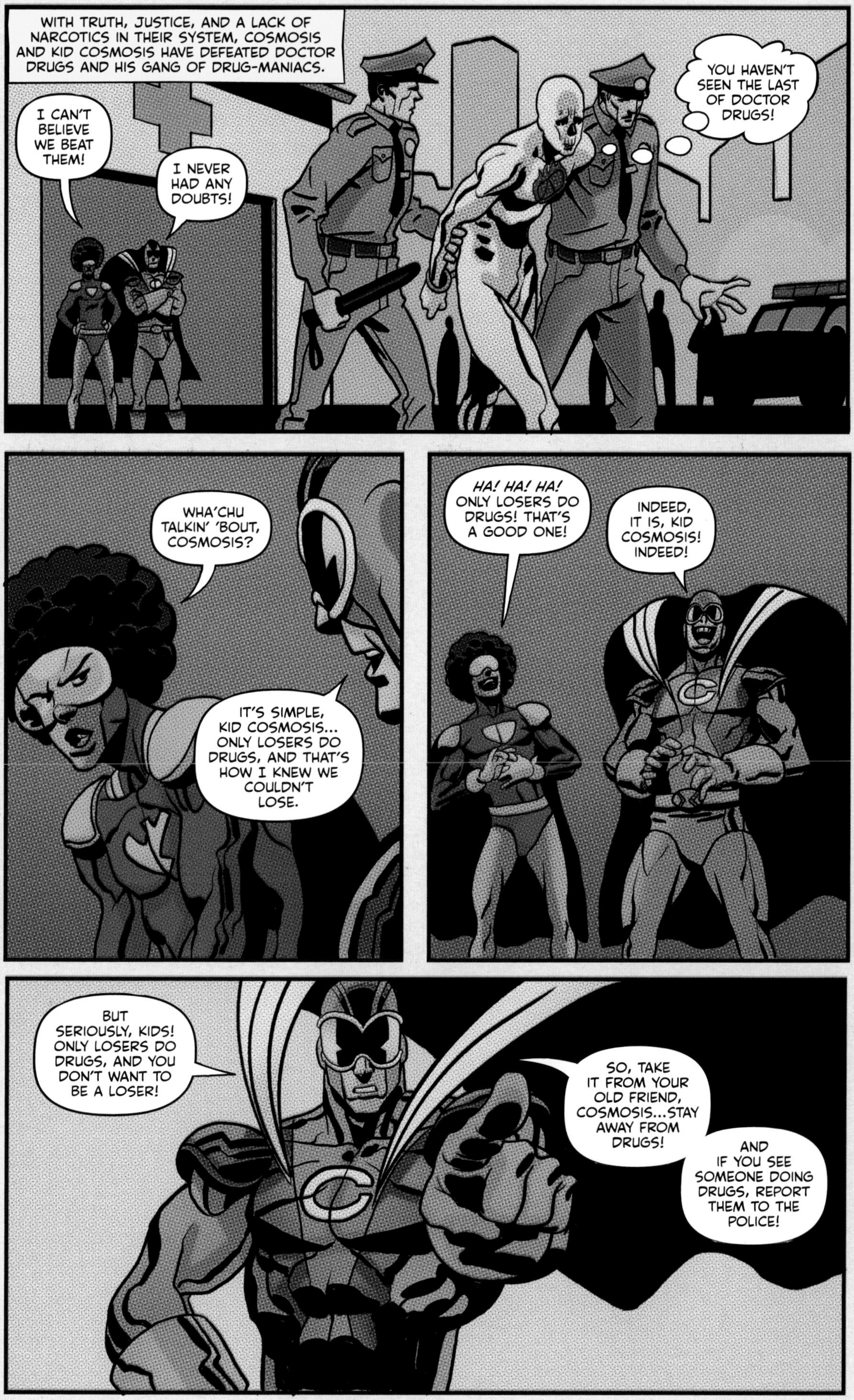
WITH TRUTH, JUSTICE, AND A LACK OF NARCOTICS IN THEIR SYSTEM, COSMOSIS AND KID COSMOSIS HAVE DEFEATED DOCTOR DRUGS AND HIS GANG OF DRUG-MANIACS.
I CAN'T BELIEVE WE BEAT THEM!
I NEVER HAD ANY DOUBTS!
YOU HAVEN'T SEEN THE LAST OF DOCTOR DRUGS!
WHA'CHU TALKIN' 'BOUT, COSMOSIS?
IT'S SIMPLE, KID COSMOSIS... ONLY LOSERS DO DRUGS, AND THAT'S HOW I KNEW WE COULDN'T LOSE.
HA! HA! HA! ONLY LOSERS DO DRUGS! THAT'S A GOOD ONE!
INDEED, IT IS, KID COSMOSIS! INDEED!
BUT SERIOUSLY, KIDS! ONLY LOSERS DO DRUGS, AND YOU DON'T WANT TO BE A LOSER!
SO, TAKE IT FROM YOUR OLD FRIEND, COSMOSIS...STAY AWAY FROM DRUGS!
AND IF YOU SEE SOMEONE DOING DRUGS, REPORT THEM TO THE POLICE!

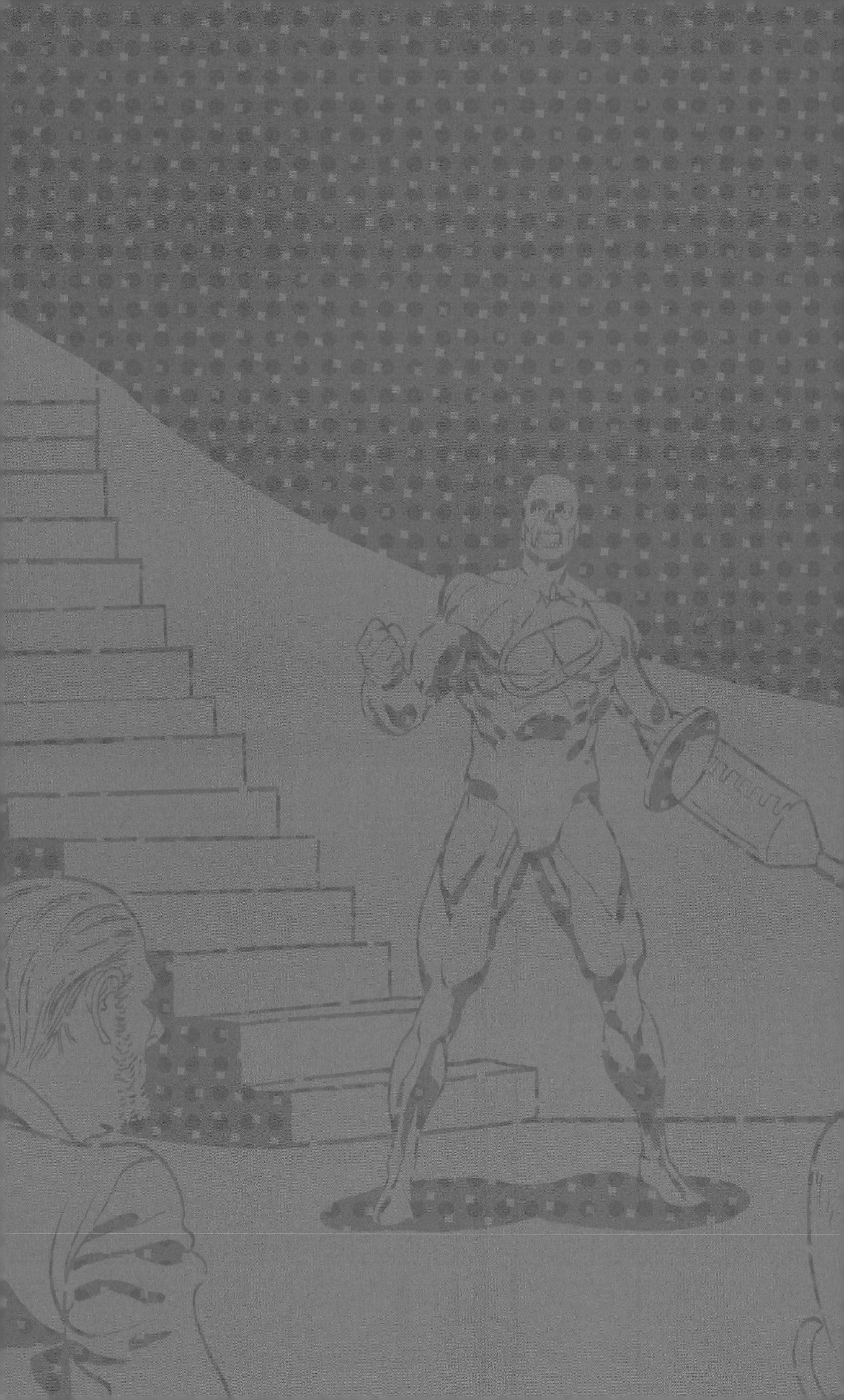

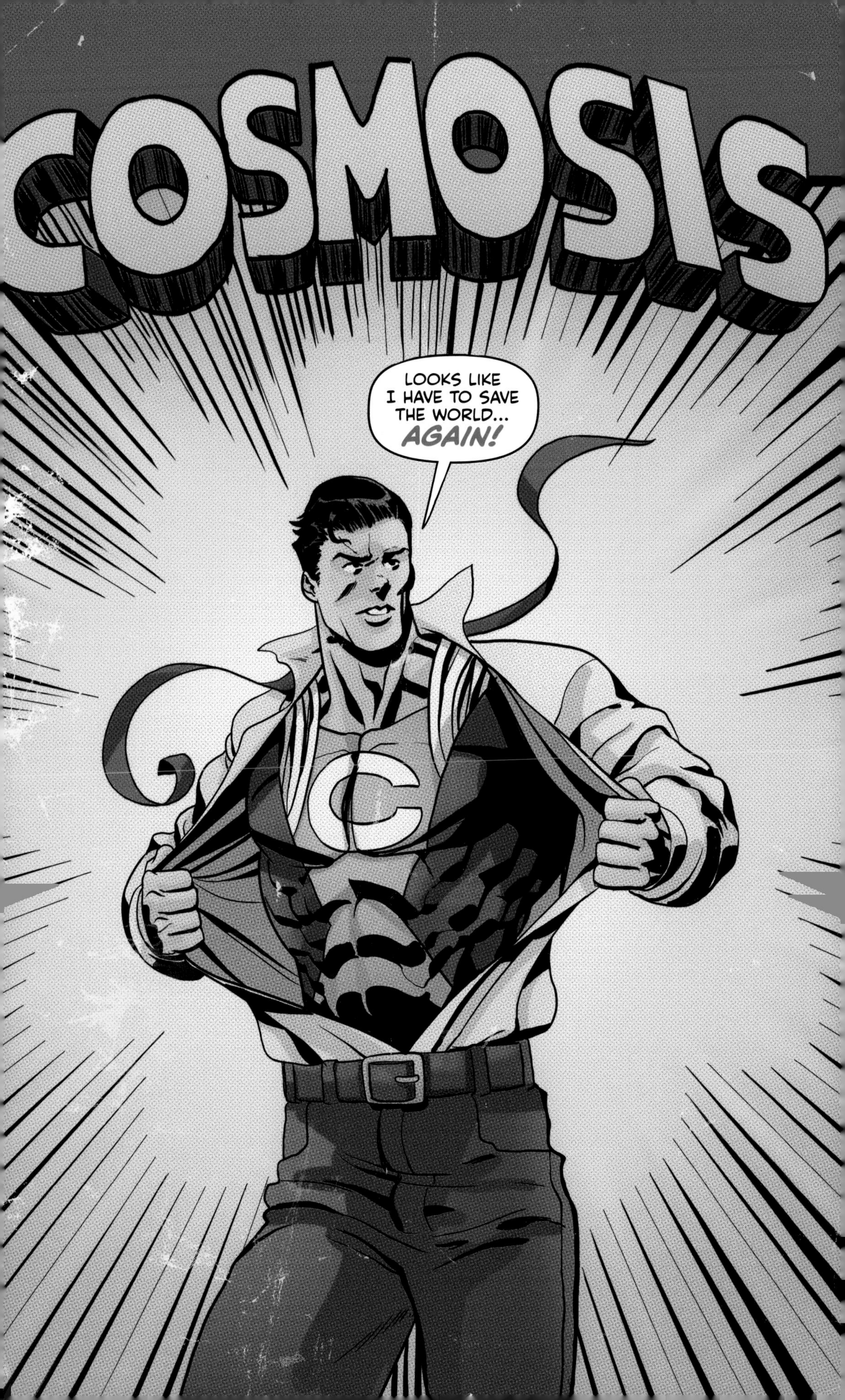
COSMOSIS
LOOKS LIKE I HAVE TO SAVE THE WORLD... AGAIN!

AT THE HEADQUARTERS OF THE INTERNATIONAL ASSOCIATION OF SPACE EXPLORATION (I.A.S.E.), DR. OWEN FELDBERG DILIGENTLY SEARCHES FOR THREATS TO HUMANITY. IT IS DIFFICULT WORK, BUT IT IS NECESSARY.

HOLY SMOKES! MY MONITORS HAVE DETECTED A THREAT TO HUMANITY!

I MUST ALERT COSMOSIS!

MEANWHILE, COSMOSIS VISITS WITH A FAN WHO IS RECOVERING FROM SURGERY. THE JOVIAL CELEBRATION IS CUT SHORT BY AN UNEXPECTED MESSAGE.

COME IN, COSMOSIS! THIS IS DR. FELDBERG! DO YOU COPY?!

WHAT'S UP, DOC?

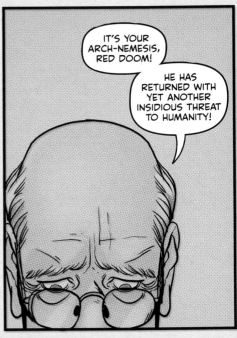

IT'S YOUR ARCH-NEMESIS, RED DOOM!

HE HAS RETURNED WITH YET ANOTHER INSIDIOUS THREAT TO HUMANITY!

AND SO, COSMOSIS RUSHES OFF TO SAVE THE DAY.

I'M ON IT, DOC!

BE CAREFUL, COSMOSIS!

SORRY ABOUT THAT HASTY DEPARTURE, TIMMY! I HAVE TO SAVE THE WORLD FROM A DEADLY THREAT!

GOSH, COSMOSIS, SOUNDS DANGEROUS! GOOD LUCK!

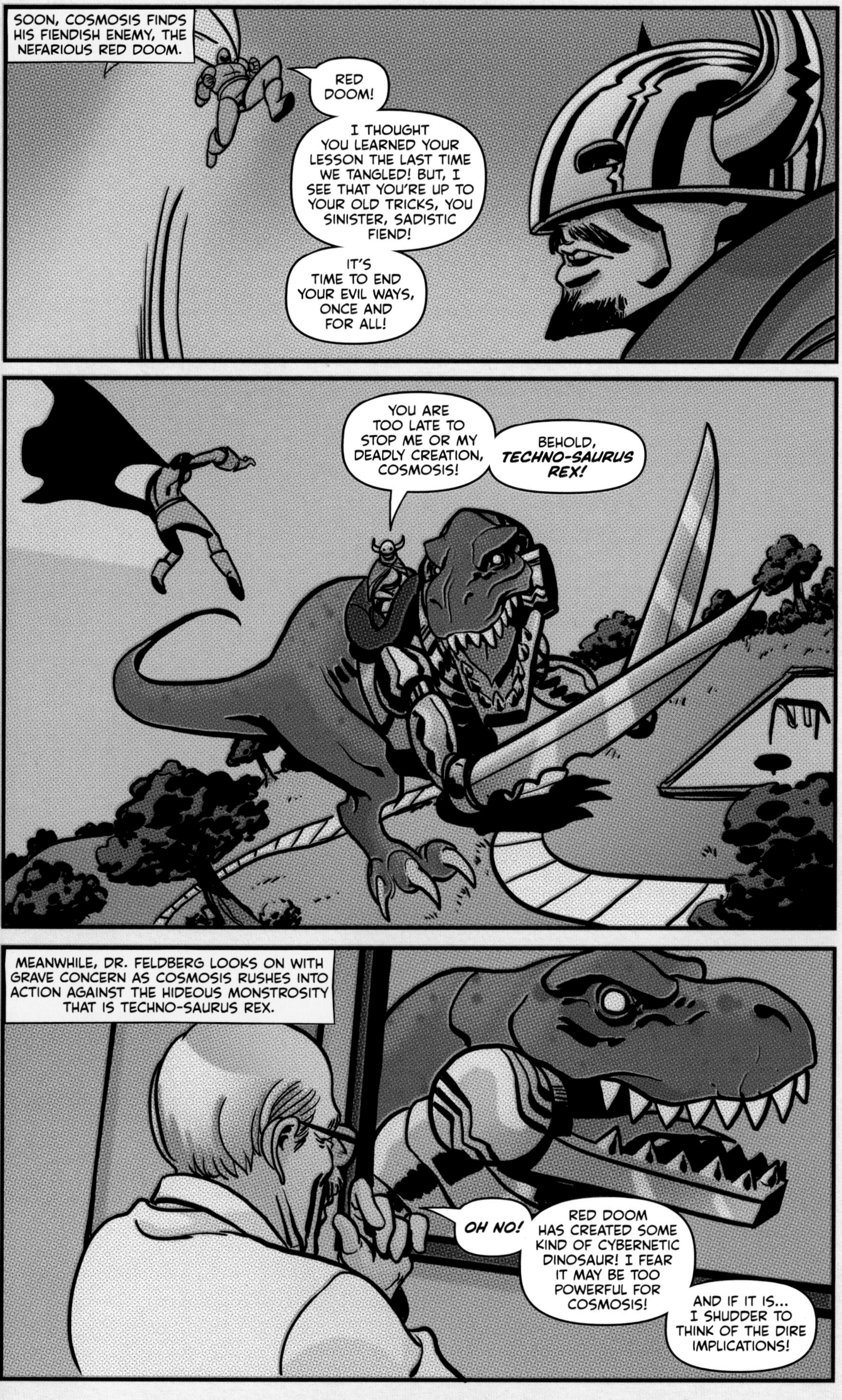
SOON, COSMOSIS FINDS HIS FIENDISH ENEMY, THE NEFARIOUS RED DOOM.
RED DOOM!
I THOUGHT YOU LEARNED YOUR LESSON THE LAST TIME WE TANGLED! BUT, I SEE THAT YOU'RE UP TO YOUR OLD TRICKS, YOU SINISTER, SADISTIC FIEND!
IT'S TIME TO END YOUR EVIL WAYS, ONCE AND FOR ALL!
YOU ARE TOO LATE TO STOP ME OR MY DEADLY CREATION, COSMOSIS!
BEHOLD, TECHNO-SAURUS REX!
MEANWHILE, DR. FELDBERG LOOKS ON WITH GRAVE CONCERN AS COSMOSIS RUSHES INTO ACTION AGAINST THE HIDEOUS MONSTROSITY THAT IS TECHNO-SAURUS REX.
OH NO!
RED DOOM HAS CREATED SOME KIND OF CYBERNETIC DINOSAUR! I FEAR IT MAY BE TOO POWERFUL FOR COSMOSIS!
AND IF IT IS... I SHUDDER TO THINK OF THE DIRE IMPLICATIONS!

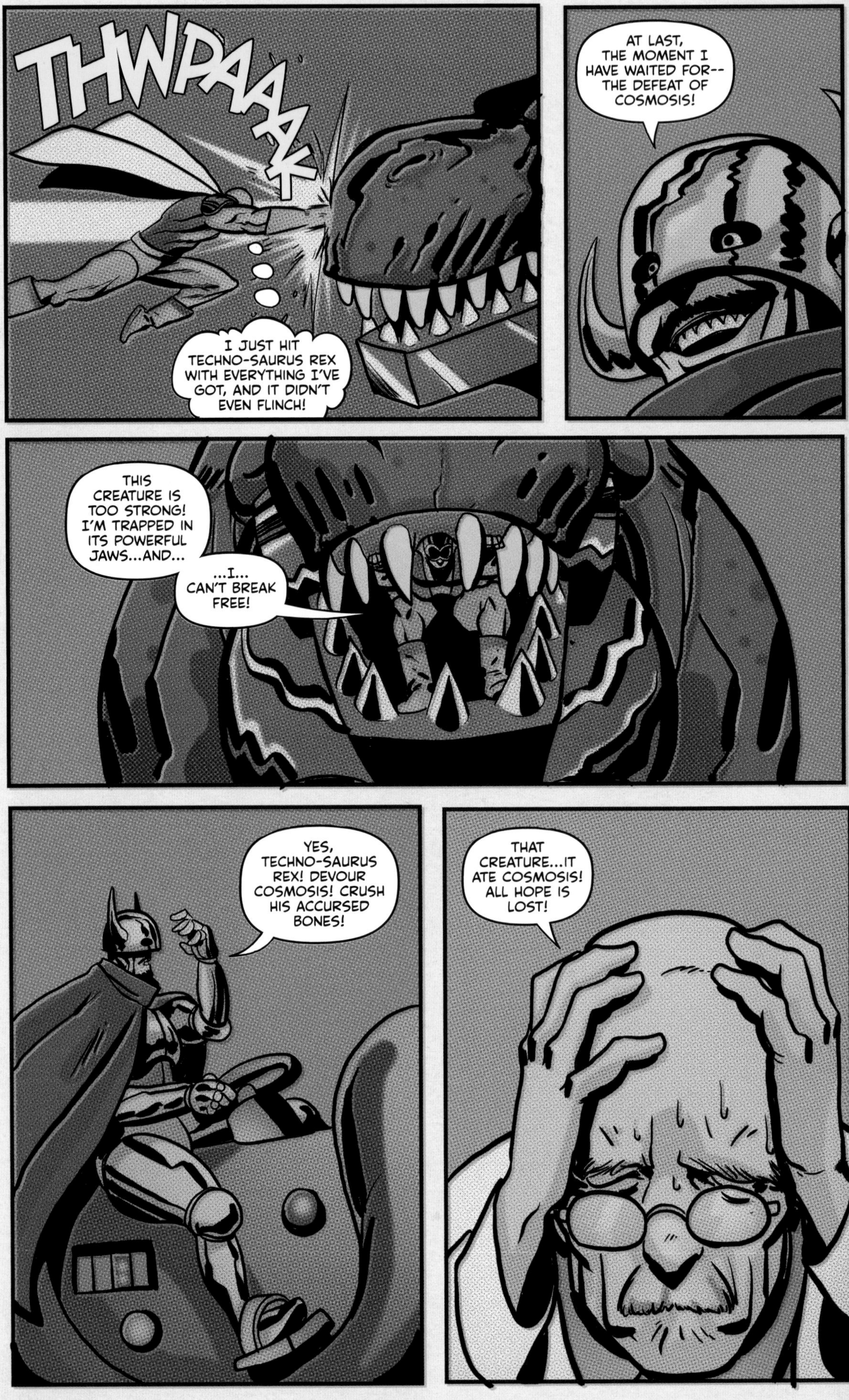
THWPAAAK
I JUST HIT TECHNO-SAURUS REX WITH EVERYTHING I'VE GOT, AND IT DIDN'T EVEN FLINCH!
AT LAST, THE MOMENT I HAVE WAITED FOR-- THE DEFEAT OF COSMOSIS!
THIS CREATURE IS TOO STRONG! I'M TRAPPED IN ITS POWERFUL JAWS...AND...
...I... CAN'T BREAK FREE!
YES, TECHNO-SAURUS REX! DEVOUR COSMOSIS! CRUSH HIS ACCURSED BONES!
THAT CREATURE...IT ATE COSMOSIS! ALL HOPE IS LOST!

INDEED, ALL HOPE DOES APPEAR TO BE LOST, AS GIANT CYBERNETIC JAWS SEEMINGLY TEAR COSMOSIS TO SHREDS.

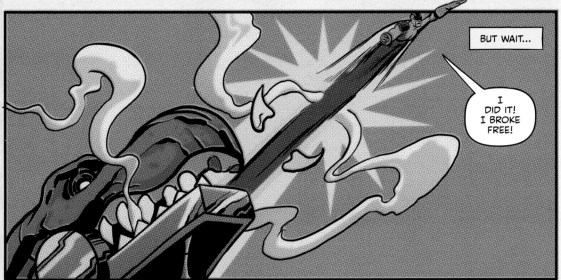

BUT WAIT...

I DID IT! I BROKE FREE!

CURSE YOU, COSMOSIS!

YOU KNOW WHAT, RED DOOM?!

THIS IS GETTING OLD!

STAY AWAY FROM ME!

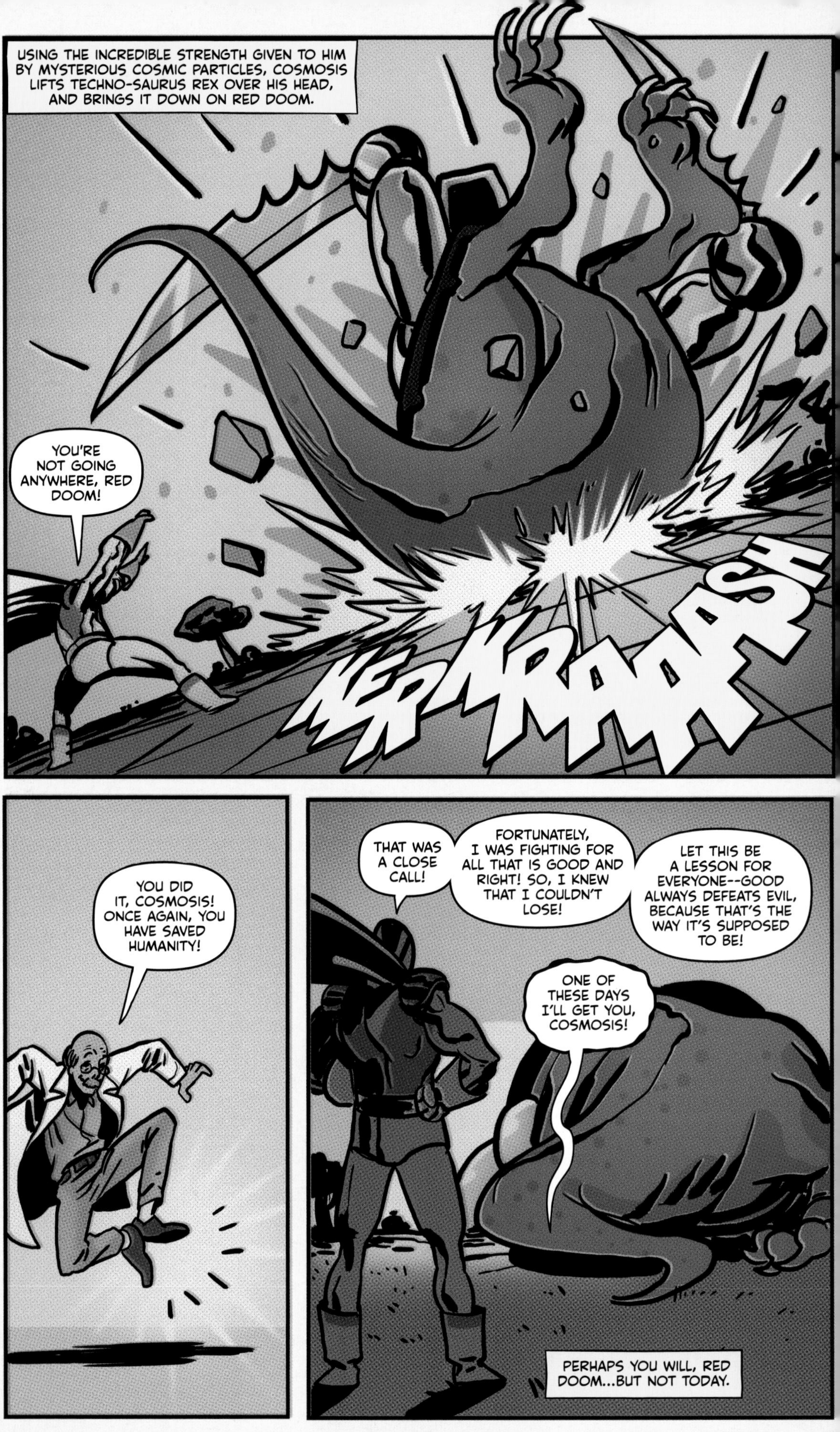
USING THE INCREDIBLE STRENGTH GIVEN TO HIM BY MYSTERIOUS COSMIC PARTICLES, COSMOSIS LIFTS TECHNO-SAURUS REX OVER HIS HEAD, AND BRINGS IT DOWN ON RED DOOM.
YOU'RE NOT GOING ANYWHERE, RED DOOM!
KERKRAAASH
YOU DID IT, COSMOSIS! ONCE AGAIN, YOU HAVE SAVED HUMANITY!
THAT WAS A CLOSE CALL!
FORTUNATELY, I WAS FIGHTING FOR ALL THAT IS GOOD AND RIGHT! SO, I KNEW THAT I COULDN'T LOSE!
LET THIS BE A LESSON FOR EVERYONE--GOOD ALWAYS DEFEATS EVIL, BECAUSE THAT'S THE WAY IT'S SUPPOSED TO BE!
ONE OF THESE DAYS I'LL GET YOU, COSMOSIS!
PERHAPS YOU WILL, RED DOOM...BUT NOT TODAY.

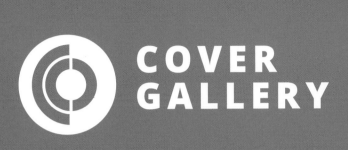

COVER GALLERY

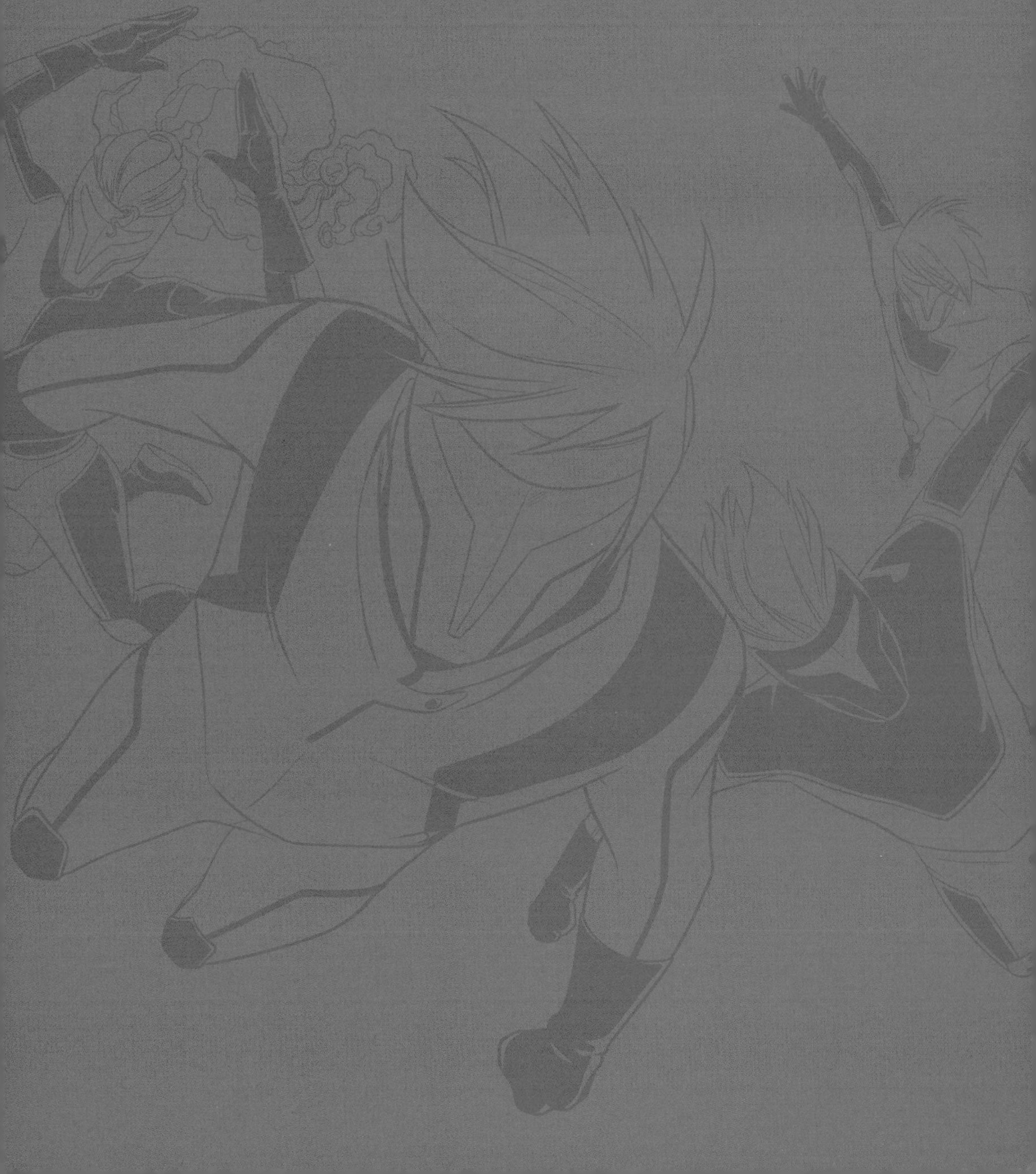

Art by **ANTHONY PIPER**

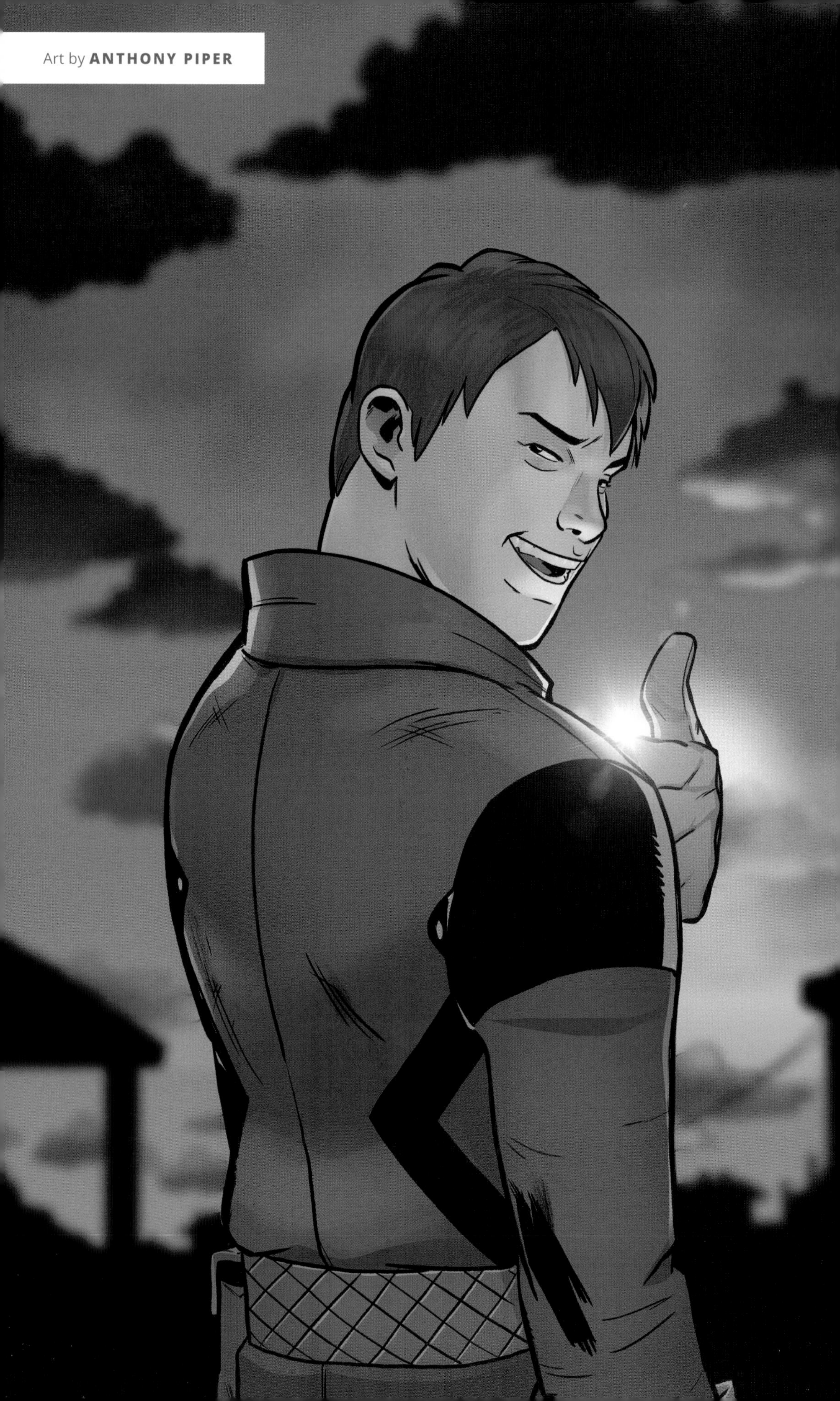

Art by **ANTHONY PIPER**

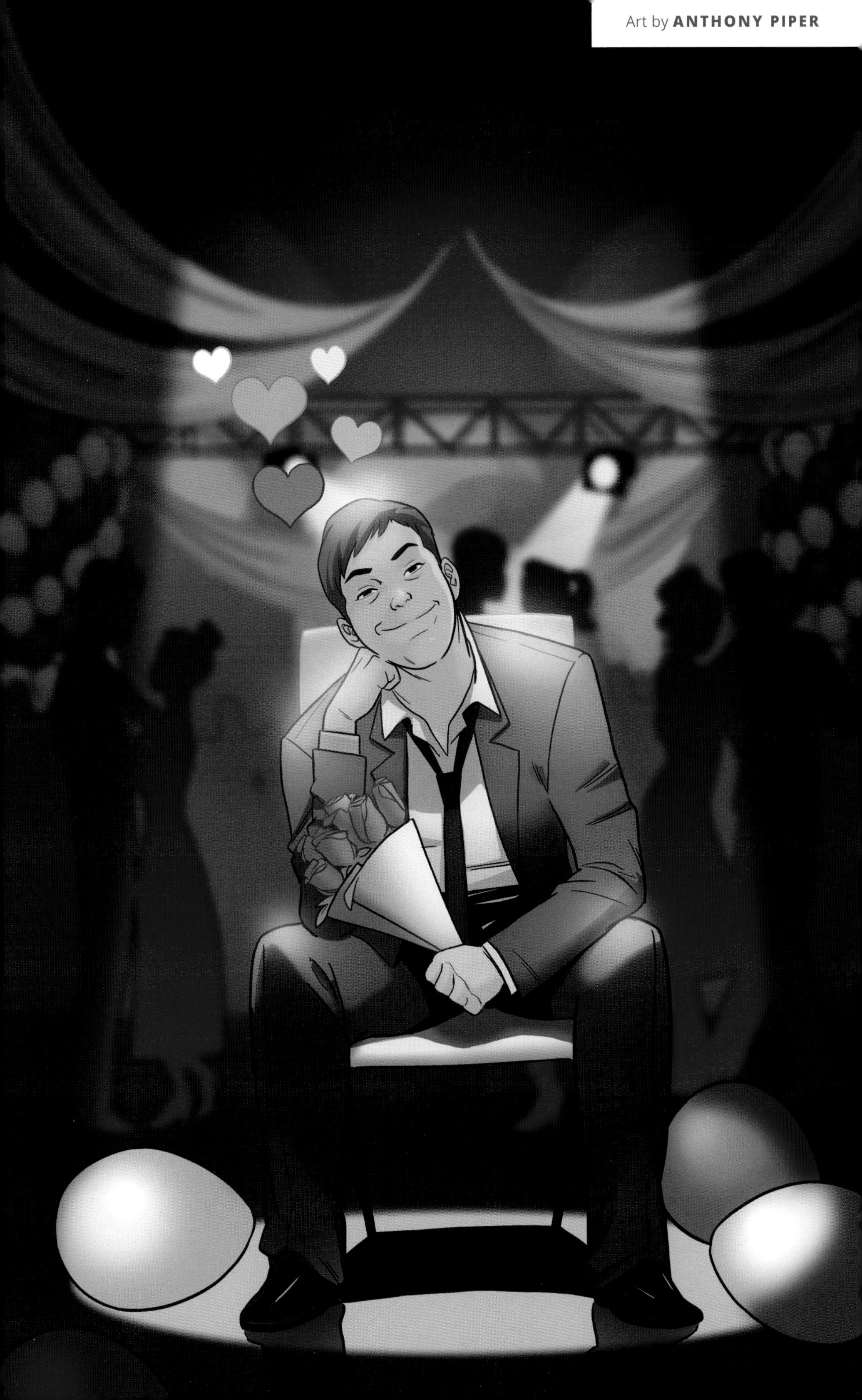

Art by **ANTHONY PIPER**

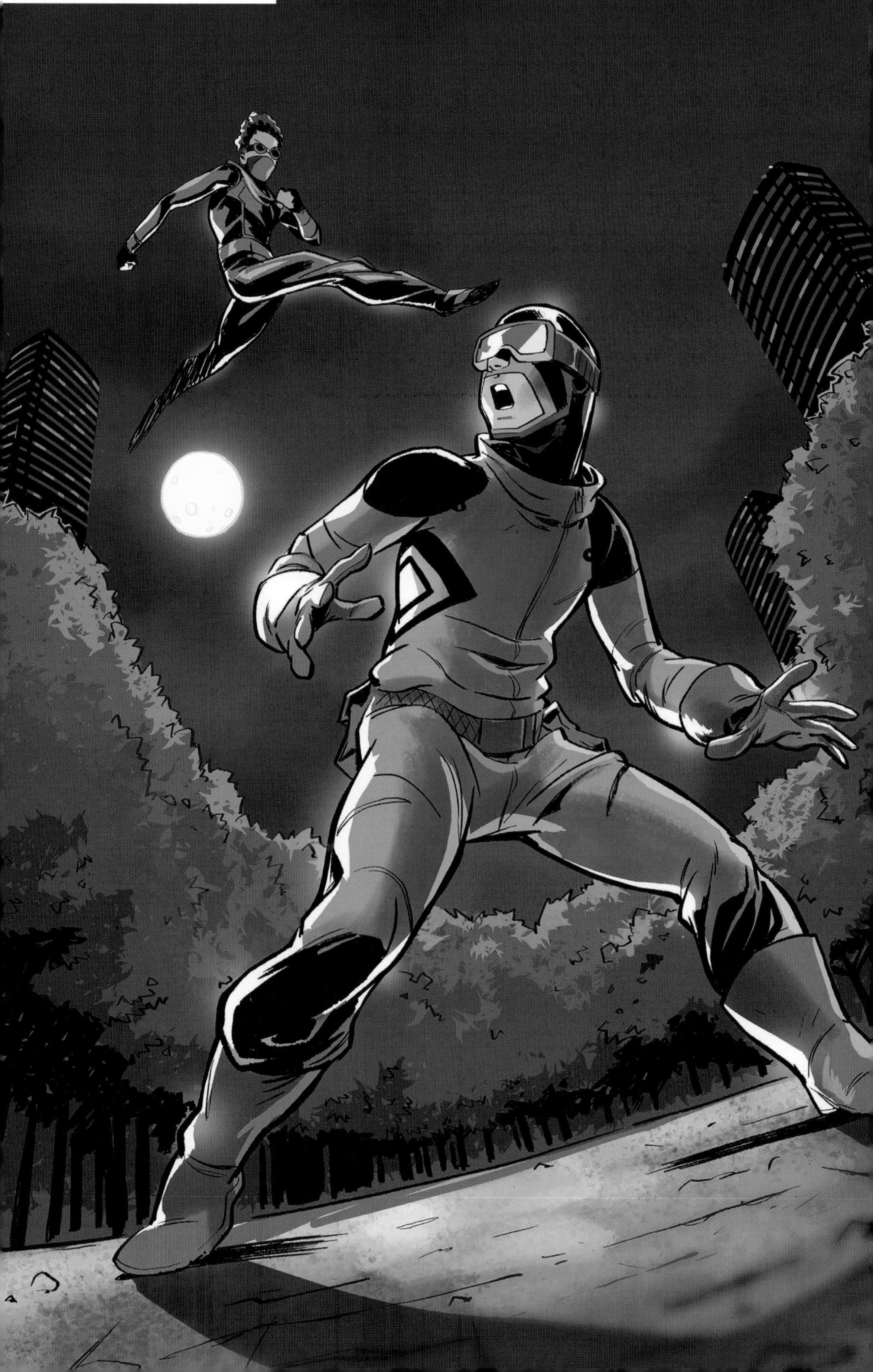

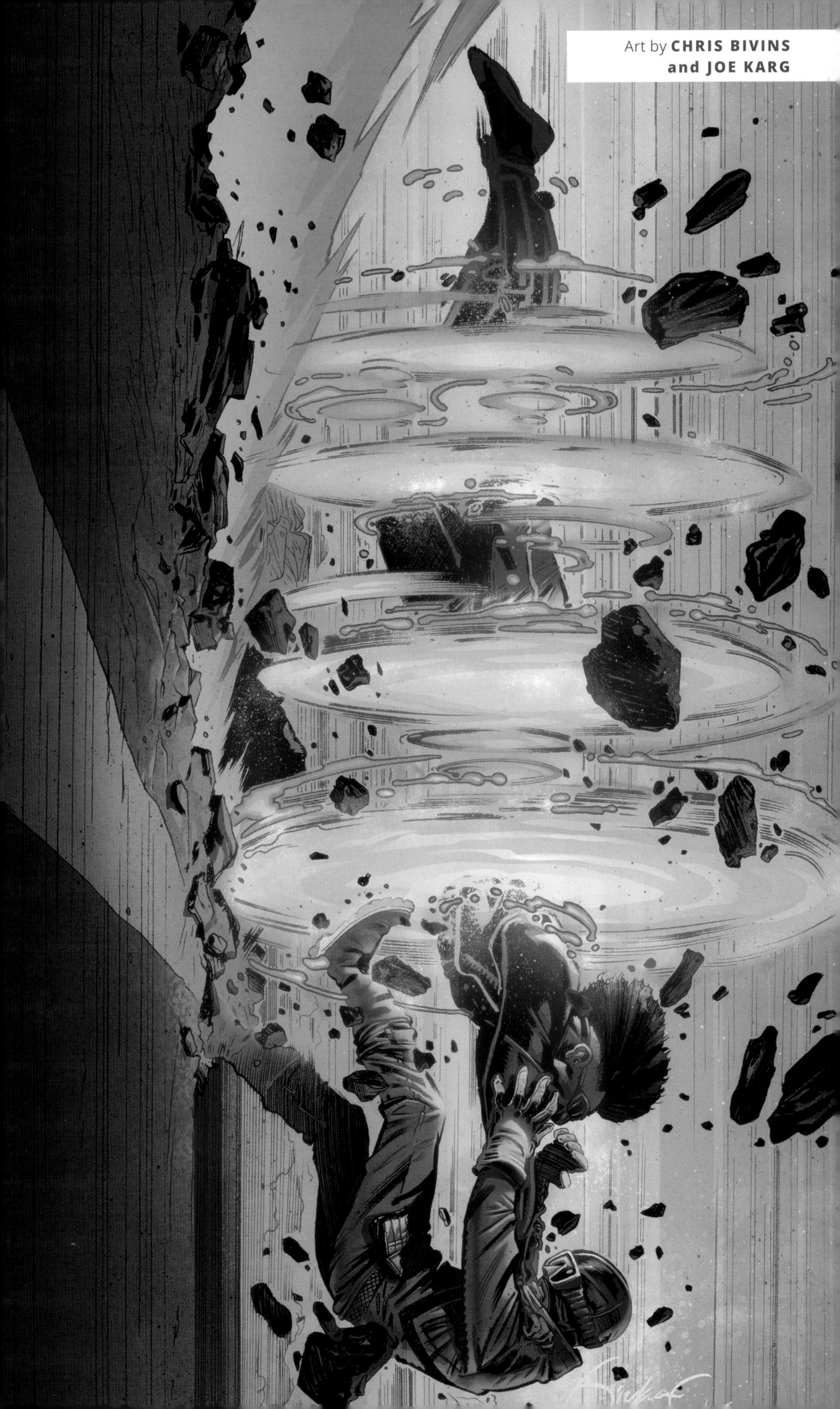

Art by **CHRIS BIVINS and JOE KARG**

Art by **CHRIS BIVINS and JOE KARG**

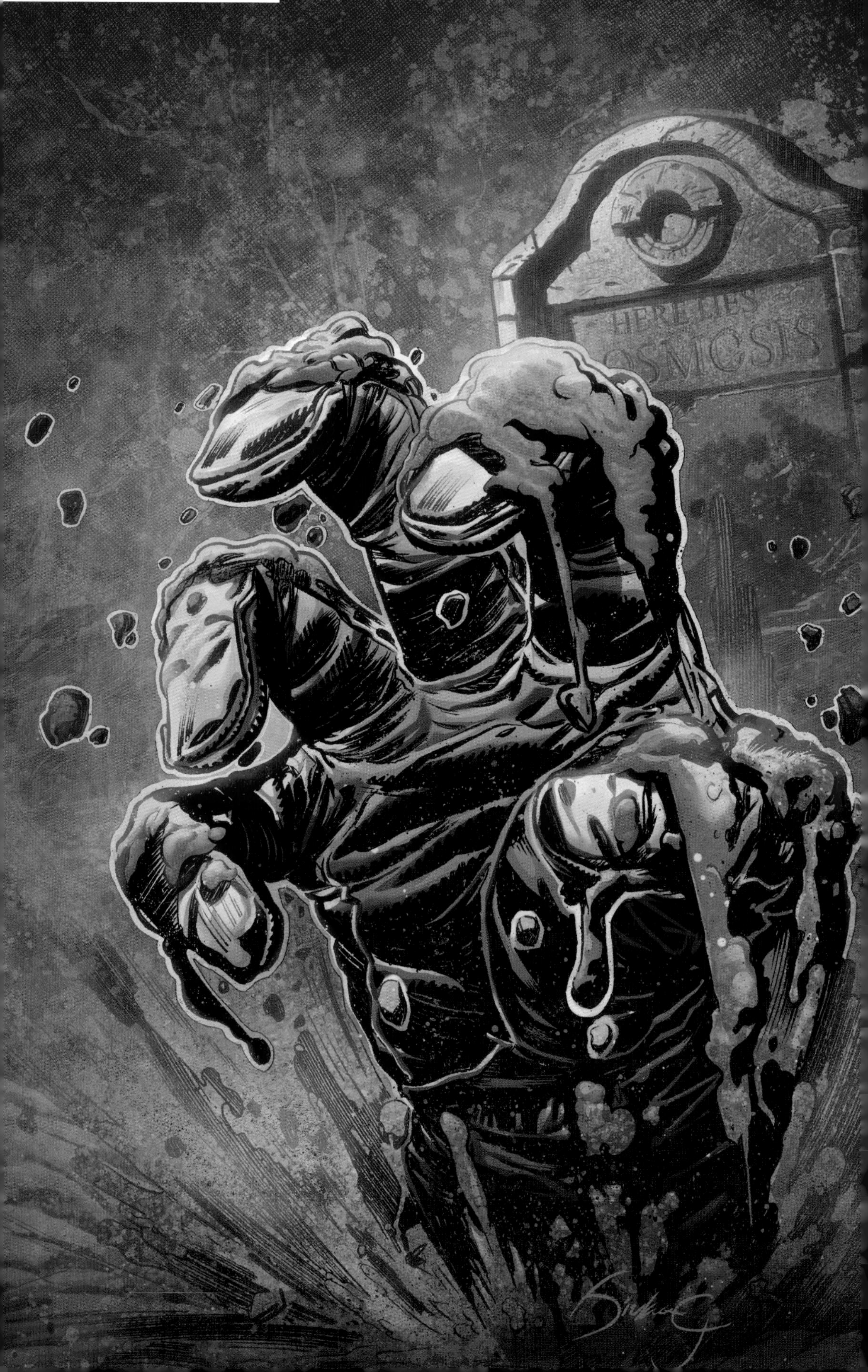
HERE LIES
OSMOSIS